New Jersey Bible Records

Volume 2
Salem and Cumberland Counties

Edited by
Anna Miller Watring

HERITAGE BOOKS
2020

HERITAGE BOOKS

AN IMPRINT OF HERITAGE BOOKS, INC.

Books, CDs, and more—Worldwide

For our listing of thousands of titles see our website
at
www.HeritageBooks.com

Published 2020 by
HERITAGE BOOKS, INC.
Publishing Division
5810 Ruatan Street
Berwyn Heights, Md. 20740

Originally published 2002

International Standard Book Number
Paperbound: 978-1-68034-495-0

CONTENTS

PREFACE

Many of these Bible Records were compiled by Genealogical Records Committee, Sewel, New Jersey (Mrs. Walter A. Simpson, Chairman) and presented by Red Bank Chapter, D.A.R., Pitman, New Jersey. These include the enormous work done by Timothy Chalkley Matlack of Morrestown and members of the Red Bank Chapter. Following the death of of Mr. Matlack in 1945, the Chairman of Genealogical Records of Red Bank Chapter was able to make a copy of his Bible records. In 1951 the chapter made the records available to various sources.

Other records were made available by Ann Whitall Chapter, D.A.R., of Woodbury, New Jersey, and consisted of records belonging to members of the Chapter, and Bibles held by the Gloucester County Historical Society. These records were generally made available by the Chapter in 1949.

Cape May County Bible Records were compiled in four volumes by the Cape May Patriots Chapter. Volume one was compiled by Miss Hattie Van Gilder, Chairman Genealogical Records, Cape May Patriots Chapter and presented by the Chapter in 1939. Volume Two was later presented by Cape May Patriots Chapter in 1940. These were compiled by Lila M. Gandy, State Chairman of Genealogical Records, New Jersey and Norman Harvey Vanaman, Acting Organizing President of Cape May Chapter, S.A.R. Volume Three was also compiled by Miss Lila M. Gandy and Norman Harvey Vanaman. Volume Four was compiled by Charlotte Kimball Stevens, Chairman of Genealogical Records and presented in 1947.

For the most part Ms. Watring has selected only the early records for publication, primarily those which pre-date 1900. The records cover the counties of Atlantic, Burlington, Cape May, Cumberland, Gloucester, and Salem and are now published in two volumes.

We wish to acknowledge the work of Mr. Matlack and the many individuals responsible for preserving this marvelous collection. We are most grateful for their work.

F. Edward Wright
Publisher

ABBREVIATIONS

The following abbreviations are used:

abt. - about
Apr - April
Aug - August
b/o - brother of
b. - born
bapt. - baptized
bur - buried
d. - died
d/o - daughter of
Dec - December
dy(s) - day(s)
dau. - daughter
f/o - father of
Feb February
h/o - husband of

Jan - January
Jul - July
Jun - June
m/o - mother of
Mar - March
mar - married
mo(s). - month(s)
N.S. - new style calendar
Nov - November
O.S. - old style calendar
Oct - October
s/o - son of
Sep - September
w/o - wife of
yr(s). - year(s)

Standard Postal Abbreviations

SALEM COUNTY

Abbott Family Bible
John Baskett, Printer to the University
Oxford, 1726

George Abbott and his two brothers emigrated from England to New England. George and his wife Mary moved to the township of Elsinborough in Salem County, NJ, about 1690.

Children of George and Mary Abbott: Benjamin Abbott b. the 2nd of the 1st mo, 1699/1700; Hannah Abbott b. the 30th of the 9th mo, 1702; George Abbott b. the 13th of the 10th mo, 1704; Sarah Abbott b. the 16th of the 2nd mo, 1706/7; Rebecca Abbott b. the 10th of the 6th mo, 1709; Samuel Abbott b. the 26th of the 6th mo, 1712; Mary Abbott b. the 26th of the 8th mo, 1714.

Samuel Abbott, 6th child of George and Mary Abbott, mar Hannah Foster, dau of Josiah and Amy Foster.

Josiah Foster was b. the 4th mo. 1682.
Amy Foster was b. the 4th mo, 1685.

Josiah and Amy Foster mar the 3rd mo, 1706.
Their children: William Foster b. the 13th of the 12th mo, 1707; Rebecca Foster was b. the 1st of the 10th mo, 1708; Hannah Foster was b. the 21st of the 10th mo, 1715; Josiah Foster was b. the 15th of the 6th mo, 1720.

Children of Samuel and Hannah Abbott: George Abbott b. the 29th of the 11th mo, 1734/5; William Abbott b. the 4th of the 4th mo, 1737; Rebecca Abbott b. the 26th of the 10th mo, 1740.

William Abbott, 2nd child of Samuel and Hannah, mar Rebecca Tyler, dau of William and Elizabeth Tyler, who was b. the 8th of the 2nd mo, 1743.

Children of William and Rebecca Abbott: Samuel Abbott b. the 27th of the 11th mo, 1763; George Abbott b. the 27th of the 9th mo, 1765; Josiah Abbott b. the 23rd of the 9th mo, 1768.

Samuel Abbott, 1st child of William and Rebecca, mar Mercy Gill, dau of John and Amy Gill, who was b. the 9th of the 9th mo, 1764 and d. the 1st of the 2nd mo, 1779.

Children of Samuel and Mercy Abbott (his 1ˢᵗ wife): William Abbott b. the 22nd
of the 7th mo, 1734/5; Rebecca Abbott b. the 29th of the 7th mo, 1794;
Hannah Abbott b. the 3rd of the 7th mo, 1796; Sarah Abbott b. the 8th of
the 10th mo, 1798.

Children of Samuel and Martha Abbott (his 2nd wife): Mary Abbott b. the 20th
of the 1st mo, 1810; Lydia Abbott b. the 21st of the 1st mo, 1813; Samuel
Abbott b. the 14th of the 3rd mo, 1815; George Abbott b. the 13th of the
7th mo, 1817; Martha Abbott b. the 4th of the 11th mo, 1819.

Martha Abbott, 2nd wife of Samuel Abbott, dau of Samuel and Mary Ann
Ogden, was b. the 2nd of the 2nd mo, 1779.

Samuel Ogden b. the 5th of the 8th mo, 1745 and d. the 21st of the 4th mo,
1821.
Mary Ann Ogden b. the 19th of the 10th mo, 1752 and d. the 18th of the 11th
mo, 1818.

Martha Abbott, 3rd d/o Samuel and Martha, mar Samuel S. Willits of
Haddonfield, NJ.
George Abbott, 2nd s/o Samuel and Martha, mar Ruth S. Baker, d/o George M.
And Ruth Baker of New Bedford, MA, on 9 Oct 1845.
Samuel Abbott, eldest s/o Samuel and Martha, mar Sarah Wistar, eldest d/o
Caspar and Rebecca Wistar, on 6 May 1846.

Samuel A. Willits, only s/o Samuel Willets and Martha Abbott, was b. 23 Jul
1843.

Children of George and Ruth S. Abbott: Henry B. Abbott b. 5 Aug 1846;
Charles T. Abbott b. 4 Dec 1848; George Abbott b. 2 Sep 1849; William
Abbott b. 2 Sep 1852; Joseph B. Abbott b. 26 Feb 1857; William Abbott b.
13 Feb. 1868.

George Abbott, Jr, s/o George and Ruth S. Abbott, and Elizabeth Lippincott, d/o
Dr. Aquilla and Sarah Eldridge Lippincott, mar. 9 Oct. 1872.

George Abbott, s/o George and Elizabeth L. Abbott, b. 9 Dec. 1776.

Children of Samuel and Sarah W. Abbott: Mary Ann Abbott b. 24 Sep 1847;
Caspar W. Abbott b. 11 Sep 1848; Samuel Abbott b. 28 Jul 1851; Rebecca
and Catherine Abbott b. 26 Feb 1853.

Josiah Foster d. the 9th of the 1st mo, 1770, aged 88 yrs.

Amy, wife of Josiah Foster, d. the 15th of the 8th mo, 1783, aged 98-5-11.

Samuel Abbott, s/o George and Mary Abbott, d. Aged 48 yrs.

Hannah, widow of Samuel Abbott, afterward consort of Samuel Nicholson, d. in her 78th yr.

William Abbott, s/o Samuel and Hannah, d. Aged 63 yrs.

Rebecca, widow of William Abbott, d. Aged 64 yrs.

Samuel Abbott, s/o William and Rebecca Abbott, d. 14 Apr 1835, aged 72 yrs.

George Abbott, 2nd s/o William and Rebecca Abbott, d. 15 Nov 1831, in his 67th yr.

Mercy Abbott, 1st w/o Samuel Abbott, d. the 1st of the 2nd mo, 1798, in her 34th yr.

William Abbott, s/o Samuel and Mercy Abbott, d. 20 Apr 1835, in his 42nd yr.

Rebecca Abbott, d/o Samuel and Marcy his wife, d. ____.

Sarah Abbott, d/o Samuel and Mercy Abbott, d. the 12th of the 1st mo, 1799, aged 3 mo, 4 dys.

Mary Ann Abbott, d/o Samuel and Martha Abbott, d. 10 Jan 1844, aged 33-2-30.

Lydia Abbott d. 14 Jun ____, aged 33 yrs.

Martha A. Abbott d. 4 May 1848, aged 70 yrs, 10 mo.

Amy Abbott, d/o William G. Abbott d. 9 Apr 1848.

Martha Abbott d. 4 May 1848, aged 70 yrs, 10 mo.

Caspar W. Abbott, s/o Samuel and Sarah Abbott, d. 2 Oct 1849.

Wm. Abbott, s/o George and Ruth, d.30 Dec 1862, aged11 yrs.

Joseph B. Abbott, s/o George and Ruth, d. 30 Jan 1863.

Samuel Abbott, s/o Samuel and Martha, d. 15 Sep. 1885, aged 70 yrs, 6 mo.

George Abbott d. 27 Sep. 1888, aged 72 yrs.

Sarah W. Abbott 2 July 1893, aged 75 yrs.

Ruth S. (Baker) Abbott, widow of George Abbott, d. 18 Apr. 1916.

Caspar W. Acton Bible
American Bible Society 1865

Caspar W. Acton, s/o Benjamin and Sarah W. Acton was b. 18 Oct 1823.
Rachel N. Goodwin, d/o Thomas and Sarah Goodwin b. 12 Apr 1822.

Caspar W. Acton and Rachel Nicholson Goodwin mar. 6 Nov 1845.

Children of Caspar W. And Rachel N. Acton: Hannah H. Acton b. 24 Jul 1847; Letitia M. Acton b. 6 Nov 1848; Richard M. Acton b. 11 Dec 1850;

Thomas G. Acton b. 1 Jun 1852; Henry Acton b. 9 Jul 1853; George Acton b. 5 Feb 1856; Catherine W. Acton b. 9 Mar 1858; Wyatt Acton b. 6 Jan 1860; Morris G. Acton b. 23 Feb 1863.

Letitia M. Acton, d/o C. W. And Rachel N. Acton, d. 14 Aug 1849.
Thomas G. Acton, s/o C. W. And Rachel N. Acton, d. 7 Dec 1853, aged 18 mo, 1 dy.
Richard M. Acton, s/o Caspar W. and Rachel N. Acton, d. 12 May 1918, aged 67 yrs, 6 mo.
Caspar W. Acton d. 6 June 1899, at 20 past 8 in the evening, aged 76 yrs.
Rachel N. Acton d. 14 July 1899, at 12:30 midnight, aged 77 yrs.

Goodwin Records

John Goodwin, son of John and Catherine Goodwin of the Parish of St. Buttoeph in Aldgate, London, was b. the 25th of the 10th mo, 1680 and emigrated to Pennsylvania in 1701. The following year he moved to Salem, NJ and in 1715 he married Susannah Smith, the oldest daughter of John Smith of Smithfield, in London. Their children were John, Mary, Thomas and William. The two oldest died young. Their son Thomas, b. 1721, married Sarah Morris, daughter of Lewis Morris of Elsinborough, Salem County, NJ, in the year 1743. Sarah d. in 1765, leaving no children. Thomas's second wife was Sarah Smith, who lived but a few years after their marriage, and Thomas d. In 1803, aged 82 years, leaving his estate to his great nephews and nieces.

Their son William, b. 1723, married in 1744, Mary Morris, second daughter of Lewis Morris. Their children were John, Lewis, Susannah, Mary and William. Their son Lewis was b. the 9th of the 1st mo, 1794. His first wife was Rebecca James of Salem. They had two children John and Susan Goodwin. Lewis=s second wife was Rachel Nicholson, daughter of William Nicholson of Mannington. They had three children, William, Thomas and Morris Goodwin. Thomas Goodwin married Sarah Jeffries and they had three children: Edwin (Edward?), b. 19 Jun 1818 and d. 1 Oct 1822; Rachel Nicholson b. 12 Apr 1822 and d. 14 Jul 1899; Richard b. 7 Sep 1825 and d. 28 Jan 1832.

Clement Acton Bible
Colluis And Company, NY 1818

Clement Acton, s/o Benjamin and Susannah Acton, was b. the 12th of the 8th
mo, 1762.
Hannah Hall, d/o William and Hannah (Brinton) Hall was b. the 15th of the 6th
mo, 1765.

Clement Acton and Hannah Hall mar the 12th of the 12th mo, 1783.

Benjamin Acton, s/o Clement and Hannah Acton b. the 10th of the 12th mo,
1786.
Sarah Wyatt Miller, d/o Richard and Elizabeth W. Miller, b. 24 Sep. 1791(?).
Benjamin Acton and Sarah W. Miller mar the 5th of the 4th mo, 1809.
Children of Benjamin and Sarah W. Acton: Richard Miller Acton b. 4 Feb 1810;
Clement Acton b. 1 Jun 1813; Benjamin Acton, Jr, b. 18 Sep 1814, at 4:00
o'clock; Hannah Hall Acton b. 2 Oct 1816, at 10:00 a.m.; Elizabeth Wyatt
Acton b. 28 Oct 1818, a little before 10 p.m., Charlotte Acton b. 9 Jul 1821,
abt 3/4:00 p.m.; Caspar Acton b. 18 Jul 1823, abt 2:00 a.m. Letitia M.
Acton b. 17 Jul 1825, abt 3:00 a.m.; Sarah Wyatt Acton b. 3 Sep 1827,
between 7;00 and 8:00 p.m.; Catherine Acton b. 22 Jun 1829, between 1:00
and 2:00 a.m.

Richard Miller, s/o Josiah and Latitia Miller, was b. the 17th of the 1st mo,
____.
Elizabeth Wyatt Wistar, d/o Richard and Sarah (Wyatt) Wistar, was b. the 22nd
of the 12th mo, 1766.

Richard Miller and Elizabeth Wyatt Wistar mar the 10th of the 9th mo, 1788.

Hannah H. Acton and Samuel P. Carpenter mar 8 Nov 1837.

Hannah Acton d. the 9th of the 3rd mo, 1798.
Clement Acton, father of Benjamin Acton, d. in the 2nd mo, 1820, after hours of
indisposition and deep bodily suffering almost the whole time.
Richard Miller d. the 1st hour of the morning, on the 1st day of the 6th mo,
1803, at Jos. Burroughs' s.
Clement Acton, s/o Benjamin and Sarah W. Acton, d. 8 Nov 1813, after much
and long suffering.
R. M. Acton d. 17 Mar 1890.

Benjamin Acton d. Sep 1882.

Samuel and Sarah Acton Bible
J. Holbrook, Brattleborough, VT 1819

Clement Acton, s/o Samuel and Sarah Acton, b. the 11th of the 5th mo, 1797 and d. 9 Mar 1868.
Sarah Jones Acton, d/o Owen and Elizabeth Jones, b. 3 Sep 1811 and d. 5 May 1901.

Clement Acton and Sarah Jones mar 12 Mar 1835.
Children of Clement and Sarah J. Acton: Elizabeth Jones Acton b. 25 Jan 1838; Clement Acton, Jr, b. 24 May 1843 and d. 14 Feb 1874; Sarah Hall Acton b. 24 Aug 1869.

J. Bernard Williard, s/o Thomas T. and Hannah T. G. Williard, mar. 4 Nov. 1889.
Clement Acton, Jr, and Martha Ann Wills, mar 10 Oct 1866 at the home of Jacob and Rebecca Wills, Evesham.
Helen Acton and Samuel A. Tatnall mar. 15 June 1895.

Chambless Allen Bible
Bible Association of Friends in America
Philadelphia 1862

David Allen, s/o Jedediah and Mary Allen, b. the 12th of the 2nd mo, 1742 and d. the 17th of the 3rd mo, 1795, aged 53-1-5.
Rebecca Allen, w/o David Allen and d/o Samuel and Edith Thompson, b. the 10th mon, 1748, and d. 28 Jul 1809, in her 61st yr.
Jedediah Allen, s/o David and Rebecca Allen, b. 27th of the 8th mo, 1784 and d. 14 Jun 1850, aged nearly 66 yrs.
Samuel Austin, s/o Edward and Sarah Austin, b. the 22nd of the 11th mo, 1749 and d. in 1834, aged nearly 85 yrs.
Lydia Austin, d/o Peter and Elizabeth Ambler, b. The 27th of the 4th mo, 1760 and d. 24 Oct 1828, aged 68-5-7.
Sarah Austin, d/o Samuel and Lydia Austin, b. the 27th of the 4th mo, 1788 and d. 18 Nov 1824, aged 36-6-25.

Jedediah Allen and Sarah Austin mar 5 Jun 1811.

Hannah Foster Abbott, 2nd w/o Jedediah Allen and d/o Samuel (b. 1753, d. 1805) and Marcia (Gill) Abbott, b. the 4th of the 4th mo, 1796 and d. 25 Dec 1866, abt. 70 yrs.

Jedediah Allen and Hannah Abbott mar 7 Feb 1827.

Children of Jedediah and Sarah Allen: Samuel A. Allen b. 8 Aug 1812 and d. 12 Sep 1812; Samuel A. Allen b. 1 Jan 1814 and d. 8 Dec 1879; Richard Allen b. 2 Apr 1814 and d. Aug 1884; Rebecca Allen b. 8 Nov 1816 and d. 4 Sep 1900; Lydia A. Allen b. 20 Aug 1818; Jedediah Allen b. 1 Nov 1820 and d. Dec 1891; Chambless Allen b. 28 Feb 1823 and d. 15 Mar 1823.

Children of Jedediah and Hannah Allen: Hannah G. Allen b. 14 Nov 1827; Chambless Allen b. 2 Aug 1833.

Chamless Allen, s/o Jedediah T. and Hannah Allen, b. 2 Feb. 1833.
Mary W. Maskell, d/o John W. and Sarah Ann Maskell, b. 6 Feb. 1838.

Chambless Allen and Mary W. Maskell mar. 23 Apr. 1862.
Children of Chambless Allen and Mary his wife: Henry Thomas Allen b. 20 Feb 1863; Hannah Maskell Allen b. 29 Oct. 1864; John Maskell Allen b. 21 Apr 1866.

Hannah Allen, widow of Jedediah Allen, d. 25 Dec 1866 in her 71st yr.
John Maskell Allen d. 5 Mar 1891, aged 24.10.12.
Chambless Allen d. 17 June 1896, aged 62.20.15.
Mary Wood Maskell Allen d. 29 Jan 1913, aged 74.11.23.
Henry Thomas Allen d. 18 Oct 1915, aged 52 yrs.

Enoch Allen Bible
Isaac Collins, MDCCXCI

Enoch Allen, s/o Matthew and Martha Allen of Chester Twp, Burlington Co., NJ, b. The 4th of the 8th mo, 1750
Hannah Colluis, d/o Samuel and Rosanna Colluis of Waterford Twp, Gloucester Co, NJ, b. The 6th of the 1st mo, 1754.

Enoch Allen and Hannah Colluis mar the 1st of the 12th mo, 1774.

Children of Enoch and Hannah Allen: William Allen b. the 26th of the 11th mo, 1775; Martha Allen b. the 13th of the 4th mo, 1778; Hannah Allen b. the 11th of the 8th mo, 1780; Rosanna Allen b. the 20th of the 4th mo, 1783; Enoch Allen, Jr, b. the 3rd of the 5th mo, 1785; Rachel Allen b. the 4th of the 2nd mo, 1788; Priscilla Allen b. the 8th of the 12th mo, 1789.

Ann Haines, 2nd w/o Enoch Allen and dau of William and Elizabeth Haines, b. the 5th of the 6th mo, 1755.

William Allen d. 11 Nov 1819, aged 43-11-2-3.
Martha Hatton d. 12 Sep 1822, aged 44 yrs, 5 mo, lacking one day.
Hannah Moore d. 17 Jan 1808, aged 27 yrs, 11 mo.
Rosanna Coles d. 23 Mar 1862, aged 78 yrs, 11 mo.
Enoch Allen, Jr, d. 8 Apr 1831, aged 45-11-5.
Rachel Bacon d. 26 Oct 1813, aged 25-8-3-1.
Priscilla Allen d. 20 Aug 1833, aged 43-8-12.

Samuel Allen b. the 28th of the 7th mo, 1792.
Ann Allen b. the 4th of the 2nd mo, 1796.
Isaac Allen b. the 17th of the 2nd mo, 1802.
Ann Guarward d. 24 Apr 1859, aged 53-2-3-2.
Ann Allen, w/o Enoch Allen, d. 16 Nov 1832, aged 77-5-11.

Hannah Allen d. 4th of 9th mo, 1798, aged 44 yrs, 2 wks, 5 dys.
Enoch Allen d. 18th of 5th mo, 1834, aged 83.11.14.

Allen/Bacon Bible
Matthew Carey, Philadelphia, 1809

Benjamin Bacon, s/o Charles and Rebecca Bacon of Greenwich Twp, Cumberland Co, NJ, b. the 8th of the 11th mo, 1780.
Rachel Allen, d/o Enoch and Hannah Allen of Woolwich Twp, Gloucester Co, NJ, b. the 4th of the 2nd mo, 1788.

Benjamin Bacon and Rachel Allen mar 29 Apr 1804.

Children of Benjamin and Rachel Bacon: Charles Bacon b. 28 Apr 1808; Beulah Bacon b. 27 Feb 1810; Enoch Allen Bacon b. 12 Feb 1812.

Armstrong Bible
Samuel D. Burlock and Co., Philadelphia

Early Armstrong records found on loose leaves of paper in bible of John
Armstrong, b. 1832;

John Armstrong b. 7 Sep 1784 and d. 9 Jun 1860.
Mary Sifin (Siffin), w/o John Armstrong, b. 24 Dec 1786 and d. Sep 1851.
William Armstrong, s/o John and Mary Armstrong, b. 8 Oct 1808 and d. 19 Apr
1844.
William Smith. s/o _____ Smith, d. 18 Sep 1839, aged 73 yrs.

Records of William Armstrong:

John William Armstrong, s/o John and Mary Armstrong, b. 18 Oct 1808.
Phebe Ann Smith, d/o William and Elizabeth Smith, b. 1 Jan 1811.

William Armstrong and Phebe Ann Smith mar 9 Apr 1831.
Children of William and Phebe Ann Armstrong: John Sifin (Siffin) Armstrong
b. 26 Mar 1832; Eliza Armstrong b. 1 May 1834; Joseph Armstrong b. 18
Feb 1837; Thomas (Benson?) Armstrong b. 17 Aug 1842; Mary Armstrong
b. 11 Nov 1844.

William Armstrong d. 19 Apr. 1844.
Mary Armstrong d. 17 Mar 1846.
Mark Armstrong b. Jun 1815 and d. 12 Mar 1877.
Catherine Armstrong b. 26 Feb 1823 and d. 24 Mar 1855.
Phebe A. Armstrong d. 24 Aug. 1891,

Mary Siffin, w/o John Armstrong (b. 1784), was b. 24 Dec 1786 and d. Sep
1851. She was the d/o John Siffin who was a drummer in the Revolutionary
Army. He stood guard where Andre' the spy was executed. He mar Ruth
Dare and lived to a ripe old age, abt 75 yrs.
Both graves are well marked, back of the old Cohansey Baptist Church in
Roadstown.
John S. Armstrong and Eliza Nelson mar. 6 May 1857.
Their children: Elizabeth Hitchner b. 3 Mar. 1861; Phebe Smith b. 3 June 1871.
Lewis Nelson b. 27 May 1876.

John Siffin Armstrong, s/o William and Phebe Smith Armstrong, b. 26 Mar.
1832.

Eliza Nelson, d/o Dr. Jonathan and Elizabeth Nelson, b. Jan. 1840.
Eliza Nelson Armstrong d. 27 Apr. 1884.
John Siffin Armstrong d. 26 June 1912.

William Henry, s/o Sheppard and Sallie Harris, b. 10 Feb. 1870.
Phebe Smith, d/o John and Elizabeth Armstrong, b. 3 June 1871.

William H. Harris and Phebe S. Armstrong mar. 14 Jan. 1889.

Archer Bible
M. Carey, Philadelphia 1814

Thomas Thompson was b. 19 Dec 1744.
Rebecca Hedge, w/o Thomas Thompson b. 21 Mar 1751.

Thomas Thompson and Rebecca Hedge mar 30 May 1770 and lived together in
wedlock 56 yrs and 13 dys.

Children of Jacob and Mary Archer: Jacob Archer b. 14 Jun 1762 and bapt 11
Jul 17762; John Archer b. (no date) and d. of smallpox, unmarried; William
Archer b. 19 Apr 1766 and bapt 25 May 1766; Sarah Archer b. 2 Mar 1769
and bapt. 12 Mar 1769. Died w/o children; Mary Archer b. abt 1769 and d.
w/o children; Benjamin Archer b. 25 Sep 1775 and bapt 27 Oct 1775.

Sarah Lowderback, 1st w/o Benjamin Archer, d. 1 May 1800, aged 23-2-24.
Harriett Archer, d/o Benjamin and Sarah Archer was b. and d. with her mother.

Rachel Thompson, 2nd w/o Benjamin Archer and d/o Thomas and Rebecca
Thompson, b. 3 May 1790.
Dr. Benjamin Archer and Rachel Thompson mar Monday, 31 May 1813.
Fenwick Hedge Archer, s/o Benjamin and Rachel Archer, b. 7 Dec 1817.

Thomas Thompson d. 12 Jun 1826, aged 81-5-23.
Rebecca Thompson, formerly Rebecca Hedge, w/o Thomas Thompson, d. 22
Oct 1831, aged 80 yrs, 7 mo.
William Archer was bur on the Sunday before 14 Mar 1807.

Benjamin Archer d. Monday evening, 15 Dec 1845, abt 7:00 p m, and was bur
on Thurs afternoon. His disease was palsy of the right side. The funeral met
at the house at 2:00 p.m. Rev. William B. Otis read the service in St. John's

Church yard. The body was placed on the new marble shelf on the west side of the family vault by George Bowen, undertaker, the coffin being enclosed in a walnut case.

Rachel T. Archer d. at 2:00 p.m. on Fri., 30 Apr 1869, and was bur on Thur., May 4, within 3 dys of 79 yrs of age. Services at the house by Rev. William A. Holbrook and Rev. James W. Bradere at 11:00 a.m.

Fenwick Hedge Archer, s/o Benjamin and Rachel T. Archer, d. Fri. evening, 29 July, 1881, abt. 9:00 o'clock. in his 65th yr. His remains were placed in the family vault, back of St. John's Church, Salem, N. J., on Tues., 2 Aug., at 11:00 a.m. Services at the house by Rev. Benj. Bradin of Millville, N. J.

Samuel Austin Bible
M. Carey, Philadelphia 1813

In the list of marriage performed by John Ladd of Gloucester, NJ, is the following: 1748, Edward Austin, blockmaker, of Philadelphia, and Sarah Wetherby, spinster, Salem County, NJ, married, accompanied by a letter dated 6 May 1748 and signed by Edmund Wetherby, father of Sarah, giving his consent.

Samuel Austin and Lydia Ambler mar the 5th day of the 10th mo, 1785.
Samuel Austin, s/o Samuel Austin, and Lydia Ann Lloyd mar the 29th of the 3rd mo, 1815.
William Austin, s/o Samuel Austin, Jr, and Mary Ann Watson mar 23 Feb 1839.
William Austin, s/o Samuel Austin, Jr, and Mary Ann Webber mar 25 Oct 1845.

Sarah Ellett, d/o Edmund and Martha Wetherby, b. the 6th day of the 6th month, 1729.
Edmund Wetherby, s/o Edmund and Martha Wetherby, b. the 6th day of the 10th mo, 1733.
Samuel Austin, s/o Edward and Sarah (Wetherby) Austin b. the 22nd day of the 11th mo, 1749 and d. the 5th day of the 9th mo, 1834.
Lydia Austin, d/o Peter and Elizabeth Ambler b. the 27th day of the 4th mo, 1760.

Children of Samuel and Lydia Austin: Sarah Austin b. the 10th day of the 7th mo, 1786; Sarah Austin b. the 27th day of the 4th mo, 1788; Hannah Austin

b. the 24th day of the 4th mo, 1791; Samuel Austin b. the 6th day of the 11th mo, 1793.

Children of Samuel Austin, Jr, and Ann his wife: William Austin b. 11 Sep 1815; Lydia Austin b. 25 Oct 1818.

Children of William Austin and Mary Ann (Watson) his wife: Sarah Ambler Austin b. 21 Mar 1840; Samuel Austin b. 28 Aug 1841; Lydia Austin b. 14 Aug 1843.

Children of William Austin and Mary Ann (Webber) his wife: Henry W. Austin b. 19 Aug 1846; Rebecca Austin b. 18 Mar 1849; Ann Lloyd Austin b. 23 July 1851; William Austin b. 19 Aug 1854 and d. in infancy; William W. Austin b. 18 Apr 1856 and d. in infancy; Mary Augusta Austin b. 19 Jul 1857; Edward Austin b. 26 Aug 1860; John W. Austin b. 2 May 1863; Margaret W. Austin b. 29 Mar 1866.

Sarah Ellet, formerly Austin and d/o Edmund Wetherby, d. the 25th day of the 9th mo, 1767, aged 38-3-7.

Elizabeth Ellet, d/o Charles Ellet and Sarah his wife (formerly the widow of Edward Austin) d. (no date).

Edmund Wetherby d. the 4th day of the 11th mo, 1766.

Sarah Austin d. the 28th of the 10th mo, 1786, aged 3 mo, 2 wks, 4 dys.

Hannah Austin, d/o Samuel and Lydia, d. the 17th of the 7th mo, 1791, aged 2 mo, 3 wks.

Samuel Austin, s/o Samuel and Lydia Austin, d. 17 Sep 1819, aged 25-10-6.

Rebecca Watson, widow of Samuel Watson and mother of Mary Ann Austin, d. 8 Sep 1852. She was the d/o James and Ruth Trueland. James Trueland was a school teacher from Ireland.

John Lloyd, s/o William and Ann Lewis Lloyd of Shrewsbury and Philadelphia, d. 29 Jan. 1860, aged 51 yrs, at the home of his nephew, William Austin.

Ann Johnson, formerly widow of Samuel Austin, Jr., and d/o John and Patience Borden Lloyd, d. 3 Feb. 1870.

William Austin, s/o Samuel Austin and Ann Lloyd, his wife, d. 13 June 1890, aged 74 yrs.

Edward Austin, s/o William and Mary Ann Weber Austin, b. 26 Aug. 1860 and d. 18 Mar. 1910.

Mary Ann Weber Austin, widow of William Austin, d. 26 Sep. 1911.

John W. Austin, s/o William and Mary Ann Weber Austin, b. 2 May, 1863 and d. 4 Mar. 1910.

Ayars Family Bible
Esther D. Ayers - Her Book, 7 Feb. 1835
Elmer Ayers - His Book, 1845
Clemmans P. Ayers - Her Book, 1845

Robeson Ayars b. 5 Sep 1783.
Esther D. Ayars b. 7 May 1786.
Clemmans P. Ayars, d/o Robeson and Esther Ayars, b. 2 Dec 1821.
Elmer Ayars, s/o Ezekiel J. and Margaret Ayars, b. 6 Aug 1821.
A son of Elmer and Clemmans P. Ayars b. 31 Mar 1844.
Elmina Ayars, d/o Elmer and Clemmans Ayars, b. 15 Dec 1845.
Joseph Ayars, s/o Edmund and Lydia, b. 3 Aug. 1856.

Robeson and Esther D. Ayars mar 20 Apr 1820.
Elmer and Clemmans P. Ayars mar 13 Apr 1843.

Robeson Ayars d. 24 Jul 1825.
Son of Elmer and Clemmans P. Ayars d. 5 Jul 1844.
Esther D. Ayars, widow of Robeson Ayars, d. 16 Oct 1844.
Elmer Ayers d. 23 Apr. 1851.
Clemmans P. Ayers d. 1 July 1854.
Lydia D. Ayers d. 7 Feb. 1858.
Rebecca J. Ayers d. 11 Dec. 1854.

Beckett Bible
M. Carey and I. Lea, Philadelphia 1822

Peter Beckett, s/o Josiah and Ann Beckett, b. 29 Sep 1791.
Ann McDermit, d/o Cornelius and Elvira McDermit, b. 20 Jan 1790.

Peter Beckett and Ann McDermit mar 1 Sep 1813.

Children of Peter and Ann Beckett: Martha Beckett b. 21 May 1815; Charles
    Beckett b. 29 Jul 1820; Franklin Beckett b. 11 Dec 1822; David Beckett b.
    14 Sep 1827.

Charles W. Beckett d. 20 Aug 1820, aged 3 yrs, 6 dys.
Ann, w/o Peter Beckett, d. 4 Sep 1860, aged 70-7-16.
Peter Beckett d. 4 May 1874, aged 82-7-5.
David Beckett d. 13 Jan. 1888,,aged 60 yrs., 4 mo.

Martha Denelsbeck d. 11 Oct. 1900. aged 85 yrs., 5 mo.
Frederick S. Denelsbeck d. 20 Jan 1845, aged 32-8-2.

Frederick S. Denelsbeck, s/o Frederick and Mary Denelsbeck, b. 18 May 1812.

Frederick Denelsbeck and Martha Beckett, d/o Peter and Ann Beckett, mar 29
    Sep 1838.
Lydia, their dau, was b. 2 Nov 1839.
Hannah More, their dau was b. 4 Sep 1841.

Bilderback Bible
M. Carey, Philadelphia 1832

Jonathan Bilderback b. 1 Mar 1776.
Temperance, w/o Jonathan Bilderback b. 20 Aug 1783.

Children of Jonathan and Temperance Bilderback: Alpheus Bilderback b. 18
    Dec 1805; Lucy Ann Bilderback b. 22 Oct 1807; Mary Jane Bilderback b.
    10 Dec 1809; Sarah Bilderback b. 23 Oct 1811; Joseph Bilderback b. 10
    Feb 1814; Martha Bilderback b. 25 May 1816; Edward Bilderback b. 25
    May 1816.

Clement H. Bilderback, s/o Joseph and Margarett M Bilderback, b. 27 Dec.
    1809(?)
Joseph M. Bilderback, s/o Joseph and Margarett M Bilderback, b. 26 Sep. 1861.
Rachel C. Thomas b. 3 Sep 1836.

Jonathan Bilderback d. 8 Sep 1839.
Temperance Bilderback d. 24 Feb 1858.
Hope Cheesman d. 1 Aug. 1858.
Clement H. Bilderback d. 24 Aug. 1860.
Joseph Bilderback, s/o Joseph and Margarett M Bilderback d. 20 Oct 1861.
Sarah Hall, w/o Clement Bilderback, d. 25 Apr. 1868.

Bowen Bible

Family record found on an old leaf out of the book, now worn and rotten:

Children of Nehemiah and Mary Bowen: Elizabeth Bowen b. 4 Aug 1778; William Bowen b. 22 Jul 1784; Charles Bowen b. 31 Jul 1787; Hannah Bowen b. 28 Jan 1781; Abigail Bowen b. 5 Jul 1793; Polly Bowen b. 26 Sep 1795; Gracey Bowen b. 12 Jan 1801.

Children of William and Susannah Bowen: Elijah Bowen b. 10 Jan 1812; William Bowen b. 2 Apr 1814; Nancy Bowen b. 19 Apr 1816; Gracey Bowen b. 10 Aug 1818.

Burt Family Bible
George Eyre and Andrew Straham, London 1804

Many of the records are so faded as to be illegible.

Joseph Burt was b. at Wilton(?) 16 Mar 1750, s/o Joseph and Ann, maiden name Bisbough(?).
Elizabeth Axton b. Wilton Wilks(?) 12 Dec 1777, d/o Jonathan and Amea Axton, maiden name Weason.

Joseph Burt and Elizabeth Axton mar 15 Sep 1798 at St. Thomas Church, Salisbury.

Elizabeth Burt b. 20 Feb 1805, at Wilton.
John Burt b. 23 Aug 1802, at Wilton.
William Burt b. 20 Feb 1805, at Wilton.
Mary Ann Burt b. 21 Mar 1807.
Martha Burt b. 9 Mar 1809.
Henry Burt b. 5 Apr 1811.
Joseph Burt b. 1 Apr 1814, at Elkton.

John Burt mar 16 Mar 1825.
William Burt mar 14 May 182_.
Mary Ann Burt mar 1 Apr 1827.
Martha Burt mar. 17 Feb 1825.

Jonathan Butcher's Bible

Adrian Watkins, His Majesty's Printer
Edinburgh, Scotland 1756

Jonathan Butcher b. 28 Dec 1762.
Elizabeth Butcher b. 19 Dec 1764.
Thomas Butcher b. 10 Apr 1769.
Aaron Butcher b. 30 Oct 1780.
James Butcher b. 7 Mar 1783.
Phebe Butcher b. 11 Mar 1785.

Jonathan Butcher, s/o Aaron and Mary Butcher, b. 28 Dec 1762.
Rachel Butcher, w/o Jonathan Butcher and d/o James and Elizabeth Stretch, b. 4 Mar 1768.

Children of Jonathan and Rachel Butcher: Hannah Butcher b. 10 Apr 1789; John Butcher b. 9 May 1791; Ruth Butcher b. 9 Sep 1792; Jonathan Butcher b. 20 Jun 1793.

Sarahann Butcher, d/o Jonathan and Prudence Butcher, b. 12 Feb 1802.
Jervis Butcher, s/o Jonathan and Prudence Butcher, b. 29 Jul 1804.
Jonathan Butcher, s/o Jonathan and Ann Butcher, b. 29 Jan 1809.
Jonathan Butcher, s/o Jervis and Rachel Butcher, b. 15 Sep 1827.

Aaron Butcher d. 19 Feb 1786.
Rachel Butcher d. 2 Aug 1895, in her 28th yr.
Jonathan Butcher, s/o Jonathan and Rachel Butcher, d. 12 Sep 1795.
Hannah Butcher, d/o Jonathan and Rachel Butcher, d. 3 Jun 1700, aged 10 yrs, 2 mo.

Jonathan Butcher d. 10 Dec. 1816.

James Butcher's Bible
Kimber and Sharpless, Philadelphia 1824

James Butcher b. 7 Mar 1783.
Hannah Sayre b. 21 Jul 1781.

James Butcher and Hannah Sayre mar 17 Apr 1806.

Children of James and Hannah Butcher: Elizabeth Butcher b. 16 Jul 1807; Job
E. Butcher b. 18 Nov 1809; Ann Butcher b. 9 Jan 1812; Hannah Butcher b.
7 May 1813; James Butcher b. 10 Dec 1816; Robert Butcher b. 20 Dec
1819; Lydia Ann Butcher b. 20 Mar 1823.

James Butcher and Mary B. Shimp mar 26 Apr 1848.

Mary Butcher, d/o James and Mary Butcher, b. 13 Apr 1849.

James Butcher, Jr, and Barbara Carlle mar 25 Feb 1841.
Robert Butcher and Mary Ann Patrick mar 14 Apr 1842.
John Lambert and Elizabeth Butcher mar 25 Mar 1826.
John Linzey and Hannah Butcher mar 7 Apr 1832.

Ann Butcher d. 11 Sep 1812.
Job E. Butcher d. 12 Sep 1813.
James Butcher, Jr, d. 14 May 1845, aged 28-5-4.
Hannah Butcher d. 25 Dec 1843, aged 62-5-5.
James Butcher d. 24 Jan 1851, aged 67-10-7.
John Lambert d. 31 Aug. 1867, aged 68 yrs.
Robert Butcher d. 28 July 1881, aged 28-5-4.
Elizabeth Lambert d. 20 Apr. 1880, aged 73 yrs.
Mary Ann Butcher d. 25 Mar. 1864, aged 39 yrs.

Francis and Lydia Borden's Bible

Francis Borden b. the 24th day of the 12th mo, 1709/10.
Lydia Borden b. the 11th day of the 11th mo, 1713/14.
Francis Borden and Lydia Wooley were mar 3/4 Mar 1732.

Carll Bible
D. Hitt and T. Ware, New York 1815

Ephriam Carll, s/o Ephriam and Rebecca Carll, b. 30 Aug 1798.
Elizabeth Finlaw, d/o John and Rebecca Finlaw, b. 6 Sep 1799.

Ephriam Carll and Elizabeth Finlaw mar 24 Dec 1817.

Children of Ephriam and Elizabeth Carll: Rebecca F. Carll b. 8 Apr 1819; Barbara Carll b. 22 Apr 1821; Elizabeth Carll b. 4 Sep 1824.

Ephriam Carll and Mary Ann Smith mar 15 Dec 1825.

Children of Ephriam and Mary Ann Carll: Mary Carll b. 21 Aug 1826; Ephriam Smith Carll b. 23 Jan 1828; Jefse Patrick Carll b. 17 Nov 1829; Lewis S. Carll b. 20 Oct 1831; Washington Smith Carll b. 16 Aug 1834; George Grier Carll b. 28 Sep 1835; Rosanna Carll b. 23 May 1838; William Henry Harrison Carll b. 30 Mar 1840; Charles M. Carll b. 4 Jul 1842.

Edward S. Carll and Mary E. Sayre mar. 6 Jan. 1858 by the Rev. Charles Cox.

Elizabeth Carll, w/o Ephriam Carll, d. 19 Oct 1824, aged 25-1-13.
Mary Carll d. 5 Oct 1827, aged 13 mo, 13 dys.
Washington S. Carll d. 9 Sep 1834, aged 1 mo.
Rosanna D. Carll d. 11 Jul 1854, aged 16-1-18.

Mary Ann Carll, w/o Ephraim Carll, d. 27 Aug. 1869, aged 65-8-24.
Ephrain Carll, h/o Mary Ann Carll, d. 30 Sep. (no year).

Casper/Wentzell Bible
M. Carey and Son, Philadelphia 1818

John Casper and Hannah Wentzell mar 22 Jun 1799.
John Casper and Sarah Bilderback mar 8 Nov 1829.
Charles W. Casper and Lavinia D. Prior mar. 20 Jan. 1862 at Salem, N. J. by Rev. Daniel Stratton.

Thomas Casper b. 12 Jul 1802.
Hannah Wentzell b. 16 Mar 1776.
Jacob Wentzell b. 17 Sep 1778.
Mary Wentzell b. 11 Sep 1783.
John Wentzell b. 6 Nov 1786.
Charles Wentzell b. 5 Oct 1790.
Catherine Wentzell b. 1 Apr 1793.
Lewis Wentzell b. 24 Apr 1808.

Children of Charles W. and Lavinia Casper: Frank Prior b. 4 Dec. 1862; Charles Preston b. 12 Feb. 1868; Joseph b. 17 Jan. 1880.

Catherine Wentzell d. 4 Sep 1812.

Charles Wentzell d. 15 Jun 1819.

Hannah Wentzell Casper d. 24 Dec 1823.

John Casper d. 9 Jan. 1852.

Thomas J. Casper. s/o John and Hannah Wentzell Casper, d. 9 June 1868, aged 66 yrs.

Anderson/Casper Bibles

William Anderson b. 10 Mar 1768.

Mary Elwell, w/o William Anderson, b. 31 Jan 1776.

Mary Ann Anderson, d/o William and Mary Anderson, b. 19 Apr 1808.

William Anderson, s/o William and Mary Anderson, b. 30 Sep 1810.

Thomas J. Casper, s/o John and Hannah Casper, b. 12 Jul 1802.

Mary Ann Casper, w/o Joseph (?) J. Casper, d. 8 Aug. 1887, in her 80th yr.

Thomas J. Casper d. 9 Jan. 1868, in his 66th yr.

In Philadelphia, PA, on 1 Jan. 1862, Joseph Casper and Lizzie R. Gillingham mar. by Rev. George Leeds.

Mary Ann Anderson and Thomas J. Casper mar 19 Jan 1828 by Rev. George W. Janvier, in the Presbyterian Church in Pittsgrove, Salem, NJ.

In Salem, N. J., on 27 Feb. 1851, William A. Casper and Elizabeth Stretch mar. by Edward Vanmeter.

In Salem, N. J., on 4 May 1853, John Casper and Keziah H. Belden mar. by Rev. Daniel Stratton.

In Salem, N. J., on 20 Jan. 1862, Charles W. Casper and Lavinia D. Prior mar. by the Rev. Daniel Stratton.

In Philadelphia, PA, on 8 Dec. 1863, Thomas J. Casper and Emma V. Fry mar. by the Rev. J. Hyatt Smith.

In Salem, N. J., on 6 Feb. 1867, S. Clement Casper and Anna Belden Habermeyer mar. by Rev. John R. Murphy.

In Salem, N. J., on 15 Mar. 1876, James Lindzey and Hannah W. Casper mar. by the Rev. Dr. Bannard.

Children of Thomas J. Casper and Mary his wife: Annie Lurene Casper b. 7 Nov 1848; Hannah W. Casper b. 4 May 1840; Mary Ann Casper b. 28 Jan 1846; E. Davis Casper b. 4 Nov 1851.

William A. Casper b. 30 Sep 1828.

John Casper b. 24 Aug 1830.

Joseph Casper b. 20 Jul 1832.

Charles Casper b. 14 Nov 1835.

Thomas J. Casper, Jr, b. 7 Jan 1838.

Samuel Clement Casper b. 12 Dec 1842.

William Anderson d. 21 Sep 1821.

Margaret Stiles, mother of Mary Anderson, d. 18 Sep 1821. Stiles was the name of her 2nd husband.

William Anderson, s/o William and Mary Anderson, d. 11 Aug. 1855.

Mary Anderson d. 5 June 1831.

William Penn Chatten Bible
American Bible Society, New York 1848

James Chatten, s/o Nixon and Hannah Chatten, b. the 4th day of the 8th mo, 1755.

Rebecca Chattin, d/o Joseph and Rachel Nicholson, b. the 17th day of the 8th mo, 1760.

Children of James and Rebecca Chattin: John Chattin b. the 11th of the 10th mo, 1778; Bernice Chattin b. the 4th day of the 3rd mo, 1781, and mar James Alluison; Rachel Chattin b. the 7 day of the 9th mo, 1782, and mar Mark Baner; Hannah Chattin b. the 7th day of the 3rd mo, 1784, and mar Jacob Ritter; Rebecca Chattin b. the 1st day of the 4th mo, 1786 and d. the 30th day of the 5th mo, 1791; Anne Chattin b. the 3rd day of the 8th mo, 1789, and mar Joseph Lippincott; Elizabeth Chattin b. the 4th day of the 4th mo, 1792; James Chattin b. the 4th day of the 2nd mo, 1794, and mar Hannah Zane; Daniel Jones Chattin b. the 28th day of the 12th mo, 1796 and d. the 5th mo, 1798; Rebecca Chattin b. the 29th day of the 12th mo, 1803, and mar Waddington Bradway.

Children of James and Hannah Chattin: James Allinson Chattin b. (no date); Rebecca Ann Chattin b. the 23 Mar 1818; Sarah Maria Chattin b. the 3 Jul 1820; William Penn Chattin b. the 22 Jul 1822; Georgianna Chattin b. (no date); Montezuma Chattin b. (no date).

Children of Samuel and Sarah M. Wetherill: John Price Wetherill b. (no date); Samuel R. Wetherill b. (no date); Georgianna C. Wetherill b. (no date); Sarah M. Wetherill b. (no date); William Chatton Wetherill b. the 22 Feb 1852; Maria K. L. Wetherill b. (no date); Rachel Elizabeth Wetherill b. (no date).

Children of William P. and Arabella S. Chattin: Hannah Maria Chattin b. the 8th
day of the 1st mo, 1849, and mar Augustus Barber; William James Chattin
b. 17 Sep 1851 and d. 19 Aug 1855.

Children of A. S. and H. M. Barber: Wm. Chattin Barber b. 22 Sep. 1876 and d.
18 Feb. 1878; John Barber b. 22 Apr. 1878.

Jessey Chew, s/o Jessey and Mary Chew, b. 12 Nov 1773 and d. 8 Mar 1813.
Joseph R. Chew, s/o Jesse and Keziah Chew, b. 23 Apr 1800.
Maria, w/o Joseph R. Chew and d/o Andrew and Margaret Sinnickson, b. 14 Oct
1801.
Children of Joseph R. and Maria Chew: Arabella S. Chew b. 20 Jul 1823;
Charles H. Chew b. 17 Aug 1825; Henrietta Chew b. 8 Oct 1827;
Sinnickson Chew b. 27 Jan 1830; Edward Chew b. 17 May 1832; Joseph K.
Chew b. 8 Feb 1837; Keziah Chew b. 27 Sep 1839; Mary A. Chew b. 8 Dec
1840.

James Chattin d. 26 May 1816.
Rebecca Chattin d. 6 Jan 1804.
James Chattin, s/o James and Rebecca, d. 1839/40.
Hannah Chattin b. 1834/35.

Children of Job and Elizabeth Kinsey: Hannah Kinsey b. 21 Mar 1765 and d. 16
Oct 1768; Amanda Kinsey b. 9 Oct 1769 and d. 23 Jul 1775; Joseph Kinsey
b. 2 Apr 1771; Keziah Kinsey b. 3 Aug 1773 and d. 11 Dec 1826.;
Hephzebuh Kinsey b. 2 Jun 1776.

Andrew Sinnickson, father of Maria Sinnickson, w/o Joseph R. Chew, was
paymaster for Salem, Cape May and Cumberland Counties during the
Revolutionary War.

Job Dennis Bible

Ralph Allen, s/o David and Sarah Allen, b. 29 Jul 1785.
Margaret Hitchner, d/o Andrew and Sarah Hitchner, b. 1 Jun 1794.

Ralph Allen and Margaret Kitchner mar 5 Mar 1813 by Joseph Morris of Salem
Co., NJ.

Children of Ralph and Margaret Allen: Sarah Allen b. 14 Oct 1816; William Allen b. 7 Feb 1819; Benjamin Allen b. 23 Jul 1821.

Ralph Allen d. 26 Sep 1835, aged 49 yrs and 3 mo.
John Allen, s/o Ralph and Margaret Allen, d. at Baltimore on Tues, 7 Jul 1857, aged 35-11-14.

J. Fithian Smith and M. Lizzie Denn mar. 20 Feb. 1866, in Salem County, by J. R. Murphy.
Sally J. D. Smith b. 2 May 1867.

Dick Family Bible
Isaac Collins, Trenton, N. J. MDCCXCI

Samuel Dick and Sarah Sinnickson, the d/o Andrew Sinnickson of Penn's Neck, mar by the Rev. Nicholas Collin 20 Oct 1773. Dr. Samuel Dick was Col., 1st Batt., Salem Co., Militia, 20 Jun 1776. He was also a member of the General Assembly of NJ.

Children of Samuel and Sarah Dick: Rebecca Dick b. 17th day (no mo or yr given) and d. the 19th day of the 10th mo, (no yr given); Mary Dick b. 4 Sep 1775 and d. 17 Nov 1821; John Dick b. 14 Nov 1779 and d. 26 Jan 1780; Samuel Dick, Jr, b. 27 Jan 1780 and d. 7 Jun 1781; Andrew Dick b. Feb 1782 and d. 11th of same mo; Isabella Dick b. 15 Feb 1783 and d. Feb 1861; Anna Dick b. 27 Dec 1787 and d. 1861?; Samuel Stewart Dick b. 22 Nov 1790; William Dick b. 17 Oct 1793; Maria Dick b. 24 Dec. 1806 and d. 21 Apr. 1872.

Dr. Samuel Dick d. 16 Nov 1812, aged 72 yrs.

Mary Dick Bible

John Dick b. 1758.
Mary Dick b. 1756.
Jane Dick b. Nov 1778.
Alexandria Dick b. 6 Apr 1779
Eliza Dick d. (?)
Allen Dick b. 27 Dec 1783.
David Dick d. (no date given).

John and Thomas b. 22 Nov 1795
Mary and John b. 8 Aug 1792.
William A. Dick b. 4 Apr 1798.

William Allen Dick, s/o John Dick and Mary Read, b. in Edinburgh, Scotland, 1797.

William A. Dick and Mary Curry mar. 25 Mar. 1819 and said wife, Mary, d. 16 May 1820 leaving issue, a daughter.
Mary Curry Dick, d/o William A. and Mary Dick, b. 16 May 1820.

Sarah Redstreake, d/o William A. and Sarah S. Dick, b. 12 Nov. 1836.

William A. Dick and Sarah S. Redstreake mar. 5 Jan. 1822.
Their children: John R. Dick b. 7 June 1832; William A. Dick, Jr., b. 20 Oct. (no year) and lived only 4 days.

William A. Dick and Mary E. Smalley mar. 17 Oct. 1844.
Their children: Anna S. Dick b. 9 Sep. 1864; Hannah J. Dick b. 14 Feb. 1850.

Andrew Thompson and Mary Curry Dick, d/o William A. and Mary Curry Dick, mar. 9 Nov. 1837.
John Redstreake Dick, s/o William A. and Sarah S. Dick, mar. Mary C. Brown, 22 Aug. 1853.
Sarah Redstreake Dick, d/o William A. and Sarah S. Dick, mar. Jacob Raymond Allen (no date).

Children of John R. and Mary C. Dick: William Allen Dick b. 11 Jan. 1855; George Henry Dick b. 10 June 1857; John Carpenter Dick b. 26 Feb. 1859 and d. unmarried; Walter J. Dick b. 10 Oct. 1861; Allen W. Dick b. 10 Aug. 1853; Harvey Brown Dick b. 9 Apr. 1866; Milton Archer Dick b. 23 Feb. 1869; Lewis D. Dick b. 20 Sep. 1861 and d. in his teens.
Sarah Jane, d/o Andrew and Mary Thompson , b. 26 June 1836(?).
William Allen Dick, s/o John R. and Mary C. Dick, b. 11 Jan. 1855 and d. unmarried.

Sarah S. Dick, w/o William A. Dick, d. 8 Dec. 1843, aged 48 yrs. and 5 mo.
John Dick d. 4 Sep. 1862, aged 70 yrs.
William Allen Dick d. 3 Nov. 1868, aged 71-6-27.
Mary E. Dick, w/o William A. Dick, d. 17 Nov. 1909 in Salem, N. J., aged 91 yrs.

Dubois Bible
Printed in Dutch, 1706

Barnett Dubois b. 3 May 1693.
Jacomimte Dubois b. 30 Oct 1693.
Catherine Dubois b. 10 Sep 1716.
Jacob Dubois b. 9 Feb 1719.
Solomon Dubois b. 6 Sep 1721.
David Dubois b. 28 Nov 1724.
Jonathan Dubois b. 3 Dec 1727.
Isaac Dubois b. 2 Jan 1731.
Garrett Dubois b. 16 Apr 1734.
Abraham Dubois b. 16 Nov 1738.

Dubois Bible
Thomas and George Palmer for Matthew Carey
Philadelphia 1803

Solomon Dubois b. 10 Oct 1765.
Rhoda Weatherington b. 11 Dec 1767.

Garrett Dubois b. 14 May 1801.
Amaziah Dubois b. 14 Aug 1802.
Garrett Dubois, the 2nd, b. 30 Oct 1804.
Lurany Ogden Dubois b. 25 Jun 1807.
Sarah Anne Dubois b. 7 Apr 1809.

Jeremiah Dubois b. 10 Sep 1760 and d. 10 Oct 1824. Served in Capt Newkirk's
    Co., 2nd Batt., Salem Co Militia, Rev. War.

Solomon Dubois and Rhoda Weatherington mar 13 Nov 1798.
Garrett Dubois and Elizabeth Richman mar 27 Dec 1827.

Garrett Dubois b. 30 Oct 1804.
Elizabeth Richman b. 21 Dec 1806.
Eliza Dubois b. 3 Jul 1829.
Henry R. Dubois b. 2 Jun 1831.
Rhoda Dubois b. 8 Oct 1833.
Jeremiah Dubois b. 25 Jun 1836.
Lovicy B. Dubois b. 21 Mar 1840.

Sarah Richman Dubois b. 17 Aug 1843.

Lurany Ogden Dubois d. 19 May 1818.
Rhoda Dubois d. 7 Jun 1818.
Sarah Ann Dubois d. 11 Sep 1821.
Amaziah Dubois d. 16 Aug 1823.
Solomon Dubois d. 9 Feb 1839.
Garrett Dubois d. 8 Jan. 1876.
Elizabeth Dubois d. 13 June 1884.

Rhoda Weatherington b. 11 Dec 1767.
Jonathan Weatherington b. 5 Aug 1769.
Susanah Weatherington b. 10 Jul 1773.
Lydia Weatherington b. 8 Mar 1775.
Amaziah Weatherington b. 8 Mar 1778.
Anne Weatherington b. 4 Apr 1780.
Elizabeth Weatherington b. 12 Jul 1783.

Royal-Dunn Bible
Matthew Carey, Philadelphia 1805

Ebenezer Dunn, s/o John and Catherine Dunn, b. Wednesday, 7 Apr 1753.

Ebenezer Dunn and Abigail Copnew mar 11 Jun 1772.
Ebenezer Dunn and Mary Pedrick mar 26 Jul 1781.
William Royal and Sarah Dunn mar. in 1801 by William Biddle.

Children of Ebenezer and Mary Dunn: Thackara Dunn (son) b. 23 Apr 1782;
    Sarah Dunn b. 23 Jun 1784; Samuel Dunn b. Sunday, 17 Dec 1786; Elijah
    Dunn b. Friday, 3 Jul 1789; Mary Dunn b. Thursday 23 Feb 1792.

Peter Royal, s/o Henry and Susanna Royal, b. 23 Aug 1763.
Sarah Dunn, d/o Samuel and Gutieline Dunn, b. 21 Mar 1809.
Mary Dunn, d/o Samuel and Mary Dunn, b. 7 Aug 1818.

Children of Henry and Susannah Royal: Catherine Royal b. 5 Oct 1765; Mark
    Royal b. 5 Jul 1767; Henry Royal b. 13 Mar 1770; William Royal b. 21
    Nov 1776.

Peter Royal, s/o Henry and Susanna, d. (no date).

Catherine Royal, d/o Henry and his wife, d. (no date).

Henry Royal, s/o Henry and his wife, d. (no date).

Mark Royal, son of Henry and his wife, d. (no date).

William Royal, s/o Pater and Catherine Royal, d. 6 Sep 1841.

Sarah Royal, d/o Ebenezer and Mary Dunn, and w/o William Royal, d. Aug (no date).

Abigail Dunn, w/o Ebenezer Dunn, d. 5 Mar 1780.

Thackara Dunn, s/o Ebenezer Dunn and his wife, d. 16 Dec 1792.

Ebenezer Dunn, Sr, d. 2 Jul 1812.

Mary Dunn, w/o Ebenezer Dunn, d. 15 Nov 1814.

Elkinton-Thompson Bible
E. White, New York & Philadelphia 1824

John Elkinton, s/o George (1727-1809) and Sarah Elkinton b. the 9th day of the 9th mo, 1767.

Rhoda Sayre, d/o Annanias and Hannah Sayre, b. (no date).

Joel Clark, s/o Cornelius and Elizabeth Clark, b. the 25th day of the 10th mo, 1761.

Anna Dallas, d/o William and Rebecca Dallas, b. the 20th day of the 5th mo, 1764.

John Elkinton and Rhoda Sayre mar the 14th day of the 2nd mo, 1790.

Joel Clark and Anna Dallas mar the 15th of the 11th mo, 1796.

John Elkinton and Ann Clark, widow of Joel Clark, mar 3 Sep 1805.

Andrew Thompson and Anna D. C. Elkinton mar 8 Nov 1827.

John A. Elkinton, M. D., and Ann De Lamater mar 5 Oct 1830.

Andrew Thompson and Mary Harmon (?) mar 8 Aug 1843.

Edward D. Johnson and Rhoda S. E. Taylor mar 23 Sep 1841.

Dr. John E. Taylor and Sarah Pearson mar. 23 Sep. 1841.

Enoch Taylor and Ann B. Pastorius mar 25 Apr 1842.

John Elkinton, s/o George and Sarah Elkinton, b. 9 Sep. 1767.

Children of John and Rhoda Elkinton: Harriett Elkinton b. 6 Jan 1791; George Elkinton b. 29 Oct 1793; Rhoda Sayre Elkinton b. 5 Oct 1794; Joseph Pimm Elkinton b. b. 2 Aug 1796; William Elkinton b. 5 Jan 1799; John Abraham Elkinton b. 19 Oct 1801; Sarah Elkinton b. 5 Feb 1804.

Elizabeth Clark, d/o Joel and Ann Clark, b. 17 Aug 1801.

Ann Dallas Clark Elkinton, d/o John and Ann Elkinton, b. 10 Jun 1806.

Children of Andrew and Ann D. C. Thompson: Joshua Thompson b. 17 Jan 1829; John Thompson b. 10 Sep 1830; Clark Holmes Thompson b. 7 Sep 1832; Andrew Thompson b. 19 Mar 1835; Ann F. Thompson b. 26 Feb 1837; Ann D. C. Thompson b. 18 Feb 1839.

James Caldwell Elkinton, s/o John and Ann Elkinton, b. 10 Oct 1829 at 11:00 p.m.
Elizabeth Taylor Johnson, d/o Edward D. and Rhoda S. E. Johnson, b. 18 May 1821(?).
Richard Pearson Taylor, s/o John E. and Sarah Taylor, b. 1 Jul 1842.

Children of Andrew and Mary T. Thompson: David A. Thompson b. 29 May 1844; Richard Thompson b. 6 Feb 1846; Anna Thompson b. 8 Nov 1847; Rebecca Thompson b. 24 Aug 1849.

George Elkinton, s/o John and Rhoda Elkinton, d. 14 May 1793.
Rhoda Elkinton, w/o John Elkinton, d. 27 Feb 1804.
Joel Clark d. 27 Mar 1801.
Elizabeth Clark d. 16 Oct 1801.
William Elkinton d. 27 Feb 1816.
Rhoda S. Taylor, w/o Maria Taylor and d/o John and Rhoda Elkinton, d. 11 Feb 1822.
Harriett Butcher, w/o Joseph Butcher and d/o John and Rhoda Elkinton, d. 31 Dec 1832.
Rebecca Griscom d. 24 Aug 1853, aged 82 yrs.
David A. Thompson d. aug, 1847, aged 44 yrs.
Ann F. Thompson, d/o Andrew and Ann D. C. Thompson, d. 31 Dec 1838.
Ann D. C. Thompson, w/o Andrew Thompson and d/o John and Anna Elkinton, d. 7 Jul 1839.
Ann D. C. Thompson, d/o Andrew and Ann D. C. Thompson, d. 16 Jul 1839.
James Caldwell Elkinton, s/o of John A. and Ann Elkinton, d. 7 Aug 1841.
John Elkinton, s/o George and Sarah Elkinton, d. 9 May 1843, aged 75 yrs, 6 mo.
Anna Elkinton, w/o John Elkinton and d/o William and Rebecca Dallas, d. 19 Nov 1843, aged 79 yrs, 6 mo.
:
Elizabeth Bodley d. 25 Nov 1815.
Sarah Stratton b. 4 May 1801.
Jonathan D. Stratton b. 8 Nov 1804.
William L. Stratton b. 14 Mar 1808.

Joseph Stratton b. 2 Sep 1811.

Benjamin Bassett Bible
J. H. A. Frost 1827

Joseph Bassett b. 26 Jun 1765.
Mary Bassett, w/o J. Bassett, b. 26 May 1768.
Samuel Acton b. 10 Jul 1765.
Sarah Acton, w/o S. Acton, b. 6 Dec 1768.
Benjamin Bassett, s/o Joseph and Mary Bassett, b. 23 May 1801.

Mary Bassett, d/o Samuel and Sarah Acton and w/o Benjamin Bassett, d. 10
    Aug 1798.
Clement A, Bassett d. 16 Oct 1835, aged 6-9-1.

Benjamin Bassett and Mary Acton mar 5 Mar 1828.

Elwell Bible
Jasper Harding 1848

John H. Elwell, s/o Alexander and Elizabeth Elwell, b. 26 Mar 1790.
Margaret May, d/o John and Margaret May, b. 13 Mar 1790.

John H. Elwell and Margaret May mar 31 Mar 1813.
George W. Elwell and Anne Hance mar. 1 Sep. 1860.
George W. Elwell mar. (2,) Sarah Ann Dendlebeck, 4 Feb. 1860 (?).
Barbara Smith Elwell and Aaron W. Brandiff mar. 19 Sep. 1863.
Hiram Elwell and Elizabeth Dendlebeck mar. 23 Sep. 1872.

Children of John H. and Margaret Elwell: George Washington Elwell b. 17 Feb
    1817; Lewiza Elwell b. 5 Jan 1820; Margaret Elwell b. 4 Jan 1822; Hiram
    Elwell b. 22 Oct 1824; Barbara Smith Elwell b. 9 Jul 1830.

Lewiza Elwell, d/o John and Margaret Elwell, d. 22 Oct 1820.
Margaret Elwell, d/o John and Margaret Elwell, d. 9 Aug 1822.
Margaret, w/o John H. Elwell, d. 27 Nov. 1862, aged 72-8-14.
George Washington Elwell, s/o John and Margaret Elwell, d. 28 Oct. 1872, aged
    55-8-11.

John H. Elwell, s/o Alexander and Elizabeth Elwell, d. 30 May 1877, aged 87-2-4.

Fogg Bible
M. Carey and Son, Philadelphia 1818

Joseph Fogg and Hannah Hoover; Joseph, the s/o Joseph and Mary Street Fogg.
(Joseph Fogg and Mary Street mar. 11 May 1775)

Edward Fogg b. 28 May 1788.
Catherine Fogg b. 2 Dec 1788.

Children of Edward and Catherine Fogg: Lewis Fogg b. 14 Jul 1812; Mary Fogg
b. 26 Sep 1813; Casper Fogg b. 8 Feb 1815; Thomas Fogg b. Oct (no date);
Richard Fogg b. 11 Apr 1819; Edward Fogg b. 14 Sep 1822; Charles Fogg
b. 25 Jul 1825; George Hartley Fogg b. 26 Aug 1832.

Lewis Fogg, s/o Edward and Catherine Fogg, d. 19 Jul 1813.
Thomas Fogg, s/o Edward and Catherine Fogg, d. 22 Feb 1843, aged 31 yrs.
Catherine Fogg, w/o Edward Fogg, d. 18 May 1851, aged 62-5-16.
Edward Fogg d. 13 Apr 1862, aged 73 yrs, 11 mo.
Jacob Thompson d. 26 Oct 1824.
Mary Thompson d. 28 Dec 1824.
Elizabeth Thompson, d/o Jacob and Mary Thompson, d. 26 Apr 1833, aged 18-11-26.
Mary Brown d. 11 Sep. 1876, aged 62-11-15.

Joseph Fogg, s/o of Joseph and Mary Street Fogg, and Hannah Hoover
(marriage?).
(Joseph Fogg and Mary Street mar 11 May 1775)

Joseph Foster's Bible
M. Carthy and Davis, Philadelphia 1830

Joseph Foster b. 24 Dec 1787.
Jemima Harvey, his wife, b. 28 Jul 1786 and d. 28 Jul 1832.
Elizabeth Harvey b. 12 Feb 1787.
Sarah Shimp b. 23 Oct 1809.

Joseph Foster and Jemima Harvey mar 26 Dec 1807
Joseph Foster and Elizabeth Harvey mar 6 Apr 1833.
Joseph Foster and Sarah Shimp mar 5 Apr 1835.

Children of Joseph and Jemima Foster: Mary Foster b. 1 Nov 1808; Amariah
Foster b. 15 Apr 1811; John Foster b. 4 Jul 1813; Joseph Foster b. 11 Feb
1815; Sarah Foster b. 3 Jun 1816; Jemima Foster b. 24 Apr 1818;
Emmaline Foster b. 5 Jan 1825. ; Henry Foster b. 15 Aug 1827.

Vanneman-Garwood Bible
Matthew Carey, Philadelphia 1805

George Vanneman b. 1753 and d. aged 53.
Susanna Vanneman b. 1759 and d. aged 67.

John Vanneman, s/o George and Susanna Vanneman b. 24 May 1781.
Isaac Vanneman b. 19 Feb 1783.
Mary Vanneman b. 18 May 1785.
Anna Vanneman b. 11 Mar 1790.
Joseph Vanneman b. 12 Oct 1787
Joseph Vanneman b. 6 Nov 1796.
Susannah Vanneman b. 10 Sep 1793.
Rebecca Vanneman b. 29 Apr 1796.
Kezia Vanneman b. 20 Oct 1798.
Charles Vanneman b. 8 Jan 1801.
Sarah Ann Vanneman b. 21 Mar 1803.

Joseph Garwood and Rebecca C. Vanneman mar 27 Nov 1818.

Children of Joseph and Rebecca Garwood: George V. Garwood b. 10 Oct 1820;
Rachel S. Garwood b. 20 Jan 1822; Charles S. Garwood b. 1 Mar 1824;
Susanna S. Garwood b. 27 May 1826.

Mary A Garwood b. 13 Mar 1828 and d. 15 Mar. 1886
Joseph V. Garwood b. 13 Jun 1830.
Wm. S. Garwood b. 27 Jan 1832.
John T. Garwood b. 17 Jan 1834.
Anna Eliza Garwood b. 11 Oct 1836 and d. 26 Feb 1856.

Charles S. Garwood, s/o Joseph and Rebecca Garwood, d. 12 Jun 1825.

Isaac Vanneman d. 4 Oct 1784.
Anna Vanneman d. 9 Feb 1791.
Kezia Vanneman d. 13 Jul 1799.
Charles Vanneman d. 1 Oct 1801.
Rebecca Garwood, w/o Joseph Garwood, d. 24 Jan, 1864, aged 65 yrs.
Susan Scott, w/o John D. Scott, d. 18 Mar. 1865, in her 72nd yr.
Mary Wood, w/o William Wood, d. 18 Sep. 1870.

Draper-Garrison Bible
M. Carey and Son, Philadelphia 1818

Jemima Draper, d/o Edward and Amy Draper, b. 27 Oct 1758.
Ananias Garrison, s/o Benjamin Garrison, b. 25 Jun 1752.
Phebe Garrison, his wife, b. 13 Feb 1752.

Children of the above:
Benjamin Garrison b. 23 Aug 1775.
John Garrison b. 27 Apr 1777.
Phebe Garrison b. 20 Jun 1779.
Tamson Garrison b. 10 Jun 1781.
Abigail Garrison b. 13 Apr 1786.
Eunice Garrison b. 8 Apr 1788.
Dorcas Garrison b. 19 Sep 1791.

Annanias Garrison d. 20 Jan 1836.

Goodwin-Woodnutt Bible

William Goodwin and Elizabeth Woodnutt mar 30 Oct 1782.
Children of William and Elizabeth Goodwin: Prudence Goodwin b. 17 Aug
    1784; Mary Morris Goodwin b. 6 Apr 1786; Rachel Goodwin b. 25 Nov
    1787; Elizabeth Goodwin b. 25 Sep 1789; Sarah Goodwin b. 12 Jan 1791;
    Abigail Goodwin b. 1 Dec 1793.

Abigail Goodwin d. 2 Nov. 1867.
Prudence Conroe d. 11 Nov. 1866.
Jonathan Woodnutt d. 23 Jan. 1871.
Sarah Woodnutt d. 1 Feb. 1873.

Thomas Goodwin Bible

Thomas Goodwin, His Book:
My brother, William Goodwin, d. 25 Sep 1801, aged almost 78 yrs.

Susannah Smith d. 29 Jun 1798. She was the widow of Richard Smith, lately of
Alliwais (?) Creek and the mother of Thomas Hancock, now living in
Elsenboro. She was full 77 yrs of age when she died.

Thomas Hancock, His Book, 1816:

Children of William and Mary Goodwin: John Goodwin b. 19 Aug 1745; Lewis
Goodwin b. 9 Jan 1749; Susannah Goodwin b. 20 Feb 1751; Mary
Goodwin b. 17 Feb 1756; William Goodwin b. 18 Feb 1756.

Mary Goodwin, w/o William Goodwin, d. 3 Apr 1776, aged 49 yrs and near 6
mo.
William Goodwin, Sr, d. 25 Sep 1801, about 78 yrs.

Hancock records:
Children of Thomas and Mary Hancock: Morris Hancock b. 11 Jan 1777;
Thomas Hancock b. 2 Apr 1781; William Hancock b. 10 Mar 1783; Morris
Hancock b. 21 Feb 1785; Susannah Hancock b. 10 Dec 1786; Mary
Hancock b. 10 Dec 1788; Sarah Hancock b. 18 Sep 1790; Elizabeth
Goodwin Hancock b. 20 Sep 1793.

Thomas Hancock, Jr, d. Jun 1828, aged 46 yrs, 10 mo.
Thomas Hancock, Sr, d. 8 Mar 1829, aged 78 yrs.
Mary Hancock, widow of Thomas Hancock, Sr, d. 18 Feb 1834, aged 78 yrs, 1
dy.
Susannah Smith d. 29 June 1798, the widow of Richard Smith and mother of
Thomas Hancock, aged 77 yrs.

Griscom Bible
A. C. Goodwin, Hartford 1851

Andrew Griscom b. 27 Oct 1800 and d. 13 Dec. 1867.
Martha Griscom b. 11 Dec 1799 and d. 20 Aug. 1853.
Benjamin Bassett b. 20 May 1801 and d.5 Dec. 1871.
Mary A. Bassett b. 20 May 1801 and d. 3 Dec. 1883.

Barclay Griscom, s/o Andrew and Martha Griscom, b. 11 Aug 1828.
Sarah Ann Bassett, d/o Benjamin and Mary A. Bassett, b. 27 Nov 1831.

Barclay Griscom and Sarah Ann Bassett mar 5 Feb 1852.

Walter Griscom, s/o Barclay and Sarah Ann Griscom, b. 27 Oct. 1855.
Clement B. Griscom, s/o Barclay and Sarah Ann Griscom, b. 9 Aug. 1857.
Richard B. Griscom, s/o Barclay and Sarah Ann Griscom, b. 13 Nov.m1864.
Harry Griscom, s/o Barclay and Sarah Ann Griscom, b. 6 Apr. 1867.

Sarah Ann Griscom d. 8 Oct. and was bur. 12 Oct. 1910.
Walter D. Griscom d. 21 Dec. and was bur 24 Dec. 1913.
Barclay Griscom d. 15 Dec. and was bur. 18 Dec. 1915.
Clement B. Griscom d. 18 May and was bur. 21 May 1918.

Grey Family Bible
H. C. Carey and I. Lea, Philadelphia 1822

Kitturah Halsey b. 11 Dec 1773.
Samuel Gray B. 4 Mar 1774.
Children of Samuel and Keturah Gray: Sallie Gray b. Thurs., 23 Jul 1797; Jesse
    Gray b. 9 Apr 1799; Hannah H. Gray b. 16 Feb 1802; John D. Gray b. 4
    Dec 1803; Charity H. Gray b. 30 Dec 1805; Mary B. Gray b. 12 Sep 1807;
    Heturah H. Gray b. 12 Sep 1812; Charles F. G. Gray b. 14 May 1816.

Charles F. H. Gray and Mary Nelson mar 29 Dec 1842.

Children of Charles and Mary Gray: Ann Maria Sexton Gray b. 4 Apr 1845;
    Joseph Nelson b. 30 Jul 1847; Keturah Alice Gray b. 26 Feb 1849;
    Elizabeth H. Gray b. 26 Aug 1850; Ruth Nelson Gray b. 25 Mar 1852;
    Charles Gray, Jr, b. 4 Jun 1853; Samuel Nelson Gray b. Nov 1855; Harry
    Paulding Gray b. 4 Jun 1861.

Jesse Halsey b. Fri., 18 May 1739.
Charity White b. Wed., 7 Jan 1741.

Jesse Halsey and Charity White mar 14 Jan 1761.

Children of Jesse and Charity Halsey: Charity Halsey b. Fri., 18 Nov 1763; Hannah Halsey b. Sat., 31 May 1766; Jesse Halsey b. Fri., 10 Mar 1769 and d. 7 Aug 1769; Charles Fithian Halsey b. Mon., 11 Feb 1771; Kiturah Halsey b. Fri., 11 Dec 1773; Sarah Halsey b. Sat., 16 Nov 1776; Abigail Halsey b. Tues., 19 Aug 1783.

Ketturah H. Gray, w/o Samuel Gray, d. 12 Jul 1845.

Samuel Gray d. 20 Sep 1851.

Ketturah Fish d. 12 July 1865.

Samuel Nelson Gray, s/o Charles and Mary Gray, d. Oct. 1856.

Mary Nelson, w/o Charles F. H. Gray, d. 28 Aug. 1885.

Elizabeth H., d/o Charles F. H. and Mary N. Gray, d. 6 Sep. 1800.

Sinnickson-Hall Bible

Clement Hall, s/o Clement and Margaret Hall b. the 13th day of the 11th mo, 1753.

Rebecca (Kay) Hall, w/o Clement Hall and d/o Joseph and Ann Kay, b. the 2nd day of the 5th mo, 1759.

Clement Hall and Rebecca Kay mar 23 Feb 1778. Witnesses were Clement and Hannah Acton.

Children of Clement and Rebecca Hall: Joseph Hall b. 29 Mar and d. 2 Apr 1779; Ann Hall b. 30 May 1780; Margaret Hall b. 19 Apr 1782 and d. Oct 1784; Rhoda Hall (and a stillborn son) b. 13 Jan and d. 30 Jan 1784; Margaret Morris Hall b. 14 Jun 1785; Morris Hall b. 27 Mar 1787; Prudence Hall b. 1 Jun 1789; Sarah Hall b. 1 Jul 1791; Charlotte Hall b. 2 Jan and d. 4 Jan 1793; Rebecca Kay Hall b. 23 Feb 1796; Rebecca Hall b. 30 Jun 1798; Isaac Kay Hall b. 14 Aug 1800 and d. Oct 1801.

Clement Hall d. 12 Sep 1807.

Rebecca Hall d. 12 Sep 1835.

Thomas Hancock, Jr, d. Jun 1828.

Thomas Hancock, Sr, d. 8 Mar 1829.

Mary Hancock d. 18 Feb 1834.

Morris Hancock d. 28 Jan 1832.

Elizabeth Williams d. 17 Feb 1830.

Lydia P., w/o Richard Woodnutt and d/o Clement and Sarah Hall, d. 12 Jan. 1897, aged 74-11-27.

Margaret M., w/o Joseph Bilderback and d/o Clement and Sarah Hall, d. 25 Jan. 1899, aged 74 yrs.

Morris Hall's Bible
Matthew Carey, Philadelphia 1801

Morris Hall and Lydia Potts mar 1788.
Children of Morris and Lydia Hall: Clement Hall b. 27 Nov 1788, at 7:00 a.m.;
    David Hall b. 18 Feb 1790, at 9:00 a.m.; Sarah Hall b. 1 Sep 1791, at 1:00
    a.m.; John Hall b. 9 Sep 1793, at 8:00 p.m.; Lewis M. Hall b. 2 Feb 1798, at
    12:00; Thomas Hall b. 8 Dec 1799; Lydia Hall b. 19 Jul 1802.

Thomas Hall, s/o Morris and Lydia Hall, d. 28 Sep 1799(?).
Lydia Hall, d/o Morris and Lydia Hall, d. 7 Sep 1803.
Lydia Hall, w/o Morris Hall, d. 9 Aug 1818, aged 57 yrs and 3 mo.
Clement Hall, s/o Morris and Lydia Hall, d. 9 Sep 1837.
Morris Hall, Sr, d. Nov 1839.
John Hall d. 18 Mar. 1858, in his 65th yr.

Sarah Bafsett, w/o Joseph Bassett, d. 20 June 1858, in her 67th yr.

May 11, David and Ann Hall started for the back part of the state of New York.

In the back of this bible is written:
Isaac Fox and Hesziah Abbott mar 11 Mar 1788.
Hannah Fox b. 10 Sep 1793.
Margaret Fox b. 10 Oct 1794.
Elizabeth Fox b. 11 Oct 1796.
Mary Fox b. 26 Aug 1801.
Isaac Fox b. 17 Dec 1803.

Nathaniel and Mary Hall Bible
Robert Barker, London 1634
Printer to the King's Most Excellent Majesty

William Hall and Elizabeth Smith, d/o John Smith, mar. the 20th day of the 9th
    mo, 1723.
Children of William and Elizabeth Hall: Clement Hall b. the 15th day of the
    12th mo, 1724, about 4 min after 2:00 a.m.; Sarah Hall b. the 23rd day of
    the 4th mo, 1727, about 12:00; Susannah Hall b. the 24th day of the 12th
    mo, 1728; Nathaniel Hall b. the 30th day of the 1st mo, 1730; Sarah Hall b.
    the 12th day of the (?) mo, 1733; Elizabeth Hall b. the 16th day of the 8th

mo, 1735; Mary Hall b. the 18th day of the 12th mo, 1737; Edward Hall b. the 4th day of the 10th mo, 1740.

Mary Hall, w/o Nathaniel Hall, b. 1730.
1730, 10 May, Mary Hall was born, as is taken from the original.

Minutes from records of Salem Meeting, Salem, NJ: 3rd mo, 1756 - Nathaniel Hall and Mary Brick passed Meeting 3rd mo, 25th day, 1756.
Children of Nathaniel and Mary Hall: Ann Hall b. 4 Jan 1758; William Hall b. 31 Jan 1759, abt 11:00 p.m. on the 4th day of the week; Elizabeth Hall b. 19 May 1762, at 5:00 p.m., and d. 12 Sep 1763; Hannah Hall b. 14 Sep 1763, abt 9:00 a.m. on the 4th day of the week; Stephen Hall b. 24 Mar 1765, abt 1:00 a.m. on the 1st day of the week; Josiah Hall b. 9 Apr 1766, about 4:00 p.m. on the 5th day of the week; John Hall b. 9 Mar 1770, abt 5:00 p.m. on the 6th day of the week; Samuel Hall b. 2 Feb 1772, at 3:00 a.m.; Mary Hall b. 17 Apr 1774 and d. 12 Jun 1776, aged 1-1-24.

Ann Hall, d/o Nathaniel and Mary Hall, d. 11 Sep 1768, abt 9:00 a.m.
Nathaniel Hall, s/o William and Elizabeth Hall, d. 18 Jan 1784, aged 54-2-12.
Stephen Hall, s/o Nathaniel and Mary Hall, d. 26 Mar 1806, abt 1:00 a.m. on the 4th day of the week, aged 41 yrs, 2 dys.
Mary Hall, w/o Nathaniel Hall, d. 23 May 1809, abt 5:00 a.m. on the 3rd day of the week, aged 79 yrs, 13 dys.
Samuel Hall, s/o Nathaniel and Mary Hall, d. 13 Apr 1812, on the 5th day of the week, aged 30-2-28.
Josiah Hall, s/o Nathaniel and Mary Hall, d. 26 Jan 1828, in his 62nd yr.
William Hall, s/o Nathaniel and Mary Hall, d. 8 Apr 1838, aged 79-2-6.

Hancock-Stratton Bible
John Thompson, Philadelphia MDCCXCVIII.

Morris Hancock, s/o Morris and Mary Hancock, b. 21 Feb 1785.
Sarah Hancock, d/o John and Elanor Hancock, b. 5 Feb 1792.
Morris and Sarah Hancock mar 16 Jan 1812.
Children of Morris and Sarah Hancock: Eleanor Caroline Hancock b. 13 Nov 1812; Morris Thomas Hancock b. 19 Sep 1919; Mary Goodwin Hancock b. 13 May 1822; Sarah Maria Hancock b. 29 Feb 1824; Henrietta Elizabeth Hancock b. 11 Dec 1825; Thomas Hancock b. 23 Mar 1829 and d. 5 Aug 1830, abt 8:00 p.m., aged 1-4-12; John Hancock b. 13 Sep 1831.

Daniel Stratton and Eleanor C. Hancock mar 10 Oct 1837.
Children of Daniel and Eleanor C. Stratton: Morris Hancock Stratton b. 19 Jul
    1838; Daniel P. Stratton b. 19 Sep 1839 and d. 13 Jan 1901. Bur Nevada,
    MO; Henry Stratton b. 8 Jul 1842 and d. 12 Jul 1843; Eleanor Yorke
    Stratton b. 17 Aug 1854 and d. 7 Aug 1855; John Quinton Stratton b. 5 Jul
    and d. 10 Aug 1858.

Thomas S. Smith and Mary G. Hancock mar 25 Apr 1843.
Children of Thomas and Mary Smith: Thomas Smith b. 29 May and d. 20 Jun,
    1845, aged 22 days; Maria Hancock Smith b. 25 Jun 1846; Mary Smith b.
    22 Jul and d. 23 Jul 1848; Prescott Smith b. 8 Apr and d. 12 Apr 1850;
    Thomas Sinnickson b. 8 Jul 1851.

Quinton Gibbon, M. D., b. 4 Jul 1813.

Quinton Gibbon and Sarah M. Hancock mar 28 May 1845.
Daniel P. Stratton and Arabella Barnes mar.28 Nov. 1866.
Constant H. Eakin and Maria H. Smith mar. 13 Dec. 1867.
Morris H. Stratton and Ellen C. Smith mar. 7 June 1876.

Henrietta Hancock Gibbon, d/o of Quinton and Sarah M. Gibbon, b. 16 Sep
    1847.
Eleanor Hancock Stratton, d/o Daniel P. and Eleanor C. Stratton, b. 26 Apr.
    1868.
Eleanor Yorke Eakin, d/o Constant and Maria H. Eakin, b. 15 Oct. 1868 and d.
    28 Mar. 1932.
Constance Eakin, d/o Constant M. and Maria H. Eakin, b. 13 Aug. 1870.
Morris Hancock Stratton, Jr., s/o Morris H. and Ellen C. Stratton, b. 7 July
    1877.

Morris Hancock, s/o Morris and Sarah Hancock, d. 9 Feb 1827, at 20 min past
    3:00 p.m., aged 7-4-20.
Thomas Hancock, s/o Morris and Sarah Hancock, d. 5 Aug. 1830, aged 1-4-12.
Thomas Hancock, Sr, d. Sat. night, 7 Mar 1829.
Mary Hancock, widow of Thomas Hancock, Sr, d. 19 Feb 1834.
Morris Hancock, s/o the above, d. 28 Jan 1836, abt 10:00 a.m., aged 50-11-7.
Sarah Hancock, widow of Morris Hancock, d. 13 Jun 1848, aged 56-4-8.
John Hancock, s/o Morris and Sarah Hancock, d. 29 May 1849, aged 17-7-29.
Mary Goodwin, w/o Thomas S. Smith and d/o Morris and Sarah Hancock, d. 9
    May 1849, aged 33-1-10.

Henrietta Elizabeth, d/o Morris and Sarah Hancock, d. 21 Mar. 1879, aged 53-3-10.

Eleanor Caroline, w/o Rev. Daniel Stratton and d/o Morris and Sarah Hancock, d. 4 Aug. 1886, aged 73 yrs., 8 mo.

Sarah Maria, w/o Dr. Quinton Gibbon and d/o Morris and Sarah Hancock, d. 26 Feb. 1904, aged 79-11-26.

Thomas Smith d. 26 Oct. 1874, aged 62 yrs.

Rev. Daniel Stratton d. 24 Aug. 1866, aged 51-11-4.

Ellen C, Stratton, w/o Morris H. Stratton, d. 14 July 1877, aged 32 yrs., 1 mo.

Constant M. Eakin b. 2 July 1843 and d. 26 Apr. 1885.

Maria H. S. Eakin, widow of Constant Eakin, d. 12 Feb, 1917, Salem, N. J.

Harris Bible
M. Carey and Son, Philadelphia 1818

John Harris b. 10 Sep 1753.

Lydia Harris, w/o Benjamin Harris and d/o Capt. William Smith, b. 11 Feb 1764.

John Harris and Lydia Smith mar 12 Jan 1785 by Peter Peterson.

Children of John and Lydia Harris: Stretch Harris b. 25 Jan 1788; Benjamin Harris b. 27 Aug 1793; Peter Harris b. 14 Jun 1796; Lydia Harris, Jr, b. 24 Oct 1798; Elizabeth Harris b. 20 Nov 1800; Margaret Harris b. 1 Jun 1803; Clarisfa Harris b. 16 Sep 1805; Beulah Harris b. 21 Jun 1809.

Stretch Harris, s/o of John and Lydia Harris, and Rebecca Padgett mar 2 Mar 1811 by Richard Craven.

Benjamin Harris and Martha English mar 21 Mar 1822 by the Rev. John Cooper.

Peter Harris and Mary Carll mar 23 Dec 1847 by the Rev. William Brown.

Letitia T. d/o Benjamin and Martha Harris, and Thomas A. Maskell mar. 16 Mar.,1853 by the Rev. George Sleeper.

Quinton P., s/o of Benjamin and Martha Harris, and Elizabeth T. Powell mar. 14 Feb. 1855 by Friends ceremony, in the presence of Joseph Pancoast.

Martha English, d/o James and Letitia English and w/o Benjamin Harris, b. 13 Nov 1793.

Children of Benjamin and Martha Harris: Peter Harris b. 24 Jan 1823; Letitia E. Harris. b. 15 Jan 1825; Quinton P. Harris b. 28 Dec 1830.

Beulah Harris, d/o John and Lydia Harris, d. 21 May 1813, aged 3 yrs, 11 mo.

John Harris d. 29 Mar 1814, aged 60-6-19.

Peter Harris, s/o John and Lydia Harris, d. 20 Jan 1815, aged 18-7-16.

Lydia Harris, w/o John Harris, d. 28 Oct 1824, aged 60-8-17.

Margaret Sayre, w/o T. D. Sayre and d/o John and Lydia Harris, d. 20 May 1825, aged 22 yrs lacking 11 days.

Lydia Harris, d/o John and Lydia Harris, d. 18 Dec 1842, in her 45th yr.

Stretch Harris, s/o John and Lydia Harris, d. 10 Aug 1848, aged 60-6-15, within 4 days of the age his father was.

Martha, w/o Benjamin Harris and d/o James and Letitia English, d. 27 Sep. 1868, aged 74-10-14. They lived together 46 yrs., 6 mo. and 6 dys.

Benjamin Harris, s/o John and Lydia Harris, d. 14 Apr. 1872, aged 78-7-17.

John Harris, b. 1753, was a soldier in the Revolutionary War, serving 8 years and spending the winter of 1777-8 with Washington's troops at Valley Forge. He is buried in the old Baptist's Cemetery at Canton, NJ. His grave is marked.

Lydia (Lucetta) Smith, w/o John Harris, was the dau of Capt. William Smith of Quinton, NJ.

Stretch Harris Bible
H. C. Carey and I. Lea, Philadelphia 1822

Stretch Harris b. 25 Jan 1788.

Rebecca Harris b. 27 Jul 1790.

Stretch Harris and Rebecca Padgett mar 2 Mar 1811.

Children of Stretch and Rebecca Harris: Ann Harris b. 17 Jun 1813; John Harris b. 10 Aug 1815; Hiram Harris b. 5 Apr 1818; Amos Harris b. 29 Mar 1821.

Ann Harris, d/o Stretch and Rebecca Harris, Luke S. Fogg mar 8 Dec 1836.

Hiram Harris, s/o Stretch and Rebecca Harris, and Hannah Smith mar 24 Sep 1840.

Amos Harris, s/o Stretch and Rebecca Harris, and Catherine Smith mar 4 May 1843.

John Harris, s/o Stretch and Rebecca Harris, d. 2 Jul 1832, aged 16 yrs.

Ann Fogg, w/o Luke S. Fogg and d/o Stretch and Rebecca Harris, d. 17 Dec 1841, aged 28 yrs, 6 mo.

Stretch Harris d. 10 Aug 1848, aged 66-6-16.

Rebecca Harris d. 10 Dec 1856, aged 66-4-14.

Hiram Harris, s/o Stretch and Rebecca Harris d. 13 Mar. 1891, aged 72-11-8.

Jonathan Hildreth's Bible
Matthew Carey, Philadelphia 1801

Jonathan Hildreth, s/o Joseph and Lydia Hildreth, b. 12 Feb 1766.
Joanna Moore, d/o Richard and Mary Moore and gd/o of Lydia H. Fogg, b. 22 Dec 1765.
Children of Jonathan and Joanna Hildreth: Joseph Hildreth b. 10 Jul 1788; Lydia Hildreth b. 5 Aug 1789; Hannah Hildreth b. 16 May 1791; Mary Hildreth b. 11 Oct 1793; Elizabeth Hildreth b. 7 Feb 1796; Jonathan Hildreth b. 1 Mar 1800.

Ann Waddington, d/o William and Martha Waddington, b. 16 Mar 1801.
Jonathan Hildreth and Ann Waddington mar 9 May 1824.
Joanna M. Hildreth, d/o Jonathan and Ann Hildreth, b. 26 Mar 1826.

David Fogg and Hannah Hildreth mar 25 Mar 1813.
David Grier and Lydia Hildreth mar 18 Dec 1816.
Mark Stretch and Elizabeth Hildreth mar 4 Dec 1822.
Jonathan D. Grier and Lydia H. Fogg mar 28 Nov 1833.

Lydia Grier, w/o David Grier, d. 2 May 1820, aged 30-8-27.
Mary Corlisf, w/o Joseph Corlisf, d. 9 May 1824, aged 34-5-5.
Joanna Moore Hildreth, w/o Jonathan Hildreth, d. 6 Oct 1828, aged 62-9-10.
Jonathan Hildreth d. 26 Apr 1829, aged 63-2-14.
William W. Hildreth, s/o Jonathan Hildreth, Jr, and Anna his wife, d. 29 Apr 1826, aged 1-3-29.
Jonathan Hildreth, Jr, 3 Oct 1827, aged 27-7-3.
Elizabeth Stretch, w/o Mark Stretch, d. 8 Jun 1836, aged 40 yrs and 5 mo.

Jonathan Houseman's Bible
Printed 1759

Mary Oakford b. 25 Aug 1740.
Anna House b. 8 Apr 1765.
Margaret House b. 27 Jan 1768.
William House b. 18 Jul 1770.
Jane Holme, d/o William Nobitt and his wife, b. 22 Aug 1781.

William House b. 27 Nov 1771.

Sarah Wood b. 14 Jul 1772.

William House and Sarah Wood mar 29 Mar 1796.

Children of William and Sarah House: Jonathan House b. 25 Sep 1798; Mary
     House b. 2 Jan 1801.

Jonathan House, Jr, b. 10 May 1843.

Elmina Ayars b. 15 Dec 1845.

Jonathan House, Jr, and Elmina Ayars mar. 15 Nov. 1864.

Children of Jonathan and Elmina House: Elmer House b. 2 Dec. and d. 5 Dec,
     1865; George House b. 21 Aug. 1867; Frances Blackwood House b. 19 July
     1870.

George House and Rebecca Fowler mar. 21 Aug. 1892.

Jonathan Woodnott Acton and Frances Blackwood House mar. 19 July 1890.

Jacob House d. 21 Dec 1726.

Mary Holme, w/o John Holme, d. 19 Mar 1796, aged 55-5-6.

Mariam Houseman, w/o John Houseman, d. 20 Jun 1803.

John Houseman d. 5 Sep 1823, aged between 80 and 90 yrs.

Elmina House, w/o Jonathan, d. 15 Aug. 1889.

Jonathan House d. 12 Aug. 1923.

Hulick Bible
Matthew Carey, Philadelphia 1812

Cornelius Hulick b. Saturday, 2 Sep 1792.

Ann Straughan, w/o Cornelius Hulick, b. Sunday, 2 Mar 1793.

Cornelius Hulick and Ann Straughan mar 10 Oct 1816.

Children of Cornelius and Ann Hulick: Mary Hulick b. Sunday, 21 Sep 1817;
     Ann Hulick, Jr, b. Tuesday, 29 Dec 1818; George Hulick b. Monday, 20
     Dec 1819; Margaret Hulick b. Monday, 12 Feb 1821; Jacob Hulick b.
     Thursday, 31 Jul 1823; Mahalah Hulick b. 18 Apr 1826; Abbyhale Hulick
     b. 4 Oct 1827; Hannah Porter Hulick b. 16 Aug 1832.

Mary Hulick and James Sayre were mar at Pittsgrove 2 Apr 1840 by the Rev.
     Silas Eisenbrey.

Jacob Hulick, s/o Cornelius and Ann Hulick, d. Wednesday, 7 Apr 1824.

Cornelius Hulick d. 5 July 1876, aged 84-10-3.
Ann, w/o Cornelius Hulick, d. 25 Aug. 1881, aged 88-5-23.
Ann, w/o Aaron Sholders and d/o Cornelius and Ann Hulick, d. 16 Jan. 1878, aged 56-1-14.
George Martin d. 4 Apr. 1897, aged 91 yrs.
Margaret Martin d. 23 Aug. 1900, aged 79-6-11.
Mary, w/o James Sayre and d/o Cornelius and Ann Hulick, d. 17 Oct. 1904.
Abihall, w/o David Young and d/o Cornelius and Ann Hulick, d. 20 Dec. 1906, aged 79 yrs.
Mahalath Hulick, Cornelius and Ann Hulick, d. 23 Sep. 1908, aged 84 yrs.
George Hulick, s/o Cornelius and Ann Hulick, d. 16 May 1910, aged 90 yrs.
Hannah Porter Hulick, w/o Eustace Moore, d. Feb. 1916, aged 84 yrs.

Jones-Lore Bible
B. and J. Collius, Boston 1825

Older records on loose leaf in bible:

Jonathan Jones, s/o William and Elizabeth (Atkinson) Jones, b. the 25th day of the 3rd mo, 1749 and d. 20 Sep 1831, aged 82-6-1.
Mary Owen, d/o Rowland and Prudence Owen, b. the 8th day of the 9th mo, 1756 and d. 15 Sep 1849, aged 93 yrs, 7 dys.

Jonathan Jones and Mary Owen mar at Evesham Monthly Meeting, Burlington Co., NJ, 12 Apr 1775.

William Jones, s/o Jonathan and Mary Jones, b. 17 May 1776 and d. 13 Mar. 1862, aged 85-9-26.
Elizabeth Jones, d/o Jonathan and Mary Jones, b. 4 Oct 1779 and d. 3 Oct 1806, aged 27 yrs, 4 dys.
Jesse Jones b. 6 Oct 1781 and d. 4 Jan. 1864, aged 82-2-28.
Owen Jones b. 4 Feb 1787 and d. 3 June 1869, aged 82 yrs., 4 dys.
Sarah Jones b. 27 May 1789 .
Hannah T. Jones b. 27 May 1797 and d. 24 Jan 1811, aged 13-7-26.

Owen Jones, s/o Jonathan and Mary Jones, b. 5 Feb 1787.
Elizabeth Lore, d/o John and Sarah Lore, b. 26 Jul 1790.
Owen Jones and Elizabeth Lore mar 25 Oct 1808.

Children of Owen and Elizabeth Jones: Sarah Jones b. 3 Sep 1811; Jesse Jones
b. 12 Jun and d. 14 Sep 1814; Charles Jones b. 21 Jun 1817 and d. 11 Jul
1819; Owen L. Jones b. 9 Oct 1823; Elizabeth C. Jones b. 8 Apr 1827.

Owen Jones and Sarah E. Thackray mar. 1 Feb. 1877

Jesse Jones d. 14 Sep. 1814.
Charles Jones d. 11 July 1819.
Elizabeth Jones, w/o Owen Jones, d. 29 Apr. 1866, at 10 min. past 9:00 a.m.
Owen Jones d. 5 June 1869, aged 82 yrs., 4 mo.
Elizabeth C. J. Wood d. at noon, 7 Aug. 1891, aged 64 yrs., 3 dys.
Sarah Jones Acton d. 13 May 1901, aged 89-8-10.
Owen L. Jones d. 16 Jan. 1912, aged 88-3-7.

Johnson Bible

Isaac Johnson, s/o Samuel and Ann Johnson, b. 20 Jul 1787.
Isaac Johnson, father of Mayhew Johnson, M. D., b. 20 Jul 1787.
Catherine Johnson, w/o Isaac Johnson, b. 10 Jul 1790.
Nancy Johnson, d/o Catherine Johnson, b. Jan 1823.
Samuel M. Johnson b. 22 Mar 1825.
Mayhew Johnson, s/o Isaac and Catherine Johnson, b. 28 May 1828.
Isabella Tilge, w/o Mayhew Johnson, b. 4 Oct 1827.
Elizabeth Morton, w/o Mayhew Johnson, b. 8 June 1852.
John Morton, father of Elizabeth Morton, b. 23 Dec. (no year given) and d. 6
    Apr. 1877.

Nancy Johnson mar Senator Isaac Nieukirk (no date).

Keasby Bible
Isaac Collins, Trenton MDCCXCI

Edward Keasby mar Elizabeth Smart, widow of Isaac Smart and d/o Andrew
    Thompson, 26 Nov 1701.

Mary, d/o Edward and Elizabeth Keasby, b. the 3rd day of the 11th mo, 1703.
Edward b. the 3rd day of the 11th mo, 1705.
Matthew b. the 28th day of the 7th mo, 1706.
Susanna b. the 24th day of the 11th mo, 1708.

Elizabeth Bradway, w/o Edward Keasby, b. 16 Mar 1700.
Edward Keasby and Elizabeth Bradway mar 8 or 18 Feb 1725.

Edward Keasby, s/o Edward and Elizabeth B. Keasby b. 22 Mar 1826 and d. 15 Sep 1779.
Mary b. 4 Oct 1727.
Bradway b. 4 Mar 1730.

Edward Keasby mar Prudence Quinton, d/o Edward and Temperance Quinton, 1746.

Edward Quinton b. 1696 and d. 26 Mar 1756, aged 60 yrs.
Temperance Quinton b. 1702 and d. 8 Jan 1775, aged 73 yrs.
Children of Edward and Prudence Keasby: Elizabeth Keasby b. 10 Aug 1747; Edward Keasby b. 2 Dec and d. 16 Dec 1748; Matthew Keasby d. 26 Oct 1749 and was lost at sea; Sarah Keasby b. 6 Dec 1751 and d. 10 Jan 1752; Lewis Quinton Keasby b. 19 Oct 1752 and d. 23 Jul 1753; Phebe Keasby b. 16 Aug 1755 and d. 28 Jan 1812; Edward Keasby b. 12 Sep 1756 and d. in infancy; Prudence Keasby (twin) b. 12 Sep 1756 and d. 12 Sep 1794; Samuel Keasby b. 22 Nov 1758 and d. in infancy; Anthony Keasby (twin?) b. 22 Nov 1758 and d. 7 May 1811; Mary Keasby b. 17 Jan 1760 and d. in infancy.

Edward Keasby and (2nd wife) Sarah Quinton mar 15 May 1765.
Children of Edward and Sarah Keasby: Temperance Keasby b. 10 Mar 1766 and d. 11 Apr 1826; Dezil Keasby b. 22 Nov 1768 and d. 30 Dec 1837; Jesfe Keasby b. Sep 1770; Jane Keasby b. 30 Aug 1773 and d. 30 Aug 1774; Rachel Keasby b. 15 Jul 1775; Kezia Keasby b. 20 Nov 1777 and d. 24 Dec 1837.

Prudence and Sarah Quinton, 1st and 2nd w/o Edward Keasby, were sisters.
Sarah Quinton Keasby survived her husband and married a Mr. Morton. They lived in New Castle, DE, and she died 15 Sep 1812, aged 58 yrs.

Anthony Keasby, s/o Edward and Prudence Keasby, b. 2 Nov 1758.
Hannah Brick, d/o Joseph and Rebecca Brick, b. 17 Jun 1768.

Anthony Keasby and Hannah Brick mar 25 Nov 1784.

Children of Anthony and Hannah Keasby: Rebecca Abbott Keasby b. 17 Apr 1786; Prudence Quinton Keasby b. 15 May 1788; Matthew Keasby b. 25

Mar 1791; Edward Quinton Keasby b. 21 Jan 1793; Hannah Foster Keasby
b. 15 Aug 1797, at 1 o'clock and 4 min in the morning; Anthony Keasby b.
1 Apr 1800; Artemefis Keasby b. 15 May 1802, at 4:30 a.m., and d. 19 Aug
1842, aged 40 yrs and 3 mo; Ann Keasby b. 30 Jun 1808.

Snow the 8th day of May, 1803, 3 inches deep.

Anthony Keasby d. 9 May 1811, in the 53rd yr of his life.
Hannah Keasby, w/o Anthony Keasby, d. 12 Nov 1833, in the 65th yr of her
    life.
Anthony Keasby, s/o Anthony and Hannah Keasby, d .2 Jan. 1832, aged 31 yrs.,
    9 mo.
Artemefia Keasby, d/o Anthony and Hannah Keasby, d 19 Aug. 1842, aged 40
    yrs., 3 mo.
Hannah F. Van Meter, d/o Anthony and Hannah Keasby, d 10 Mar. 1871.

Kelsay Bible
Boulter Grierson, Dublin, 1768
Printer to the Kings Most Excellent Majesty

William Kelsay, s/o Rev. Robert Kelsay, b. 25 Dec 1744.
Kezia Shepard, w/o William Kelsay and d/o Rev. Job Shepard, b. 25 Jun 1744.
William Kelsay and Kezia Shepard mar 6 Jan 1766 at the house of Catherine
    Shepard, widow. The marriage was solemnized by the Rev. Robert Kelsay.
Children of William and Kezia Kelsay: Daniel Kelsay b. 19 Feb 1768; William
    Kelsay, Jr, b. 4 Nov 1769 and d. 9 Jul 1771, aged 1-8-5; Robert Kelsay b.
    18 May 1772; Mary Kelsay b. 30 Nov 1773 and d. 20 May 1775; Sarah
    Kelsay b. 7 Feb 1776; Martha Kelsay b. 6 Oct 1779; Job Kelsay b. 16 Jul
    1784; Clarisfa Kelsay b. 30 Jul 1786 and d. 12 Apr 1787, aged 8 mo, 12
    dys; William Kelsay b. 6 Aug 1788.

In the cemetery of an old Baptist yard, lying between Greenwich and Hopewell,
    Cumberland Co., NJ, are the graves of the Kelsay family, notably the Rev.
    Robert Kelsay and Miriam his wife, who were parents of William Kelsay,
    b. 25 Dec 1744.

Record from stone at graves:
In memory of the Rev. Robert Kelsay who departed this life 30 May 1789, age
    78 yrs. Minister to this church 33 yrs.

Miriam Kelsay, w/o the Rev. Robert Kelsay, who d. 8 Jan 1785, age 62 yrs.

Mary Kelsay, 1767
D. K.
Wm. K.
M. K.

William Kelsay was paymaster, also Captain, Cumberland County Militia, Rev. War.

Kelty Bible
W. and H. Merriman, Troy, New York 1846

Jonathan Kelty b. 10 Mar 1791 and mar Angelina Robinson 2 Dec 1840. Their children: Richard Kelty b. 12 Sep 1841; Benjamin R. Kelty b. 8 May 1843; Clement Kelty b. 13 Jun 1846; William R. Kelty b. 11 Feb 1848; Albert Kelty b. 10 Jul 1849 and d. 9 Sep 1853; Jonathan H. Kelty b. 29 Aug 1851.

Jonathan Kelty, Sr., d. 13 Oct. 1852 and his wife Angelina, d. 6 Aug. 1908. Richard Kelty mar. Louisa Sharp (no date). Their children were: DeWitt Clinton, Sharp. Bertis, Catherine, Elizabeth and William Robinson. Benjamin Robinson Kelty mar. Harriett Mulford in 1899. No issue. Clement Kelty mar. Kate Bullock (no date). Their children: Edith, Alice and Hannah. William R. Kelty mar. Linda Butcher. No issue. Albert Kelty never married. Jonathan Hiles Kelty mar. Sara S. Davidson 15 Feb. 1863 and had one child, Frederick B. Kelty, b. 15 Nov. 1883.

Lawrie Bible
Isaac Collius MDCCXCI

Thomas Lawrie b. 6 Oct 1763.
Ann Lawrie b. 29 Jan 1769.
Their children: Lydia Lawrie b. 13 Oct 1789; Mary Lawrie b. 2 Oct 1791; William Lawrie b. 31 May 1793, between 11 and 12 o'clock at night; Abigail Lawrie b. 11 Dec 1794; Hannah Lawrie b. 21 Nov 1796; Thomas

Lawrie, Jr, b. 13 Apr 1799; Deborah Lawrie b. 27 Dec 1800; Ann Lawrie b. 30 Apr 1803; James Lawrie b. 3 Aug 1805; Jane Lawrie b. 4 May 1807.

Mary Lawrie, d/o Thomas and Ann Lawrie, d. 22 Jul 1793 at half after six in the morning, aged 2-9-20.

William Lawrie, s/o Thomas and Ann Lawrie, d. 3 Aug 1794 at half after 9 in the evening, aged 1-2-3.

Thomas Lawrie d. 3 Oct 1815 at half past 2 in the morning, aged 52-11-28.

Ann Lawrie d. 6 Aug 1825 at half past 12 at night, aged 56-6-7.

Deborah Lawrie d. 4 Dec 1832 between 9 and 10 in the evening, aged 31-11-3.

Thomas Lawrie, Jr, d. 30 Aug 1835 about half past 9 in the morning, aged 36-4-19.

Linsey Bible
Oxford, 1784

John Dickinson and Syndonia his wife mar. 29 Feb 1768 (?).

John Linsey and Syndonia his wife mar 18 Aug 1778.

Children of John and Syndonia Linsey: A dau b. 3 Oct 1780; Jonathan Linsey b. 16 Mar 1781; Samuel Linsey b. 29 Mar 1783; Elizabeth Linsey b. 17 Feb 178_ and d. 7 Aug 1785; A son b. 13 Sep 1786; John Linsey, Jr, b. 19 May 1788; William Linsey b. 11(?) Mar and d. 22 Mar 1790; Joseph Linsey (twin) b. 11 (?) Mar 1790; Syndonia Linsey, Jr, b. 30 Dec 1791; A dau b. 20 Jan 1793.

Elizabeth Linsey d. 7 Aug. 1785.

Syndonia Huddy d. Apr ____.

Druzield Heartly d. 17 Feb 1793.

Syndonia Linsey, w/o John Linsey, d. 25 Dec 1802.

John Linsey d. 24 Jul 1803, at 7 o'clock in the afternoon.

Children of Jonathan and Sarah Linsey: William Lindsey b. 1 Nov 1803; John Linzey b. 30 Apr 1806; Ruth Lindzey b. 29 Sep 1808; Edward Lindzey b. 4 Aug 1815 and d. 16 Aug 1816; Mary Lindzey b. 22 Sep 1817.

Ruth Wood, d/o Jonathan and Sarah Lindzey, d. 19 Apr 1832.

Sarah Wood, d/o Isaiah and Ruth Wood, d. 30 Apr 1832.

James Lindsey, s/o Jonathan and Sarah20 Apr 1834.

Jonathan Lindsey, the parent, d. 1 Nov 1830.

Caleb Lippincott's Bible
M. Carey, Philadelphia 1812

Mary Lippincott, d/o Samuel Ogden and Mary Ann, his wife, b. 13 June 1771
and d. 13 Jan. 1797, aged 25 yrs., 7 mo.

Caleb Lippincott, s/o Samuel and Mary Lippincott, b. 25 Nov 1795.
Ann Thompson, d/o Joshua and Rebecca (Allen) Thompson, b. 5 May 1797.
Caleb and Ann Lippincott mar 5 Apr 1820.
Children of Caleb and Ann Lippincott: Samuel T. Lippincott b. 1 Jan 1829;
Clarkson Lippincott b. 12 May 1832; David T. Lippincott b. 7 May 1835.

Mary Jane Woolman, w/o Clarkson Lippincott and d/o James and Mary Ann
Woolman, b. 22 Sep 1842.
Clarkson Lippincott and Emma L. Pedrick mar. 24 Sep. 1863 (1st wife)
Clarkson Lippincott and Mary Jane Woolman mar. 5 Jan. 1871.

Children of Clarkson and Mary Jane Lippincott: J. Presson b. 24 June 1872;
James Woolman b. 5 Dec. 1873;Andrew Thompson b. 24 Sep. 1876; Emma
Linda b. 17 July 1879; Mary Woolman b. 27 Sep. 1881.

David A. Thompson d. 13 Aug 1847, aged 44 yrs.
David T. Lippincott d. 23 Jul 1846, aged 11-1-18.
Caleb Lippincott d. 25 Dec. 1864, aged 69 yrs., 1 mo.
Ann T. Bassett d. 6 Mar. 1870, aged 23-8-14.
James Woolman, s/o Clarkson and Mary Jane Lippincott, drowned on 19 Aug.
1877.
Clarkson Lippincott, s/o Caleb and Ann Lippincott, d. 28 Sep. 1901.
Mary Jane Lippincott, w/o Clarkson Lippincott, d. 17 Feb. 1902.

Hannah Lippincott's Bible
Kimber and Sharpless, Philadelphia

Samuel Lippincot, s/o Caleb and Hannah Lippincott, b. 28 Oct 1762.
Mary Lippincott, 1st w/o Samuel Lippincott and d/o Samuel and Mary Ann
Ogden, b. 13 Jun 1771.

Caleb Lippincott, s/o Samuel and Mary Lippincott, b. 25 Nov 1795.

Patience Lippincott, 2nd w/o Samuel Lippincott and d/o Samuel and Sarah
    Webster, b. 4 Sep 1768.

Children of Samuel and Patience Lippincott: Hannah b. 15 Jul 1802; Sarah
    Lippincott (twin) b. 15 Jul 1802; Samuel Lippincott, Jr, b. 15 Jan 1805;
    Josiah Lippincott b. 28 Dec 1807; Charles Lippincott b. 13 Nov 1809.

Christianna Lippincott, 3rd w/o Samuel Lippincott and d/o John and Mary
    Black, b. 28 Jun 1777.
Asa Moore, 1st husband of Hannah Lippincott and s/o Benjamin and Hannah
    Moore, b. 28 Jun 1788.
Samuel Duell, 2nd husband of Hannah L. Moore and s/o John and Lydia Duell,
    b. 17 Jul 1798.

Mary Lippincott d. 5 Jan 1797.
Sarah Lippincott d. 15 Jul 1802.
Patience Lippincott d. 30 Oct 1811.
Samuel Lippincott d. 9 Sep 1841.
Charles Lippincott d. 9 Jan 1845.
Christianna Lippincott d. 26 Aug 1851.
Asa Moore d, 23 July 1852.
Hannah Horner d. 16 Mar. 1858.
Caleb Lippincott d. 25 Dec. 1864.
Ann T. Moore, w/o Caleb Lippincott, d. 27 Mar. 1870.

Samuel T. Lippincott's Bible
A. Andrus and Son, Hartford 1844

Sarah Pancoast b. 15 May 1764.
Joseph Davis b. 15 Jun 1766.
Mary Davis b. 1 Nov 1770.
William Folwell b. 23 Feb 1790.
Martha C. Folwell b. 30 Mar. 1791,
Daniel C. Pancoast b. 3 Dec 1802.
Anna H. Pancoast b. 3 Sep 1807.
Ann T. Lippincott b. (no date)
William F. Pancoast b. 7 Feb 1828.
Samuel T. Lippincott b. 1 Jan 1829.
Mary D. Pancoast b. 28 Nov 1829.
Martha F. Pancoast b. 22 Dec 1831 and d. 31 Aug. 1878.

Joseph D. Pancoast b. 9 Jul 1833.
Annie E. Pancoast b. 27 Jul 1835.
Ellen Pancoast b. 20 Dec 1837.
David Pancoast, Jr., b. 30 May 1840.
William H. Pancoast b. 15 Mar 1843 and d. 14 Dec. 1888.
Charles F. Pancoast b. 8 Mar 1844.
Isabella Pancoast b. 26 May 1845.
Rebecca S. Pancoast b. 11 Jun 1847.
John Pancoast (no date)
Clement G. Lippincott b. 3 Mar. 1875.

Samuel T. Lippincott and Martha F. Pancoast mar. 6 Oct. 1858.

Caleb Lippincott d. 25 Dec. 1864, Salem, N. J., in his 70th yr.
Ann T. Lippincott Bassett d. 27 Mar. 1870.

William Lippincott's Bible
Matthew Carey, Philadelphia 1805

William Lippincott b. 1 Jan 1753.
Rebecca Lippincott, w/o William Lippincott, b. 19 Jul 1763.

William Lippincott and Rebecca, his wife, mar. 1789.
Jeremiah Jones and Rebecca Lippincott mar. 31 Mar. 1831, by Rev. Sedgwick
    Rusling.

William Lippincott, Jr, s/o William and Rebecca Lippincott, b. 2 ___ 1790.
John Lippincott b. 6 Feb 1792.
Susanna Lippincott b. 23 Feb 1794.
Rebecca Lippincott b. 10 Oct 1797.
Thomas Lippincott b. 1 Feb 1801.

George McNichol b. 19 Feb 1787.
Susanna L. Jones, d/o Jeremiah and Rebecca Jones, b. 11 Oct 1832.
Thomas and William Jones, sons of Jeremiah and Rebecca Jones, b. 20 Jul
    1834.

William Lippincott d. 16 Apr 1807.
William Lippincott, Jr, s/o William and Rebecca Lippincott, d. 27 Dec 1792
John Lippincott d. 2 Apr 1812.

Thomas Lippincott d. 20 Aug 1815.
Rebecca Drew d. 2 Feb 1842, in her 80th yr.

Mecum Bible
Kimber and Sharpless, Philadelphia

William Mecum mar Margaret Wickry (Vicary?) 23 Jul 1828.
Their children: William Mecum, Jr, b. 12 Jun 1730 around 5:00 a.m. Christened
in Penn's Neck Church (St. George's) on the 21st of above said month and
year; Margaret Mecum b. 5 Nov 1735 about 7:00 a.m. and christened the
9th of the same month.

Dorcas Gibson, d/o Joseph Gibson, b. 1 Aug 1732 and d. 31 Jan 1755, aged 22-
5-20.

William Mecum mar Doras Gibson 17 Aug 1751.
Their children: Joseph Mecum b. 20 Mar 1753; William Mecum b. 24 Jan 1755
and d. 13 Aug 1757, aged 2-6-11.

William Mecum mar Eleanor Sinnickson mar 22 Nov 1761.

Records from St. Georges Church Yard, Churchtown, Salem Co., NJ:

Children of William and Eleanor Mecum: Sarah Mecum b. 19 Sep 1767 and d. 1
Nov 1835; Margaret Mecum b. 23 Aug 1770 and d. 30 Apr 1846; William
M. Mecum b. 22 Nov 1772 and d. 24 Dec 1805; Rebecca Mecum b. 7 Oct
1774 and d. 5 Feb 1795; George Washington Mecum b. 10 Oct 1777 and d.
6 Sep 1803; Andrew Mecum b. 23 Feb 1780 and d. 14 Oct 1814; Eleanor
Mecum b. 23 Feb 1780 and d. 14 Oct 1814 (this entry may be an error);
Eleanor Mecum b. 6 Feb 1782 and d. 27 Aug 1848.

Eleanor Mecum, w/o William Mecum, d. 28 Mar 1783, aged 40-3-5.
Andrew Sinnickson, of Lower Penn's Neck, d. Sunday, 22 Aug 1790, in his
72nd year (A PA Gazette clipping in the record).

James Mecum, s/o Andrew and Nancy Wright Mecum b. 9 Dec 1809.
Lydia Ann Harrison, d/o Josiah and Isabella Dick Harrison, b. 26 Jan 1812.

James W. Mecum and Lydia Ann Harrison mar in St. John's Church, Salem, NJ,
24 May 1841, by the Rev. Edward G. Prescott, Rector.

Their children: Isabella Harrison Mecum b. 8 Apr 1842; George Mecum b. 20 Apr 1844; Ellen Mecum b. 1 Jul 1846; James H. Mecum b. 12 Apr 1849; Maria Harrison Mecum b. 6 Jan 1852; Charles Mecum b. 15 Jan 1855.

Charles Mecum and Margaret Howard Sinnickson mar. in St. John's Church, Salem, N. J., 29 May 1890, by the Rev. C. M. Perkins, Rector.

William Mecum, b. 12 Jun 1730 and d. 21 Mar 1790, served as Major, 1st Batt., Salem Co. Militia, revolutionary War. Appointed 20 Jun 1776.

Miller Bible
R. White, Huthuison and Dwier, Hartford 1836

Josiah Miller, s/o Richard and Elizabeth W. Miller, b. 24 Aug 1799.
Hetty H. James, d/o Samuel L. and Mary James, b. 20 May 1798.
Josiah Miller and Hetty H. James mar 18 Feb 1823 by the Rev. Mr. Otis.
Their children: Richard Miller b. 6 Dec 1823; Samuel L. J. Miller b. 10 Feb 1825; Wyatt W. Miller b. 1 Nov 1828.

"Died, in Sculltown, Salem Co., on 4th day, morning, 20th, 1824, Gideon Scull, Sen."
Hannah Scull Carpenter d. 1828, in the 26th yr of her life.
Cousin William J. Waynman d. 8 May 1835, Knoxville.
Aunt Sarah Schull d. 22 Apr 1836, in her 77th yr.
{Sarah Scull, widow of Gideon Scull, d. 23 Apr 1836, in her 75th yr}
Uncle James d. 24 Feb 1838, in his 75th yr.
Ann Hall d. 17 Aug 1840, in her 84th yr.
Mary H. James d. 20 Jul 1843, aged 68 yrs.
Paul Schull d. 10 Feb 1844, in his 50th yr.
Samuel L. James d. 22 Feb 1845, aged 77 yrs.
Sarah Scull d. 15 Feb 1845, in her 45th yr
Cousin Abigail S. Waynman d. 1853, aged 55 yrs.
Cousin Sallis W. Carpenter d. Sep. 1854.
Elizabeth Miller d. 30 July 1858, in her 29th yr.
Hetty H. White, w/o David Reeves, d., at Phoenixville, PA, Thursday, 2 Jan. 1868, aged 69-7-13.
Josiah Miller d. 24 Aug. 1880, aged 34 on the day of his death.

Morris Bible
M. Carey, Philadelphia 1815

Christopher Morris b. 5 Dec 1768.
Lydia Morris b. 25 Aug 1774.

Martha Morris b. 26 Nov 1793.
William Morris b. 28 Oct 1795.
Rachel Morris b. 29 Oct 1797.
Elizabeth Morris b. 16 Oct 1799.
John Morris b. 9 Sep 1802.
Rebecca Morris b. 7 Jun 1804.
Mary Morris b. 26 Aug 1807.
John Morris b. 26 May 1809.
Charlotte Morris, d/o E. Morris, b. 29 ___ 1815.
Elizabeth Morris, w/o William Morris, b. 3 Feb 1796.

William and Elizabeth Morris mar 19 Mar 1814.
Children of William and Elizabeth Morris: John Morris b. 21 Jul 1814; Lydia
    Morris b. 6 Oct 1815; Josiah Morris b. 2 Jul 1817; William M. Morris b. 1
    May 1819; Samuel Morris b. 10 Jan 1821; Elizabeth Morris, Jr, b. 22 Feb
    1823; Mary Amanda Morris b. 17 Oct 1824; Hannah Morris b. 2 Jul 1831;
    Rebecca Morris (twin) b. 2 Jul 1831; Wesley Pitman Morris b. 17 Aug
    1832; Emma Jane Morris b. 16 Aug 1835.

James B. Hunt and Lydia R. Morris b. 3 Apr 1845.

William M. Hunt, s/o James B. Hunt and Lydia R. Hunt b. 11 Jan 1846.

John W. Morris and Mary Stretch mar. 23 Apr. 1846.
Joseph B. Wiley and Mary Amanda Morris mar. 29 Mar. 1847,
Josiah Morris and Margaret Rice mar. (no date).
John Newell and Emma J. Morris mar. 20 Oct. 1859.
Clement Hall and Elizabeth Morris mar. 12 Dec. 1867.

Lydia Morris d. 9 Jun 1809.
Mary Morris d. 2 Oct 1815.
Rebecca Robbins d. 13 Oct 1821.
Christopher Morris d. 19 Oct 1821.
Hannah Morris, d/o William and Elizabeth Morris, d. 13 Jul 1831.
Rebecca Morris, d/o William and Elizabeth Morris, d. 13 Jul 1831.

Wesley Pitman Morris, s/o William and Elizabeth Morris, d. 22 Aug 1832.
William M. Hunt, s/o James B. and Lydia R. Hunt, d. 30 Jan 1846.
Elizabeth Morris, widow of W. Morris, d. 15 Oct. 1847.
Mary Amanda Wiley d. 3 Jan. 1893.

Muckleroy-Ward Bible
Joseph Galbbreath, Glasgow MDCCLXXII

_____ _____, d/o James and Kesia, b. the last of Feb. 1769.
Maryann and Ann Muckelroy b. 2 Jan 1782 and d. two days after.
William McElroy, s/o John and Mary Ann McElroy, b. Oct 1748, abt 3 o'clock
     in the morning. John McElroy, Jr, s/o John and Mary Ann McElroy, b. 15
     Nov 1750 and d. 17 Jun 1752.
Martha Mountain, d/o John and Maryann Mountain, b. 25 Apr 1759 and d. 13
     Sep 1759.
Maryann Mountain, d/o John and Maryann Mountain, b. 15 Mar 1762, abt 9
     o'clock in the evening.
Isabella Parrett, d/o Richard and Maryann Parrett, b. 9 Oct 1780, abt 8 o'clock in
     the morning.
Isabella Parrett, d/o Richard and Maryann Parrett, b. 27 Sep 1782, abt 12 o'clock
     in the day.
John Muckelroy, s/o William and Rachel Muckelroy, b. 23 Mar 1783, at 8:00
     o'clock in the evening.

William McElroy, h/o Rachel Muckelroy, d. 24 Feb. 1784, aged 35-3-24.
John Mountain d. 23 Dec. 1784.
Mary Parrott d. 15 Feb. 1785, aged 22-11-4.
John Mountain Parrott d. 9 Jan. 1785, aged 5 wks. and 3 dys.

Children of Robert and Elizabeth Ward: David Ward b. 3 Sep. 1788; James
     Ward b. 25 July 1791; William Ward b. 3 Oct. 1793; Mary Ward b. 3 Jan.
     1797; Mary Ann Ward b. 14 Sep. 1800; Isabella Ward b. 12 Sep. 1803,

Mary Ann Parrott, d/o Richard and Mary Parrott, b. 17 Mar. 1779, abt.1:00 in
     the morning.

Daniel Tracey, s/o Daniel and Martha Tracey, d. 2 Apr. 1752, aged 32 yrs.
Martha Tracey, w/o Daniel Tracey, d. 26 Dec. 1752, aged 52 yrs.
Thomas Tracey, s/o Daniel and Martha Tracey, d. 23 Feb. 1771, aged 28 yrs.

Elizabeth Lawrence, w/o Daniel Lawrence, d. 2 May 1779, aged 53 yrs. and 1
    mo.
John Patterson, s/o John and Elizabeth Patterson, d. 12 May 1779, aged 27 yrs.

Mulford Bible

Lewis Mulford b. 29 Aug. 1720 and d. 4 July 1802.
Tamson Mulford b. 14 Dec. 1719 and d. 10 Feb. 1800.
John Mulford b. 2 Dec. 1842 and d. 5 Oct. 1822.
William Mulford b. 23 Dec. 1744 and d. 19 Oct. 1809.
Elizabeth Mulford b. 15 July 1746 and d. 26 Apr. 1827.
David Mulford b. Jan. 1748.
Jonathan Mulford b. 21 Oct. 1749 and d. 1 Apr. 1836.
Lewis Mulford b. 20 Aug. 1752 and d. 20 Oct. 1820.
Furman Mulford b. 5 Feb. 1756 and d. 26 May 1827.
Samuel Mulford b. 18 Oct. 1757 and d. 5 Oct. 1800.
Enoch Mulford, s/o David Mulford, b.26 July 1773.

David Mulford and Mary Sayre mar. 27 June 1775.
Ephraim Mulford and Ruth Wheaton mar. 15 Mar. 1804.
Thomas Mulford and Phebe Butcher mar. 12 Apr. 1804.
Charles Hannah and Mary Mulford mar. 16 Nov. 1805.
Asa Couch and Rebecka Mulford mar. 16 Oct. 1816.

David Mulford Bible
L. Ashmead and Co., Philadelphia 1803

David Mulford and Mary Sayre mar. 27 June 1775.
Ephraim Mulford and Ruth Wheaton mar. 15 Mar. 1804.
Thomas Mulford and Phebe Butcher mar. 12 Apr. 1804.
Charles Hannah and Mary Mulford 16 Nov. 1805.
Asa Couch and Rebecka Mulford mar/ 16 Oct. 1816.

Children of David and Mary Mulford: Hannah Mulford b. 21 June 1776;
    Ephraim Mulford b. 16 Aug. 1778; Mary Mulford b. 27 Oct. 1780;
    Thomas Mulford b. 19 Dec. 1782; Nancy Mulford b. 19 Jan. 1785; David
    Mulford b. 19 July 1787; Sarah Mulford b. 17 Jan. 1790; William Mulford
    b. 29 Feb. 1792; Rebeckah Mulford b. 15 June 1794; John Mulford b. 6
    Oct. 1796; Elizabeth Mulford b. 24 Aug. 1799.

Isaac W. Mulford, s/o Ephraim and Ruth Mulford, b. 26 July 1805.

Children of Richard and Luceta Mulford: Mulford b. 6 Feb. 1831; Phebe
    Mulford b. 3 Feb. 1832; Ann Maria Mulford b. 27 July 1835; Mary
    Mulford b. 17 Mar. 1839; Martha Mulford b. 4 Jan. 1843.

Children of Charles and Mary Hannah: Gilbert Hannah b. 10 Oct. and d. 22
    Nov. 1806, aged 1 mo. and 12 dys; James M. Hannah b. 14 Sep. 1807.

Children of Thomas and Phebe Mulford: Hanna Mulford b. 20 Jan. 1895;
    Richard Mulford b.3 Dec. 1807; Charles H. Mulford b. 27 Feb. 18010;
    Mary Mulford b.31 July 1815; Mary S. Mulford b. 24 July 1817.

David Mulford Couch, s/o Asa and Rebecka Couch, b. 11 July 1817.

Hannah Mulford d. 22 Sep. 1778, aged 2-3-1.
Nancy Mulford d. 14 July 1786, aged 1-4-25.
Sarah Mulford d. 4 Jan. 1792, aged 1-11-11.
John Mulford d. 30 Mar. 1797, aged 5 mo. and 24 dys.
Mary Hannah d. 16 Sep. 1807, aged 26-10-20.
David Mulford d. 3 Aug. 1810, aged 23 yrs. and 15 dys.
Mary Mulford, w/o David Mulford, d. 19 Feb. 1825, aged 67 yrs., lacking 10
    dys.
Mary Mulford, d/o Richard and Luceta Mulford, d. 3 Mar. 1831, aged 23 dys.
David Mulford, Sr., d. 2 Nov. 1832, aged85 yrs. and 9 mo.
Thomas Mulford, Sr., d. 4 Feb. 1834, aged 51-1-6.
Richard Mulford d. 12 Apr. 1874, aged 66-4-9.

Captain William Smith's Records

Cap't. William Smith, s/o the Emigrant Peter Smith and Elizabeth, his wife, b.
    10 Dec. 1742 and d. 26 Apr. 1820. He mar., 18 Jan. 1764, Sarah Stretch,
    who was b. 24 Oct. 1744.
Their children:
Lydia Lucretia Smith b. 11 Feb, 1764 and mar., 12 Jan. 1785, John Harris.
Oliver Smith b. 18 Apr. 1865 and mar., 5 June 1787, Hannah Sims.
Phineas Smith b. 17 Oct. 1768 and mar. Tamson Moore.
Hannah Smith b. 14 Sep. 1779 and mar. James Sims.
Milisent Smith b. 25 Dec. 1772 and d. young.

Sarah Smith b. 17 Oct. 1778 and mar. John Blackwood.
Mary Smith b. 18 Mar. 1779 and d. young.
Washington Smith b. 22 June 1780 and mar., 15 Feb. 1803, Mary Patrick.
Elizabeth Smith b. 27 Apr. 1782 and mar. Abner Simpkins.

Oliver Smith and Hannah Sims mar. 5 June 1787.

Oliver Smith Bible
Matthew Carey, Philadelphia 1801

Oliver Smith and Hannah Sims mar. 5 June 1787.
Edward Gibbs and Clarace Smith mar. 2 Sep. 1812.
David Platts and Lydia Smith mar. 16 Mar. 1820.

Oliver Smith b. 18 Apr. 1865.
Hannah Sims b. 29 Nov. 1766.
Clarace Smith b. 16 Aug. 1787.
Lydia Smith b. 8 Dec. 1788.
Sarah Smith b. 7 June 1791.
William Smith b. 16 Sep. 1794.
Oliver Smith, Jr., b. 6 Feb. 1802
James Smith b. 16 Feb. 1811.

Children of William and Rebecca Smith: Rebecca Smith b. 24 June 1824; Mary
    Smith b. 9 Oct. 1826; Hannah Smith b. 26 June 1828; Charles L. Smith b. 8
    Mar. 1832.

Sarah Smith, d/o Oliver and Hannah Smith, d. 12 Feb. 1818, aged 27-8-5.
Hannah Smith, w/o Oliver Smith, d. 10 Oct. 1818, aged 51-18-1-4.
Clarace Smith, d. 30 Aug. 1824, aged 37 yrs., 14 dys.
William Smith, Jr., d. 26 Apr. 1820, aged 77-4-2.
Oliver Smith, d. 26 Mar. 1833, aged 76-11-8.
Lydia Smith, d/o Oliver and Hannah Smith, d. 4 Nov. 1836, aged 47-10-3-5.
Hannah S. English, d/o William Smith, d. 19 July 1858.
Mary C. Patrick, d/o William Smith, d. 4 Feb. 1850, aged 23-5-26.
William Smith d. 28 Jan. 1870, aged 75-9-12.
Rebecca Smith, w/o William Smith, d. 31 Aug. 1877.
Mary S. Bullock, d/o Hannah S. English, d. 18 Jan. 1878.

Nicholson Bible
Jasper Harding, Philadelphia 1846

Daniel, s/o William and Sarah Nicholson, b. 19 Jan. 1786.
Mary Chambers, d/o Walter and Hope Chambers, b. 16 Sep. 1797.

Daniel Nicholson and Mary Chambers mar. 4 Aug. 1816.
Their children:
Rachel P. Nicholson b. 30 Apr. 1817 and d. 13 Oct. 1891.
George W. Nicholson b. 26 June and d. 2 July 1818.
Homer J. Nicholson b. 29 Oct. 1819 and d. 8 Dec. 1880, aged 61-1-8.
Rebecca Ann Nicholson b. 4 Feb. 1822.
Anna E. Nicholson b. 21 Aug. 1824 and d. 25 Oct. 1849, aged 25-2-4.
William T. Nicholson b. 17 Apr. 1826.
Sarah Ann Nicholson b. 23 Sep. 1827 and d. 27 Oct, 1828, aged 1 yr. and 29
    dys.
Edward H. Nicholson b. 3 Apr. 1831 and d. 1 Mar. 1914.
Ruth B. Nicholson b. and d. (no date given)
Mary C. Nicholson b. and d.15 Aug 1831.
George W. Nicholson b. 9 Oct. 1832.
Elizabeth A. Nicholson b. and d. 11 June 1835.
Caroline Amanda Nicholson b. 7 Sep. 1836.
Hiram Nicholson b. 11 Sep. and d. 12 Dec. 1838, aged 3 mo. and 1 dy.

Daniel Nicholson d. 23 Feb. 1846, aged 61-1-4.

Ogden Bible
Oxford, England 1770

David Ogden's Book by Will of his father, 23 Apr. 1821.
Wharton Ogden's Book by Will of his father, 2 July 1825.

Samuel Ogden b. 8th of 5th mo., 1745 and d. 21st of 4th mo 1821.
Mary Ann Hoofman b. 19th of 10th mo., 1752 and d. 18th of 1st mo., 1818.
Their children:
Mary Ogden Lippincott b. 13th of 6th mo., 1771 and d. 13th of 1st mo., 1797.
Esther Ogden Davis b. 15th of 2nd mo., 1773 and d. 1st of 8th mo., 1845.
Joseph Ogden b. 7th of 8th mo., 1775 and d. 20th of 11th mo., 1863.
Martha Ogden Abbott b. 2nd of 2nd mo., 1779 and d. 4th of 5th mo., 1848.
Hannah Ogden Townsend b.21st of 6th mo., 1781.

Ann Ogden Street b. 22nd of 11th mo., 1783 and d. 31st of 8th mo., 1861.
Sarah Ogden Holmes b. 22nd of 7th mo., 1787 and d. 26st of 2nd mo., 1829.
Samuel Ogden b. 29th of 4th mo., 1790 and d. 8th of 4th mo., 1852.
John Ogden b. 20th of 6th mo., 1792 and d. 4th of 9th mo., 1877.
David Ogden b. 19th of 2nd mo., 1796 and d. 2nd of 7th mo., 1825.

Ogden Bible
Kimber and Sharpless, Philadelphia 1824

John Ogden b. 20 Jun 1792.

Charles S.. Ogden b. 13 Feb 1820 and d. 26 May; 1844, aged 24 yrs.
Mary Ann Ogden b. 10 Jun 1821.
Martha Ogden b. 9 Dec 1823 and d. 19 Jan 1825, aged 13 mo, 10 dys.
Martha H. Ogden b. 1st day of the week, Jan 1826.
David H. Ogden b. 6 Dec 1827
Anna M. Ogden b. 6 Jun 1830.

Children of John and Abigail Ogden, his 2nd wife: Elmira T. Ogden b. 1 Jan 1833; Sarah Jane Ogden b. 23 Dec 1834; Joseph H. Ogden b. 12 Mar 1837; George P. Ogden b. 15 Oct 1839; David Ogden b. 22 Apr 1844.

John Ogden and Anna Howey mar at Piles Grove Meeting 31 Dec 1818.
Clayton C. Atkinson and Abigail J. Antrim mar. 24 Sep. 1818.
Joseph Robins and Sallie J. Ogden mar. 25 Dec. 1856.
George P. Ogden and Sallie P. Rose mar. 6 Mar. 1862.
John Ogden and Emily Deroit mar. 22 Apr. 1896.

Clayton C. Atkinson, s/o John and Mary Atkinson, b. 3 Mar. 1797.
Abigail Antrim, d/o Benajah and Bernice Antrim, b. 20 May 1801.

Children of Clayton C. and Abigail Atkinson: John C. Atkinson b. 10 Feb 1820; Joshua E.
Atkinson b. 10 Sep 1823; Benajah Atkinson b. 12 Nov 1825.

Emily W. Ogden, d/o Charles and Tamar Ogden, b. 22 Sep 1843.

John, s/o George and Sallie L. Ogden, b. 8 Dec. 1862.
Alfred, s/o George and Sallie L. Ogden, b. 12 Oct. 1867.

Children of Joseph and Annie Ogden: Charles Groff Ogden, b. 12 Oct. 1866;
Elmira Townsend Ogden, b. 13 Dec. 1868; Jesse Tyson V14 Dec. 1870;
Lizzie Logan Ogden, twins, b. 7 May 1874.

Martha Ogden, 1st deceased d/o John and Ann Ogden, d. 19 Jan. 1825, aged 13
mo., 10 dys.

Clayton C. Atkinson, s/o John and Mary Atkinson, d. 14 Mar 1828.
Charles L. Ogden, s/o John and Ann Ogden, d. 26 May 1844, aged 24 yrs.
Tamar A. Ogden Thompson, w/o Charles Ogden, d 18 July 1856, aged 32 yrs.
Sallie J. Ogden, w/o Joseph Robins, d. 22 Nov.1859, aged 25 yrs,
Abigail Ogden, 2nd w/o John Ogden, d. 28 Dec.1861, aged 62 yrs.
Elmira L. Ogden d. 10 Oct. 1863, aged 37 yrs.
Freddie, s/o George and Sallie Ogden, d. 26 June 1869, aged 1-8-14.
Elmira T. Ogden d. 3 Oct. 1869, in her 36th yr.
Emily W. Ogden d. 18 July 1873, aged 33 yrs.
Martha F. Ogden, d/o George and Sallie Ogden, d. 23 Feb. 1874, aged 4 yrs., 6
mo.
Mary Tyson Ogden d. 26 Sep. 1874.
Emily W. Ogden, d/o Charles and Tamar Ogden, d. 18 July 1874.
John Ogden d. 4 Sep. 1877, aged 86 yrs.

Joseph D. Pancoast Bible
S. Andrus and Son, 1844

David D. Pancoast and Ann H. Davis mar 8 Feb 1827.

Joseph Barnes and Phoebe Ann High mar 18 Jun 1831.
Joseph D. Pancoast and Mary Jane Barnes mar. 26 Feb. 1857.
John Pancoast, s/o Edward Pancoast, b. 17 Mar 1765 and d. 18 Jul 1831.
Sarah Pancoast, d/o Bradway Keasby, b. 15 Jun 1766.

Joseph Davis b. 15 Jun 1776 and d. 24 Feb. 1837.

Mary Davis, w/o Joseph Davis, b. 1 Nov 1770 and d. 14 Dec. 1849.

Joseph Barnes, s/o Jonathan and Rebecca Barnes, b. 2 Mar 1796 and d. 21 Oct.
1863.

Phoebe Ann High, d/o Lot and Mary High, b. 24 Mar 1814 and d. 2 Mar 1849.

Mary Jane Pancoast, d/o Joseph and Phoebe Barnes, b. 2 Nov 1836 and d. 21 Mar. 1930

Joseph D. Pancoast, s/o David and Ann H. Pancoast, b. 9 Jul 1833 and d. 7 Dec. 1879.
David C. Pancoast, s/o John and Sarah Pancoast, b. 13 Dec 1802 and d. 26 Nov. 1881.
Ann H. Pancoast, d/o Joseph and Mary Davis, b. 3 Sep. 1807 and d. 11 Dec. 1878.

Isabell Stottsenburg b. 20 June 1867.
Morris Hall Pancoast b. 27 Apr. 1877.

Children of Joseph D. and Mary Jane Pancoast: Louis Pancoast b. 11 May 1859 and d. 9 May 1901; David Archer Pancoast b. 8 May 1868; Mary David Pancoast b. 24 May 1870; Charles Fithian Pancoast b. 19 Sep. 1875 and d. 24 Mar. 1928; Morris Hall Pancoast b. 27 Apr. 1877.

Isabella Pancoast's Bible
William W. Harding, Philadelphia 1862

John Pancoast b. (no date).

Sarah Keasby, b. 15 May 1764.
Joseph Davis b. 15 June 1776.
Mary Haines, w/o Joseph Davis, b. 1 Nov. 1778.

David C. Pancoast b. 13 Dec 1802.
Ann H. Davis b. 3 Sep 1807.
David C. Pancoast and Anna H. Davis mar at Friend's Meeting House, Woodstown, 2 Aug 1827.
James D. Lawson and Mary D. Pancoast mar. 27 Feb. 1851.
Joseph D. Pancoast and Mary J. Barnes mar. 26 Feb. 1867.
Samuel T. Lippincott and Martha F. Pancoast mar. 28 Apr. 1859.
Joseph W. Scull ans Isabell Pancoast mar. 2 June 1889.
Enoch C. Stottsenberg and Annie E. Pancoast mar. 28 Apr. 1859.
David Pancoast and Elizabeth B. Hurley mar. 14 Mar. 1867.

Children of David and Ann Pancoast: William F. Pancoast b. 7 Feb 1738; Mary Pancoast b. 28 Nov 1829; Martha F. Pancoast b. 22 Dec1831; Joseph D.

Pancoast b. 9 Jul 1833; Ann E. Pancoast b. 27 Jul 1835; Ellen Pancoast b. 20 Dec 1837; David Pancoast b. 30 May 1840; William Henry Pancoast b. 16 Mar 1843; Charles F. Pancoast b. 8 Mar 1844; Isabella Pancoast b. 26 May 1846; Rebecca Spicer Pancoast b. 11 Jun 1847.

William F. Pancoast, s/o David C. and Anna H. Pancoast, d. 30 Aug 1831, aged 3-6-23.

Joseph Davis d. 24 Feb 1837, over 70 years.
Ellen Pancoast, d/o David C. and Ann H. Pancoast, d. 19 Jul 1838, aged 6 Mo, 29 dys.
Rebecca Spicer Pancoast, d/o David C. and Ann H. Pancoast, d. 15 Aug 1847, aged 7 wks.
Mary Davis, w/o Joseph Davis, d. 14 Dec 1849.
Martha F. Lippincott, w/o S. T. Lippincott, d. 31 Aug. 1878.
Anna H. Pancoast, w/o David C. Pancoast, d. 11 Dec. 1878.
Joseph D. Pancoast, s/o David C. and Ann H. Pancoast, d. 7 Dec. 1879.

Finlaw/Corlifs Bible
Matthew Carey, Philadelphia 1812

John Finlaw and Rebeckah Carlifs mar 15 Feb 1796.
Joseph Carlifs and Mary Hildrith b. 9 Jan 1817.
Ephraim Carll and Elizabeth Finlaw mar 24 Dec 1817.
Edward Hancock and Claaracy Finlaw mar 11 Feb 1819.

William Plummer and Rebecca Carll mar 21 Feb 1839.
William Smith and Rebecca Finlaw mar 15 Feb 1826.

Samuel Patrick and Mary C. Smith mar 9 Jan 1845.

Anthony English and Hannah Smith mar 27 Jan 1848.
Samuel Patrick and Rebecca F. Smith (2nd wife) mar 17 Jun 1852.
Charles Leslie Smith and Rebecca J. Wood mar. 18 Jan. 1857.

John Finlaw b. 13 Dec. 1770.

Children of Daniel and Rebeckah Corlifs: Elenor Corlifs b. 9 Apr 1790; Mary Corlifs b. 5 Sep 1791; Joseph Corlifs b. 27 Oct 1793.

John and Rebekah Finlaw: David Finlaw b. 15 Nov 1796; Elizabeth Finlaw b.6
Sep 1799; Claaracy Finlaw b. 6 May 1803; Rebeckah Finlaw b. 22 Mar
1805.

Children of Ephraim and Elizabeth Carll: Rebecca Carll b. 8 Apr 1819; Barbara
Carll b. 22
Apr 1821; Elizabeth Carll b. 14 Sep 1825.

Children of Edward and Claaricy Hancock: John F. Hancock b. 7 Dec 1819;
Elizabeth Ann
Hancock b. 9 Mar.1824; Ann Hancock b. 21 Feb 1828.

Children of William and Rebeckah Smith: Mary C. Smith b. 9 Oct 1826;
Hannah S. Smith b.

26 Jun 1828; Charles Leslie Smith b. 8 Mar 1832; Rebecca F. Smith b. 24 Jun
1834.

John Finlaw d. 9 Oct 1840, aged 69-9-26, and was bur in the Baptist Burial
Ground in Alloway's Creek.

Hannah S. English, d/o William Smith, d. 19 July 1858, aged 30 yrs.
William Smith d. 28 June 1870, aged 75-9-12.
Rebecca Smith, w/o William Smith and d/o John and Rebecca Finlaw, d. 31
Aug. 1877, aged 72-5-9.
Claracy, d/o John and Rebecca Finlaw, d. 8 Aug. 1874, aged 71-3-2.
Charles Leslie Smith d. 22 Mar. 1898, aged 66 yrs.
Elizabeth Hogbin, d/o William Hogbin, d. 3 Mar. 1858, in her 20th yr.

Patrick Bible
Collius and Company, New York 1816

Jesse Patrick b. 9 Jan 1790.
Ann Hancock b. 8 Sep 1791.
Jesse Patrick and Ann Hancock mar 11 Oct 1810.
Their children: Elizabeth H. Patrick b. 18 Sep 1811; Abner Patrick b. 8 Dec
1813; John Patrick b. 9 Oct 1815; Jesse Patrick, Jr, b. 4 Nov 1817; Ephriam
Patrick b. 30 Nov 1819; Samuel Patrick

b. 5 Nov 1822; Jesse Patrick b. 19 Dec 1824; Edgar Patrick b. 22 May 1827;
Ann Elizabeth Patrick b. 15 Apr 1829; Mary Patrick b. 25 Mar 1831.

Children of Ephriam and Margret Patrick: John H. Patrick b. 15 Mar 1842;
Susanna D. Patrick b. 23 Dec 1844; Ann Elizabeth Patrick b. 16 Jan 1847.

Jesse Patrick d. 31 Aug 1819, aged 1-9-27.
Elizabeth Patrick d. 19 Aug 1821, aged 9 yrs, 9 mo.
Edgar Patrick d. 31 Jul 1828, aged 1-2-9.
Jesse Patrick, Sr, d. 23 Jul 1834, aged 44-6-14.
Elizabeth Dubois d. 3 May 1854, aged 25 yrs. and 18 dys.
John H. Patrick d. 17 Oct. 1859, aged 44 yrs. and 8 dys.
Ann Ashton, relict of Jesse Patrick, d. Mar. 1885, aged 93 yrs. and 6 mo.
Samuel Patrick d. 10 Apr. 1901, in his 79th yr.

Patterson Bible
Jasper Harding and Son, Philadelphia 1857

James Patterson, s/o John Patterson, emigrant, b. 1749 and d. 1806. He mar.,
1771, Martha Kent, b. 1751, d. 1806.

James Patterson, s/o above John Patterson, b. 14 Apr. 1792 and d. 5 May 1865.
He mar., Nov. 1817, by Rev. John Walker, Prudence Mulford, d/o Jacob
Mulford, b. 3 June 1791 and d. 1 Jan. 1844.

William Patterson b. 29 Nov. 1818 and d. 27 Aug. 1900. Mar., 28 May 1846, by
Rev. J. Helm, in Old Presbyterian Church, Salem, N. J., Amelia Ramsey, b.
27 June 1823 and d. 6 Aug. 1886; Jacob Mulford Patterson b. 25 Aug. 1825
and d. 18 Apr. 1885. Mar. 21 July 1854, Clementine P. Lloyd.

Children of above: George Rumsey Patterson b. 2 Mar. and d. 29 Aug. 1849;
Anna Rumsey Patterson b. 29 Nov. 1850; James Kent Patterson b. 28 Aug.
1823(?) and d. 7 Nov. 1889; Henry Ware Patterson b. 9 Nov. 1855 and d.
31 Jan. 1924; Jacob Mulford Patterson b. 25 Aug. 1825, d. 18 Apr. 1885
and mar., 21 July 1854, Clementine F. Lloyd; Theophilus Patterson b. 18
Oct. 1827, d. 7 Sep. 1894 and mar., 8 June 1858, Caroline Rowe, b. 24 Feb.
1829 and d. 11 July 1925; Mary Jane Patterson b. 17 Aug. 1831, d. 14 Oct.
1884 and mar., 26 Nov. 1866, John C. Cooke.

Job Ware b. 4 Dec. 1761, d. 19 Mar. 1806 and Mae. Hannah ....

Bacon Ware, s/o Job Ware, b. 16 Mar.1794, d. 10 Mar. 1853 and mar., 9 Feb.
   1820, Anna Jane Rumsey, b. 28 Dec. 1796 and d. 26 Oct. 1853, d/o
   Benjamin Rumsey and Mary Clark.
Children of Bacon and Anna Jane Ware:
George Clark Ware b.27 Mar. 1821, d. 30 Dec. 1866 and mar. Margret Wooton.
Henry Burtt Ware b. 24 Aug. 1825, d. 23 July 1875 and mar. Sarah Gilmore
   Cattell, b. 16 Aug. 1825 and d. 23 July 1910, d/o Thomas W. Cattell.
Richard Baxter Ware b. 19 Mar. 1827 and mar. 9 June 1858, Hannah Frances
   Allen, b. 7 July 1826 and d. 9 Sep, 1900.

Children of Henry Burtt and Sarah Gilmore Ware:
Anna Rumsey Ware b. 18 Feb. 1857; Thomas Bacon Ware b. 23 June 1859;
   Henry Orso Ware b. 30 July 1861 and d. 17 Mar. 1868; Alexander Cattell
   Ware b. 27 Nov. 1863.

Children of Richard Baxter and Hannah Frances Ware: Charles Wood Ware b. 6
   July 1861; Allan Bacon Ware b. 6 July 1861 and d. Dec. 1925; Harriet
   Archer Ware b. (no date); George Janvier Ware b. 27 July 1863.

Rumsey Family Bible
American Bible Society 1847

Benjamin Rumsey b. 26 Jan 1772 and d. 1 Apr 1802.
Mary Clark b. 1 Jan 1774 and d. 3 Apr 1817.
Benjamin Rumsey and Mary Clark mar 9 Feb 1820 [Obvious error]
Their children: Charles Rumsey b. 24 Apr 1795 and d. 4 Sep 1841; Anna Jane
   Rumsey b. 28 Dec 1796 and d. 26 Oct 1853; George Clark Rumsey b. 24
   Nov 1798 and d. 21 Dec 1851; Eliza Brown Rumsey b. 24 Jan 1801 and d.
   18 Sep 1805.

Benjamin Rumsey was the son of Col. Charles Rumsey, who was the son of
   William Rumsey, a son of Charles Rumsey, an emigrant from Wales.
   Settled St the head of Bohemia River, Maryland. Home called Bohemia
   Manor.

Col. Charles Rumsey, s/o William Rumsey, was b. at Bohemia Manor, Cecil
   Co., Maryland, 1736 and d. 1780. He mar Abigail Caner in1672(?). He was
   a Col. in the Maryland Line of the Continental Army, Revolutionary War.

Richman Bible
Matthew Carey, Philadelphia 1801

Michael Richman and Rebecca Keen mar 19 Dec 1754.

Rebecca Keen, d/o Mounce and Elizabeth Keen and w/o Michael
Richman, b. 13 ___ 1731.
Their children: Nehemiah Richman b. 22 Oct 1755; Elizabeth Richman b. 12
    Feb 1757; Sarah Richman b. 18 Oct 1758; Moses Richman b. 13 Feb 1761;
    Rebecca Richman b. 28 Jan 1763; Jeremiah Richman b. 28 Nov 1764;
    Magdalen Richman b. 1 Sep 1766; James Richman b. 1 Mar 1768;
    Margaret Richman b. 11 Jan 1770.

Children of Nehemiah and Mary Richman: Charlotte Richman b. 15 Aug 1792;
    Moses Richman b. 28 May 1794; Moses Richman b. 28 May 1797;
    Nehemiah Richman, Jr, b. 16 Jun 1799.

Harrison Johnson and Emily Richman mar on the evening of 13 Mar 1845, by
    the Rev. G. W. Janvier.
Harriet McCollister Richman mar William Allen 25 Sep 1823.
Harriet McCollister Richman Allen mar (2nd) Charles Wood 3 Apr. 1828.
Joseph L. Richman and Margaret Jane Van Meter mar 18 Feb 1841.
Hannah Frances Allen, d/o William and Harriett Allen, mar. Richard Baxter
    Ware (no date).
William Allen Wood mar. Sabina S. Snyder 25 Oct. 1854.
William Allen Wood mar. Sarah Richman (2nd wife) 29 Feb. 1872.

William Allen s/o Benjamin and Hannah Allen, b. 8 Mar 1798.
Charles Wood b. 17 Jan 1799.
Moses Richman and Phebe DuBois mar the evening of 18 Mar 1817 by Rev.
    Mr. Janvier.
Elijah Bowen Richman, s/o Moses Richman and Phebe DuBois. b. 29 Dec 1817
Emily Richman, d/o Moses Richman and Phebe DuBois, b. 19 Sep 1820.
Hannah Frances Allen, d/o William and Harriet McColister Richman Allen, b. 7
    Jul 1824 and mar Richard Baxter Ware.
William Allen Wood, s/o Charles and Harriet Wood, b. 29 Sep1829 and d. 27
    June 1906.
Sarah Richman b. 4 Mar 1842.
Harriett McCollister Richman b. 31 May 1802.
Hannah Moore Richman b. 31 May 1894.
Rebecca Keen Richman b. 12 Dec 1808.

James Pennington Richman, s/o Joseph L. Richman and Margaret Jane Van
    Meter, b. 5 Jan 1841(?).

Michael Richman d. 12 May 1773.
Jeremiah Richman d. 9 Jul 1773.
Moses Richman, Sr, d. 17 Feb 1790.
Rebecca Richman d. 10 Sep 1791.
Charlotte Richman, d/o Jeremiah and Mary Richman, d. 23 Sep 1794.
Mary Richman, w/o Nehemiah Richman, d. 13 Jan 1795.
Moses Richman, s/o Nehemiah and Hannah Richman, d. 31 Mar 1816.
Elizabeth Richman, or Rose, d/o Michael and Rebecca Richman, d. 9 Jan 1818.
Hannah Richman, w/o Nehemiah Richman, d. 29 Jan 1823 at 20 min past 3;00
    p.m.
Nehemiah Richman d. 20 Feb 1826 at half past 3:00 p.m.
Moses Richman, Jr., d. 27 Aug. 1862, in Pittsgrove, in his 65th yr.

Harriett McCollister Wood, d/o Nehemiah and Hannah Richman, d. 26 Mar.
    1889, aged 37 yrs.
Hannah Moore Wood, d/o Nehemiah and Hannah Richman, d. 3 Mar. 1895,
    aged 91 yrs.

Capt. Abner Penton Bible
Matthew Carey, Philadelphia 1805

Abner Penton, s/o Abner and Rebecca Penton, b. 8 Mar 1741.
Ann Penton, w/o Abner Penton and d/o Job and Phebe Smith, b. 2 Feb 1744.

Abner Penton, Alloways Creek, and Ann Smith, Alloways Creek, mar. 25 Aug
    1764.
Their children: Burton Penton b. 16 Oct 1765; Abner Penton b. 21 Jan 1767;
    Phoebe Penton b. 7 Feb 1768; Rebecca Penton b. 12 Apr 1769; Daniel
    Penton b. 28 Sep 1770; Jeremiah Penton b. 26 Nov 1771; Susannah Penton
    and her sister (twins?) b. 2 Feb 1773; William Penton b. 13 Sep 1774; Mary
    Penton b. 11 May 1776; Ann Penton b. 27 May 1778; Sarah Penton b. 8
    Nov 1779; Temperance Penton b. 13 Feb 1782; Rebecca Penton b. 12 Apr
    1784; Smith Penton b. 2 Jan 1788.

Jane Penton, w/o Daniel Penton and d/o Matthew and Elizabeth Morrifson, b. 12
    Jul 1782.

Jane Morrifson and Daniel Penton mar 12 Mar 1807.
Their children: Elizabeth Penton b. 24 May 1810?; Jane Penton b. _ Mar 1813.

Sarah Penton, w/o Daniel Penton and d/o John and Hannah Cooper, b. 1 Oct
1773.
Their children: Sarah Penton b. 27 Nov 1816; Hannah Penton b. 20 Nov 1818;
Daniel Cooper Penton b. 30 Jun 1820.

John Gregory, s/o William and Catherine (Dunham) Gregory, b. 13 Feb 1811.

Hannah C. Hitchner, d/o Daniel and Sarah Penton, d. 22 Feb. 1886.
Elizabeth Gregory, widow of John Gregory, and d/o d/o Daniel and Jane
Penton, d. 8 Jan. 1898, aged 88 yrs.
John Gregory, h/o Elizabeth Gregory, d. 29 May 1887, aged 76 yrs.

Robins Bible
M. Carey, Philadelphia 1815

Nathaniel Robins, s/o Nathaniel and Mary Robins, b. 14 Mar 1790.
Harriet V. Robins, d/o James and Anne Vernon, b. 23 Sep 1791.
Nathaniel Robins and Harriet Vernon mar in 1815.
Their children: Mary Robins b. 5 Dec 1815; Margaret Robins b. Sep 1817;
James V. Robins b. 7 Jul 1819; Vanroona Robins b. 5 May 1821; Ezekiel
Robins b. 6 Aug 1823.

Hannah L. Robins, d/o Thomas and Ann Lawrie, b. 21 Nov 1796.

Nathaniel Robins and Harriett L. Allen mar in 1825.
Their children: Nathaniel Robins, Jr, b. 3 Sep 1826; Ann L. Robins b. 28 Apr
1828; Joseph A. Robins b. 1 Nov 1830.

Joseph Allen, s/o Ner. and Hope Allen, b. 21 Jan 1796.

Joseph Allen and Hannah Lawrie mar. in 1819.

Sarah Ann Allen, d/o Joseph and Hannah Allen, b. 22 Jun 1820.
Horace Robbins, s/o Joseph and Sarah J. Robbins, b. 22 Feb. 1858.
Emma B. Robbins, d/o Joseph and Margaret C. Robbins, b. 1 Apr. 1870.

Mary Robins, Sr, w/o Nathaniel Robins, d. 24 Aug 1821.

Nathaniel Robins, Sr, d. 18 Apr 1825.

Harriet Robins, w/o Nathaniel Robins, d. 4 Nov 1823, aged 30-1-11.

Vanroom Robins, s/o Nathaniel and Harriet Robins, d. 16 Aug 1824, aged 1-3-11.

Ezekiel Robins d. 6 Aug 1824, aged 1 yr, 10 dys.

James V. Robins, s/o Nathaniel and Harriet Robins, d. 1815.

Nathaniel Robbins, Jr., s/o Nathaniel and Mary Robins, d. 28 Mar. 1869.

Hannah L. Robbins, w/o Nathaniel Robbins, d. 7 Apr. 1882, in her 69th yr.

Joseph A. Robbins, s/o Nathaniel and Hannah J. Robins, d. 30 June 1890, at Swan Lake, South Dakota.

Robinson Bible
M. Carey, Philadelphia 1815

Benjamin Robinson b. 7 Feb 1764.

Elizabeth, w/o Benjamin Robinson, b. 23 Dec 1780.

Their children; Joseph Robinson b. 20 Mar 1805; Mary Robinson b.15 Aug 1807; William Robinson b. 4 Nov 1809; Angeline Robinson b. 2 Dec 1812 and mar Jonathan Kelty, 2 Dec 1840; Caroline Robinson b. 1 Jul 1816; Emeline Robinson b. 31 May 1819; John Robinson b. 15 Jun 1822.

John Robinson d. 14 Oct 1822.

Benjamin Robinson d. 2 Sep 1823.

Elizabeth Robinson d. 27 Sep 1850.

Thompson Bible
H. C. Carey and J. Lea, Philadelphia 1822

William Thompson b. 6 May 1746.

Mary, w/o William Thompson, b. 30 Oct 1751.

Their children: Margaret Thompson b. 13 Sep 1772; James Thompson b. 20 Sep 1774; Isaac Thompson b. 18 Oct 1776; William Thompson b. 13 Jan 1779; Elizabeth Thompson b. 23 Dec 1783.

Margaret Thompson, d/o William and Mary Thompson, d. 10 Oct 1773.

Isaac Thompson d. in 1786.

William Thompson, the younger, d. in 1806.

Mary Thompson, w/o William Thompson, d. 5 Oct 1814

William Thompson d. 31 Dec 1838.

Davenport Bible
Thomas Basket, Oxford, England 1756

Samuel Davenport b. 5 Sep 1750.
Hannah Simpson b. 25 Nov 1755.
Their children: Thomas Davenport b. 15 Sep 1779; Priscilla Davenport b. 7 Feb
1782; Ann Davenport b. 25 Jul 1784; Beulah Davenport b. 23 Nov 1786;
Sarah Davenport b. 30 Oct 1789.

Ann Cavmer, 2nd wife of Samuel Davenport, b. (no date).

Their children: Patience Davenport b. 3 May 1799; Franklin Davenport b. 26
Jun 1801; Rebeckah Davenport b. 17 Feb 1803.

Sheppard Bible
John Bill and Christopher Barker
Printers to the Kings Most Excellent Majesty

Children of David and Sarah Sheppard: Phillip Sheppard b. __ Aug. 1721;
Ephraim Sheppard b. 21 May 1723; David Sheppard b. 15 ___ 1725;
Joseph Sheppard b. 8 Sep 1728; Pheby Sheppard b. 21 May 1730; ____
Sheppard (a son) b. 20 May 1732.

Sarah Sheppard b. 24 Jun 1732 and d. 24 ___ 1783.
David Sheppard b. 10 Mar 1757.
Ruhama Sheppard b. 10 May 1762.

Joseph Sheppard, our Grandfather, b. 8 Sep 1728. Our Grandmother's name was
Mary. Their children, as follows: Ruth Sheppard b. 5 Jun 1758; Lydia
Sheppard b. 29 Apr 1760; William
Sheppard b. 28 Jan 1762; Ruth Sheppard b. 17 Dec 1763; Isaac Sheppard b. 30
Sep 1765; Mary Sheppard b. 14 Jan 1768; Sarah Sheppard b. 20 Feb and d.
16 Sep 1770; Lucy Sheppard b. 10 Oct. 1773; William Sheppard b. 22 Nov
1775 and d. 11 Jun 1775(?); Lydia Sheppard b. 19 Jul 1789(?).

Shepherd Bible
Andrew Anderson 1676
Printer to his Most Sacred Majesty

David Sheppard b. 16 mar 1757 and d. at Morris .(?) with smallpox.
David Sheppard b. 5 Jun 1758, mar Phebe Ludlam 27 May 1783.
Our oldest child, Sarah, b. 25 Jun 1784, mar William Walker and d. 14 Feb
    1814, having 4 children.
Joseph Sheppard, our second child, b. 29 Jan 1786 and mar H. H. Budd 23 Jan
    1813.
Providence L. Sheppard b. 21 Feb 1788 and mar Mary Letson in the autumn,
    1813.
William and David Sheppard b. 8 Apr 1790. David, M. D., d. 4 Jun 1814.
Ercurious Sheppard b. 14 Nov 1793.
Martha L. Sheppard b. 13 Feb 1817.
Charles b. 27 May and d. Sep (no year given).
Ebenezer Sheppard b. 23 Jul 1796 and d. 1 Jun 1814.

The offspring of David and Miriam Smith, Mary H. Sheppard, b. 21 Aug 1800.
Isaac Alpin Sheppard b. 21 Aug 1806.

Henry Sinnickson Bible
Kimber & Sharpless, Philadelphia 1824.

Jonathan Dallas b. 11 Jul 1762.
Elizabeth Clark, w/o Jonathan Dallas b. 2 Oct 1767.
Susan Dallas b. 23 Jun 1792 and d. 3 Jul 1824.

John M. Sinnickson b. 2 Dec 1793.
Ann Dallas Sinnickson, d/o Jonathan Dallas, b. 11 Mar 1800.
John M. Sinnickson and Ann Dallas mar 20 Oct 1819.
Their children: Elizabeth Sinnickson b. 23 Apr 1822; Henry Sinnickson b. 25
    Feb 1824; Dallas Sinnickson b. 26 Apr 1828.

John Johnson and Elizabeth Sinnickson mar. 15 Apr. 1851 by the Rev. John
    Kidney.
Dallas and Mary Sinnickson mar. 23 Nov. 1869.
Henry Sinnickson and Harriet A. Wells mar. 2 Mar. 1864, in Woodbury, N. J.,
    by Rev. S. J. Baird, D. D.

Children of Henry and Harriet Sinnickson: Elizabeth J. Sinnickson b. 21 Jan. 1865 and d. 10 Nov. 1830; Frank A. Sinnickson b. 30 Dec. 1866 and d. 23 Mar. 1921; Henry W. Sinnickson b. 2 Jan. 1869; Mary D. Sinnickson b. 2 July 1875.

Children of Dallas and Mary Sinnickson: Henry Hall Sinnickson b. 17 Oct. 1860; Anna D. Sinnickson b. 27 Nov. 1862; Mary Adeline Sinnickson b. 4 Sep, 1865.

James Dallas Johnson b. 7 June 1874.

Elizabeth Randolph, mother of John M. Sinnickson, d. 17 Feb 1805.
Elizabeth Broadley d. 25 Nov 1815.
John W. Sinnickson d. 11 Apr. 1877.
Henry Sinnickson b. 1824 and d. 12 Oct. 1908.
Harriet A. Sinnickson b. 1838 and d. 2 Aug. 1825.
Frank Acton Sinnickson b. 1866 and d. 28 Mar. 1821.
Elizabeth Johnson Sinnickson Carr, widow of George Wentworth Carr, b. 1865 and d. 10 Nov. 1830.

Sinnickson Bible
M. Carey, Philadelphia 1813
Records of John Sinnickson, b. 1789

Robert Johnson mar Margaret Morgan 18 Dec 1752.
Margaret Johnson, d/o Robert and Margaret Johnson,, b. 2 Aug 1756.

Robert Johnson mar Jane Gibbon 3 Nov 1767, having only one child, Robert G. Johnson, b. 22 Jul 1771.
Captain Andrew Sinnickson mar Margaret Johnson 26 May 1779 by the Rev. Wm. Caxton.

John Sinnickson b. 9 Jul 1789.
Mary Clarissa Sinnickson b. 29 Dec 1790. (1st wife, Howell).

John Sinnickson and Mary C. Howell 3 Mar. 1814 by the Rev. J. Shepherd.
Their children: Harriett Howell Sinnickson b. 29 Nov 1814; Robert Johnson Sinnickson b. 3 Mar 1816; Thomas Sinnickson b. 29 Sep 1818; Stillborn son 25 Sep 1820; William Henry Sinnickson b. 11 Jan 1822.

John Sinnickson and Rebecca K. Hall mar. 23 Sep. 1826 by Joseph Watson, Mayor of Philadelphia.

Children of John and Rebecca Sinnickson: John Howard Sinnickson b.14 Jul 1827; Mary Elizabeth Sinnickson b. 23 Feb 1830; Clement Hall Sinnickson b. 16 Sep 1834.

Harriet H. Sinnickson mar Jonathan Ingham 7 Aug 1838.

Thomas Sinnickson mar Adeline M. Wood, d/o John Wood. Aug. 1848.

Children of Thomas and Adeline Sinnickson: John Wood Sinnickson b. 1849; Mary Howell Sinnickson b. 16 Jan 1853.

J. Howard Sinnickson and Sarah Elizabeth Foreman, d/o John Foreman of Freehold, N. J., mar. 9 Dec. 1854.

Mary E. Sinnickson and Dallas Sinnickson mar. 23 Nov. 1859.

Clement H. Sinnickson and Sarah M. Smith, d/o Louis Smith, mar. 18 June 1862.

Margaret Morgan Johnson, w/o Robert Johnson, d. 24 Nov 1757, aged 23-7-17. (1st wife)

Jane Gibbon d. 4 Nov 1792, aged 36 yrs, 3 mo. (2nd wife)

Robert Johnson d. 28 Dec 1796, aged 69 yrs, 11 mo.

John Sinnickson d. 27 Mar. 1862, aged 73-8-18.

Andrew Sinnickson d. 23 Jul 1819, aged 70-4-17.

Mary Clarissa Sinnickson, w/o John Sinnickson, d. 26 Jan 1822, at half hour bef. 1:00 a.m.

Robert J. Sinnickson, s/o John and Mary Sinnickson, d. Jan 1839, aged 22 yrs, 9 mo.

William Henry Sinnickson, s/o John and Mary Sinnickson, d. 23 Jul. 1844, aged 22-6-11.

Harriet Howell, w/o Jonathan Ingham and d/o John and Mary C. Sinnickson, d.16 May 1877, aged 63-5-17.

Rebecca K. Sinnickson, w/o John Sinnickson, d. 26 Feb. 1882.

Thomas Sinnickson, s/o John and Mary Sinnickson, d. 23 Apr. 1894.

Adeline M. Sinnickson, w/o Thomas Sinnickson, d. 4 June 1895.

John Wood Sinnickson, s/o Thomas and Adeline Sinnickson, b. 1849 and d. 9 July 1911.

Mary Howell Sinnickson, d/o Thomas and Adeline Sinnickson, d. 9 May 1921.

Howell Records

Mary A. Howell d. 1 Jun 1785, aged 20 yrs.
Doc t. Ebenezer Howell d. 22 Jan 1791, aged 43 yrs.
William Parrot d. 11 Apr 1804, aged 52 yrs.
Clarissa Burroughs d. 22 Aug 1843, aged 37 yrs. She was the sister of Ebenezer
    Howell. Her 1st husband was Wm. Parrott, her 2nd, Edward Burroughs.

Clement and Rebecca K. Hall Bible

Clement Hall. s/o Clement and Margaret Hall, b. 13 Nov 1753.
Rebecca Hall. w/o Clement Hall and d/o Joseph and Ann Kay, b. 2 May 1759.
Clement Hall and Rebecca Kay mar. 23 Feb 1887, Salem County, NJ. Clement
    Acton, Hannah Acton, witnesses.
Births of their children; Joseph Hall b. 29 Mar 1779; Ann Hall b. 30 May 1780;
    Margaret Hall b. 19 Apr 1782; Rhoda Hall b. 13 Jan. 1784, a stillborn son
    b. the same time; Margaret Morris Hall b. 14 Jun 1785; Morris Hall b. 27
    Mar 1787; Prudence Hall b. 1 Jun. 1789; Sarah Hall b. 1 July 1791;
    Charlotte Hall b. 2 Jan. 1793; Deborah Kay Hall b. 23 Feb. 1796; Rebecca
    Hall b. 30 June 1798; Isaac Kay Hall b. 14 Aug. 1800.

Deaths of their children:
Joseph Hall d. 2 Apr 1779.
Margaret Hall d. __ Oct 1784.
Rhoda Hall d. 30 Jan 1784.
Charlotte Hall d. 4 Jan 1793.
Isaac Kay Hall d. __ Oct 1801.
Clement Hall d. 12 Sep 1801.
Rebecca K. Hall d. 12 Sep 1835.
Deborah K. Hall d. 6 Oct 1862.

Sinnick Sinnickson Bible
Mark Baskett   1768
Printer to the Kings Most Excellent Majesty

Sinnick Sinnickson, s/o John and Ann Sinnickson, b. 5 Oct 1739.
Mary Sinnickson, d/o Nicholas and Elizabeth Philpot, b. 1 Feb. 1744 and d. 10
    Aug. 1799, aged 55 yrs and 6 mo.

Their children: John Sinnickson b. 25 Dec 1762; Andrew Sinnickson b. 21 mar 1764; Ann Sinnickson b. 20 Jan 1767; William Sinnickson b. 30 May 1769; Elizabeth Sinnickson b. 12 Feb 1772.

Garrison Records

Children of Gamaliel and Mary Garrison: Nicholas Garrison b. 25 Mar 1777; Phebe Garrison (twin) b. 25 Mar 1777; Nehemiah Garrison b. 22 Jul 1779; Mary Garrison b. 13 Jul 1782; Daniel Garrison b. 26 Apr 1785.
Ann Paullin, d/o Enos and Ann Paullin, b. 26 Oct 1788.
Daniel Garrison, s/o Gamaliel Garrison, d. 3 Apr 1803, aged 18 yrs, 23 dys

Smith Bible
Mathew Carey, Philadelphia 1806

Seth Smith, s/o Solomon and Sarah Smith, b. 5 May 1768.
Benjamin Smith b. 25 Aug 1770.
Sarah Smith b. 11 Nov 1772.
Elizabeth Smith b. 20 Oct 1774.
Charity Smith b. 13 Aug 1777.
Solomon, 3 Mar 1780.
Margaret Smith, 13 Oct 1782.
William Smith, 3 Mar 1785.
Abel Smith, 21 May 1786.

Hannah Acton b. 17 May 1785.
William Smith and Hannah Acton mar 21 Mar 1807 at Salem, NJ, by John Firth, J.P.
Their children: Benjamin Smith b. 18 Dec 1807; Edward Smith b. 3 Mar 1811; Samuel Smith b. 19 Dec 1813.

Hannah Smith d. 15 Dec 1826.
William Smith d. 30 May 1825.

John Smith Bible
Mathew Carey, Philadelphia 1806

John Smith, s/o John and Melecent Smith b. 4 Feb 1774.
John Smith and Mary Sinnickson mar 14 Nov 1805 by the Rev. Mr. Fetters.
Their children: Robert Johnson Smith b. 29 Mar 1807, Easter Sunday;
    Margarettte Johnson Smith b. 22 Mar 1810; Thomas S. Smith b. 29 Jul
    1812; Mary S. Smith b. 1 May 1815.

The Rev. Edward Goldsburg Prescott, of Boston, Mass., mar. Margaretta
    Johnson Smith, of Salem, N. J., 23 Apr. 1840, at St. John's Church by the
    Bishop of the Diocese, the Rev. G. W. Brown.

Mary Sinnickson Stoughton, d/o Olivor B. and Mary S. Stoughton, b. 1 Jan
    1845.
Margaretta Prescott Stoughton, d/o Oliver B. and Mary S. Stoughton, b. 18 mar
    1847.
Augustus Bissell Stoughton b. 1 Jun 1849.
Cylinda Bissell Stoughton, d/o Mary S. Stoughton, b. 15 Dec 1850.
Maria Hancock Smith, do Thomas S. and Mary Smith b. 25 Jun 1846.
Thomas Sinnickson Smith, s/o Thomas S. and Mary S. Smith, b. 8 Jul 1851.

Robert Johnson Smith, s/o John and Mary Smith, d. 8 Aug 1808, aged 16 mon,
    10 dys.
John Smith, s/o John and Melicent Smith, d. 11 Dec 1845, in his 72nd yr.
Augustus Bissell Stoughton, s/o Oliver B. and Mary S. Stoughton, d. 7 Feb
    1850, aged 8 mo and 7 dys.
Cylinda Bissell Stoughton, d/o Oliver B. and Mary S. Stoughton, d. 4 Nov 1852,
    aged 1-10-2-5.
Oliver B. Stoughton d. 7 Aug. 1866, in his 75th yr.
Thomas S. Smith d. 26 Oct. 1874, in his 63rd yr.

Thomas S. and Mary G. Smith Bible
R. H. Butler & Co., Philadelphia 1846

Thomas S. Smith, s/o John and Mary Smith, b. 29 Jul 1812.
Mary Goodwin Hancock, d/o Morris and Sarah Hancock, b. 30 May 1822.
Thomas S. Smith and Mary G. Hancock mar 25 Apr 1843.

Their children: Morris Smith b. 27 Apr 1844; Thomas Smith b. 29 May 1845; Maria Hancock Smith b. 25 Jun 1846; Mary Smith b. 22 Jul 1848; Prescott Smith b. 8 Apr 1850; Thomas Sinnickson Smith b. 8 Jul 1851.

Morris, s/o Thomas S. and Mary G. Smith, d. 27 Apr 1844.
Thomas Smith, s/o Thomas S. and Mary G. Smith, d. 20 Jun 1845.
Mary, d/o Thomas S. and Mary G. Smith, d. 23 Jul 1848, aged 1 day.
Prescott, s/o Thomas S. and Mary G. Smith, d. 12 Apr 1850, aged 4 dys.
Mary G. Smith d. 8 July 1856, aged 34 yrs.
Thomas S. Smith d. 26 Oct. 1874, aged 62 yrs.
Thomas S. Smith, Jr., d. 9 Dec. 1881, aged 30 yrs.
Constant M. Eakin d. 26 Apr. 1885.

Morris Hancock, s/o Thomas and Mary Hancock, b. 21 Feb 1785.
Sarah Hancock, d/o John and Eleanor Hancock, b. 5 Feb 1792.

Morris Hancock and Sarah Hancock mar 16 Jan 1812.

Morris Hancock d. 28 Jan 1836, aged 51 yrs.
Sarah Hancock d. 13 Jun 1848, aged 56 yrs.

John Smith, s/o John and Melicent Smith, b. 4 Feb 1774 and d. 11 Dec 1845, aged 72 yrs.
Mary Sinnickson, d/o Andrew and Margaret Sinnickson, b. 27 Aug. 1781. They mar 14 Nov 1805.
Eleanor Yorke Eakin, d/o Constant M. and Maria H. Eakin, b. 15 Oct 1868 and d. 28 Mar. 1932.
Constance Dumine Eakin, d/o Constant M. and Maria H. Eakin, b. 13 Aug. 1870.

Nelson Family Bible
J. Holbrook's Stereotyped Copy, 6th Edition
Brattleborough, VT 1817

Gabriel Nelson and Sarah his wife mar 1 Jan 1779.
Gabriel Nelson d. 10 Dec 1788.
Sarah Nelson, w/o Gabriel Nelson, d. 20 Feb 1805.
Their children: Davis Nelson b. 1 Jul 1779; Anthony Nelson b. 15 Jan 1782; Hannah Nelson b. 16 Apr 1784; Jonathan Nelson b. 15 ___ 1785; Phebey Nelson b. 29 Apr 1788.

Davis Nelson and Frances Miller mar 21 Oct 1802.
Their children: John M. Nelson b. 31 May 1803; William H. Nelson b. 24 Nov 1804; Eliza M. Nelson b. 14 Nov 1806.

William H. Nelson, s/o Davis and Frances Nelson, mar Joel Greer b. 3. Jul 1838. He built the Nelson House, once famous hotel in Salem, NJ.

Frances Nelson, w/o Davis Nelson, d.17 Sep 1838, aged 56 yrs.
Phebey Nelson, d/o Gabriel and sarah Nelson, d. 4 May 1807.
Jonathan Nelson, s/o above, d. 2 Apr 1814.
Anthony Nelson d. 11 Aug 1834, aged 52 yrs, 6 mo.
Sarah Nelson, w/o Anthony Nelson, d. 1 Dec 1842, aged 59 yrs.
Dr. John M. Nelson, s/o Davis and Frances Nelson, d. 2 Sep 1845, in his 43rd yr.
William H. Nelson d. 14 Jan. 1865, aged in his 63rd yr.
Eliza M. Waddington d. 15 Mar. 1869, in her 63rd yr.

Holy Bible
Isaac Collins, Trenton, New Jersey 1791

Mary Street and Joseph Fogg mar 11 May 1775.

Children of Joseph and Mary Fogg: Sarah Fogg b. 1 Jun 1776; Lydia Fogg b. 27 Sep 1777; Joseph Fogg, Jr, b. 28 Oct 1785.

David Stretch and Mary Stretch mar 1787.

Children of David and Mary Stretch: Hannah Stretch b. 8 Jan 1788; Jonathan Stretch b. 3 Mar 1790; Nathaniel Stretch b. 9 Feb 1792; David Stretch b. 8 Mar 1795; Mark Stretch b. 13 June 1797; Joel Stretch b. 17 Nov 1799.

Mary C. Sprogell Yorke Bible
Thomas Baskett, London
Printers to the King's Most Excellent Majesty

Mary Robeson, d/o David and Elenor Robeson, b. 20 Jun 1722.
Georgiana Bryan (?) Farquhar, d/o George and Elizabeth Farquhar, b. 1 Mar 1795 at 10:00 in the morning.

Children of Thomas and Martha Yorke: Stephen Yorke b. 3 Dec 1735 at 9 of the
clock at night; Edward Yorke b. 20 Sep 1738 at ¾ past 7 in the evening.

Children of Thomas and Margaret Yorke: Thomas Yorke, Jr, b. 26 Nov 1740 at
9 in the evening; Andrew York b. 26 Nov 1742 at half past 2 in the
morning.

Children of Thomas and Mary Yorke: Robeson Yorke b. 16 Dec 1743; Martha
Yorke b. 11 Jun 1747; Margaret Yorke b. 22 Mar 1749 at 3:00 in the
afternoon; Samuel Yorke b. 22 Mar 1753 9:00 at night; Mary York b. 22
Mar 1735? At 1:00 in the afternoon.

Thomas, s/o Edward and Sarah Yorke, b. 22 Jun 1763 at 2:00 in the morning.

Thomas Yorke, Esq, d. 24 Jun 1764 and was buried the 27th following at
Perkiomen Church.
David Robeson d. 26 Mar 1764.
Elinor Robeson d. 13 Jan 1778.
Ludonick Sprogells d. 12 Feb 1781.
Edward Yorke d. 12 Apr 1781.
Margaret Morgan d. 19 Oct 1784 in her 36th year.
Doctor Robeson Yorke d. 7 Jan 1786 in his 43rd year.

Andrew Yorke Bible   1791

Andrew Yorke d. in his 50th year and was buried in the church yard at Salem on
23 Mar 1794.
Elinor Yorke, widow of Andrew Yorke, d. in her 56th year and was buried in the
church yard at Salem on 24 Jan 1802.
Andrew Yorke, s/o Andrew and Elinor Yorke, d. in his 27th year and was buried
in the church yard at Salem on 12 Oct 1806.

Thomas Yorke and Margaret Robeson, his 2nd wife, were married by the Rev.
Mr. Ross of Oxford, in the county of Philadelphia, by whom he had issue,
Thomas Yorke, now of London, and Andrew his brother.

Andrew Yorke married Eleanor Cox by the Rev. Mr. Wrangel of Wicacoa, by
whom he had issue:

Christian b. 17 May 1767 and d. July 1769.

Lewis, b. 19 Feb 1770 at Alloways Creek, Salem County.

Marget, b. 26 Apr 1772 and d. Mar 1773.

Eleanor, b. 20 Feb 1774 and d. 21 Oct 1840.

Martha, b. 7 Jan 1778 and d. 22 Dec 1815.

Andrew, b. 5 Sep 1779.

Mary, b. 4 Dec 1781 and d. 1784.

Thomas, b. 1 Oct 1785 and d. 28 Jun 1820, aged 34 years.

Thomas J. Yorke Bible

Thomas Jones Yorke, s/o Lewis and Mary Yorke, b. at Hancock's Bridge, county of Salem, NJ, on 25 Mar 1801 at about 4:00 p.m.

Mary Ann Smith, d/o Jonathan and Elizabeth Smith, b. at New Hope, Bucks Co., PA on 1 Jul 1803.

Thomas Jones York and Mary Ann Smith were married at the residence of Louis P. Smith on Wed. evening, 7 Apr, 1830 by the Rev. Henry M. Mason, Pastor of St. John's Church, Salem, NJ.

Louis Eugene Yorke, s/o Thomas J. and Mary Ann Yorke, b. Thursday, 13 Dec 1832, at 3:00 in the afternoon.

Mary Ann, w/o Thomas Jones Yorke, d. on Sun, 15 Jun 1834, at 3:00 p.m.

Margaret Johnson Sinnickson, d/o Thomas and Elizabeth Sinnickson, b. at Salem on 26 Jan 1814.

Thomas Jones Yorke and Margaret Johnson Sinnickson were married at the residence of her father Thomas Sinnickson in Salem, on Wed. evening, 28 Nov 1838 by the Rev. Edward G. Prescott, Pastor of St. John's Church.

Their children: Mary Adelaide Yorke b. 25 Sep 1839, at half past 9:00 a.m; Elizabeth Sinnickson Yorke b. Sat. morning, 20 Feb 1841, at 40 minutes before 1:00; Thomas Jones Yorke b. at Salem on Sun. night, 10 Jun 1843, at a few minutes before 12:00; Margaret Johnson Yorke b. at Salem on Thurs, 20 Mar 1845, at 3:00 a.m; Caroline Perry Yorke b. at Salem on Tues, 26 Jun 1849, at a quarter before 2:00.

William F. Allan and Caroline P. Yorke mar. at St. John's Church, Salem, N. J., on Thurs., 20 Apr 1871, by the Rev. Dr. Garrison.

D. W. C. Clement and Mary Adelaide Yorke mar. at the residence of her father, t. Jones Yorke, in Salem, on Mon., 24 Apr. 1861, by the Rev. Thomas T. Ballopp, Rector of St. John's Church, sd city.

Lieut. Col. Louis Eugene Yorke, Asst' Inspector General, 15th Corps (Capt., 13th U. S. Infantry), and Mary Taylor Miller mar. at the residence of her grandfather, Griffin Taylor, at Clifton, near Cincinnati, Ohio, at 1:30 P.M., 1 Nov. 1864, by the Rev. Samuel Clements, rector of Clifton Chapel.

Joseph B. Parker, a Surgeon in the U. S. Navy, and Margaret Johnson Yorke mar. on Thurs., 15 Oct. 1868, at St. John's Church, Salem, N. J., by the Rev. Wm. A. Holbrook, Rector.

Louis Eugene Yorke, s/o Thomas J. and Mary Ann Yorke, d. at Cincinnati, Ohio, 4 Apr. 1882, in his 81st yr.

DeWitt Clinton Clement, s/o Samuel and Eliza Clement, d. in Salem, N. J., 10 Jan. 1833, in his 57th yr.

Margaret Johnson Yorke, widow of Thomas J. Yorke and d/o Thomas and Elizabeth Sinnickson, d. in Salem, N. J., 9 Jan. 1900, aged 86 yrs.

Thomas Jones Yorke, Jr., s/o Thomas Jones and Margaret Johnson Yorke, d. in Salen, N. J., 3 Dec. 1913, aged 70 yrs.

Dr. Joseph B. Parker, U. S. N., d. in Philadelphia, on 21 Oct. 1915, aged 74 yrs.

Margaret J. Yorke, w/o Joseph B. Parker, d. 20 Aug. 1920, aged 70 yrs.

William Frederick Allen, h/o Caroline P. Yorke, d. at South Orange, N. J., 11 Nov. 1915, aged 69 yrs.

Elizabeth Sinnickson Yorke, d/o Thomas and Margaret J. S. Yorke, d. in Salem, N. J., 7 Feb. 1925, aged 84 yrs.

Samuel Allen Bible

Samuel Allen, s/o Jedediah and Mary Allen b. 11 Dec 1762, at Mannington, Salem Co., NJ, and mar., 15 Sep 1785, Mary Brown.

Their children: Maria Allen b. 25 Jun 1786 and d. 20 Aug 1787; Rebecca Allen b. 28 Oct 1787 and d. dec 1808; Maria Allen b. 16 Jul 1789 and d. 31 Jul 1790; Robert Allen b. 17 Nov and d. 30 Nov 1790; Robert Allen b. 23 Jul 1793 and d. 12 Dec 1815.

Mary Allen, w/o Samuel Allen, d. 22 Nov 1795, aged 32 years and some months.

Kitty Vaughn Allen, d/o Richard and Jane Cox, b. at Mt. Holly, NJ, 22 Oct 1781. Married 5 Sep 1799, and d. 28 Mar 1844.

Children of Samuel and Kitty V. Allen: Maria Louisa Allen b. 22 Aug 1800 at
Mt. Holly and d. 13 Nov 1838; Richard Cox Allen b. 12 Jul 1802 at Mt
Holly and d. 26 Aug 1858; Samuel Allen, Jr, b. 23 Dec 1804 at Philadelphia
and d. 8 Jun 1842; William Allen b. 6 Dec 1809 at Philadelphia and d. May
1830; Edward Allen b. at Philadelphia 26 Feb 1811 and d. 25 Jun1838;
Katherine Cox Allen b. at Philadelphia 20 Nov 1812; Chamless Allen b. at
Philadelphia 27 Apr 1814 and d. 2 May 1816; Jane Ross Allen b. at
Philadelphia 5 Apr 1820.

Catherine R. Allen, d/o William and Ann Rosell, b. at Mt Holly, NJ, 24 Oct
1805. Married to Samuel Allen, Jr, 3 Dec 1827.
Their children: William Rosell Allen b. at Philadelphia 29 Dec 1828. Married to
Elizabeth Frazier Head 3 Dec 1863 and d. 27 Jan 1872; Anna Eliza Allen b.
at Mt Holly 1 Aug 1830; Marian Wilmer Allen b. at Philadelphia Dec 1833
and d. 17 Sep 1834; Charles Cariol (?) Allen b. at Mt Holly 20 Sep 1839
and d. 13 ___ 1843 at Mt Holly.

Elizabeth Frazier Allen, d/o Joseph and Ann Frances Head, b. at Boston 22 May
1832.
Samuel Allen, s/o Samuel and Catherine R. Allen, b. at Mt. Holley, 22 Aug.
1842 and d. 13 ....1857.
Charlotte Louisa, d/o Wm. R. and Eliz. F. Allen, b. at Mt. Holley, Friday, 30
Dec. 1864.
Nathan Myers, s/o Wm. R. and Eliz. F. Allen, b. at Mt. Holley, Sunday, 14 Oct.
1866.

Morris Hancock Bible

Morris Hancock, s/o Thomas and Mary Hancock, b. 21 Feb 1785.
Sarah Hancock, d/o John and Eleanor Hancock, b. 5 Feb 1792.
Morris Hancock and Sarah his wife mar 16 Jan 1812.
Eleanor Caroline Hancock, d/o Morris and Sarah Hancock, b. 30 Nov 1812.
Thomas Hancock, s/o Morris and Sarah Hancock, b. 23 Mar. 1829.
John Hancock, s/o Morris and Sarah Hancock, b. 30 Sep 1831.
Morris Thomas Hancock, s/o Morris and Sarah Hancock, d. 9 Feb 1827 at 20
min past 3:00 p.m., aged 7-4-20.
Thomas Hancock, s/o Morris and Sarah Hancock, d. 5 Aug. 1830, about 8:00 in
the evening, aged 1-4-12.

Eleanor C. Hancock and Daniel Stratton mar 10 Oct 1837 by Rev. A. Herberton.

Their children: Morris Hancock Stratton b. 19 Jul 1838; Daniel P. Stratton b. 19
    Sep 1839 and d. 13 Jan 1901. Bur at Nevada, MO; Henry Stratton b. 8 Jul
    1842 and d. 12 Jul 1843, New Bern, NC; Eleanor Yorke Stratton b. 17 Aug
    1854 and d. 7 Aug 1855.

Thomas S. Smith and Mary G. Hancock mar 25 Apr 1843 by Rev. James I.
    Helm.
Their children: Morris H. Smith b. 28 Apr 1844; Thomas Smith b. 29 May and
    d. 20 Jun 1845, aged 22 days; Maria Hancock Smith b. 25 Jun 1846; Mary
    Hancock Smith b. 22 Jul and d. 23 Jul, 1848; Prescott Smith b. 8 Apr and d.
    12 Apr, 1850; Thomas Sinnickson Smith b. 8 Jul 1851.

Quinton Gibbon, b. 4 Jul 1813, and Sarah L. Hancock mar 28 May 1845 by Rev
    James I. Helm

Children of C. M. and Elenor. H. Shartel: Daniel Stratton Shartel b. 9 Dec. 1892
    and d. 9 Dec. 1892, in Nevada, Mo.; David Stratton Shartel b. 4 Dec. 1893;
    .... Stratton Shartel b. 26 Dec. 1895, in Nevada, Mo.; Eleanor Yorke
    Shartel b. 2 June 1898 at Nevada, Mo.

Children of Daniel P. and Arabel Stratton: Eleanor Hancock Stratton b. 26 Apr.
    1868; Rebecca Barnes Stratton b.5 May 1874, at Stockton, Mo.; Arabel
    Stratton b.15 Dec. 1875 and d. 28 Aug. 1876, at Stockton, Mo.; Daniel
    Stratton b.2 May 1878, at Stockton, Mo.; Henrietta Gibson Stratton b.20
    Dec. 1881, at Stockton, Mo.; Joseph Barnes b. 18 Sep. 1884, at Nevada,
    Mo.

Children of Constant M. and Maria H. Eakin: Eleanor Yorke Eakin b. 15 Oct.
    1868; Constance DuMiny Eakin b. 13 Aug. 1870.

Henrietta Hancock Gibbon, d/o Quinton and Sarah M. Gibbon, b. 16 Sep 1847
    and d. Nov. 1946.
Morris Hancock Stratton, s/o Morris H. and Ellen C. Stratton, b. 7 July 1877.
Constance Eakin, d/o I. F. and R. S. Barr, b. 12 Nov. 1900, at Nevada, Mo.

Children of George B. and Constance Duminy Runsey: Constance Connarroe b.
    Sun., 1 Dec. 1907; Eleanor Margaret b. Mon., 11 Jan. 1909 ay Salem, N. J.;
    Alice Mary Eakin b. 20 Aug. 1911, at Salem, N. J., and d. 14 Oct. 1916.

Children of William Alderman and Henrietta G. S. Jaquette: William Alderman b. Sat., 26 Mar. 1910, at West Philadelphia; Henrietta Arebel b. 23 Sep. 1911.

Virginia Barnes, d/o Daniel and Jessie T. Stratton b. Sat., 27 June 1909, at Neosho, Mo.

Daniel P. Stratton and Arabel Barnes mar. 28 Nov. 1866, by Rev. C. R. Gregory.

Constant M. Eakin and Maria H. Smith mar. 30 Dec. 1867, by Rev. Mr. Noble.

Morris H. Stratton and Ellen C. Smith mar. 7 June 1876, by Rev. C. S. Stephenson, Rector of St. Mary's, Mott Haven, New York.

Cassius M. Shartel and Eleanor H. Stratton mar. 3 Oct. 1889 at Nevada, Mo., by the Rev. Dr. Edmondson.

James Francis Barr and Rebecca Barnes Stratton mar. 6 June 1898, at Nevada, Mo, by the Rev. T. M. Corneilison.

Morris H. Stratton, Jr., and Elsie D. Tyson mar. 19 Jan. 1905, at Salem, N. J., by Rev. Frank La Barrer.

George B. Rumsey and Constance DuMiny Eakin mar. 13 Dec. 1806, at Salem, N. J., by the Rev. V. Lauderbough.

William Alderman Jaquette and Henrietta Gibbon mar. Fri., 14 June. 1907, in Cincinnati. Ohio, by Rev. Wallace Gordon.

Daniel Stratton and Jesse Josephine Graves mar. 18 Dec. 1907, at Neosho, Mo.

Joseph Barnes Stratton and Myrtle Montgomery mar. 9 Jan. 1911, at Centralia, Ok., by Rev. R. H. Horton.

Mary Hancock, widow of Thomas Hancock, Sr, d. 19 Feb 1824.

Thomas Hancock, Sr, d. Sat. night, 7 Mar 1829.

Morris Hancock, s/o Thomas and Mary Hancock, d. 28 Jan 1836 about 1:00 a.m, aged 50-11-7.

Sarah Hancock, widow of Morris Hancock, d. 13 Jun 1848, aged 56-4-8.

John Hancock, s/o Morris and Sarah Hancock, d. 29 May 1849, aged 17-7-29.

Mary Goodman, w/o Thomas S. Smith and d/o Morris and Sarah Hancock, d. 9 July 1856, aged 33-1-10.

Rev. Daniel Stratton d. 24 Oct. 1866, aged 51-11-4.

Thomas S. Smith d. 26 Oct. 1874, aged 62-2-27.

Ellen C., w/o Morris H. Stratton, d. 14 July 1877, aged 32 yrs., 1 mo.

Henrietta Elizabeth , d/o Morris and Sarah Hancock, d.21 Mar. 1879, aged 53-3-20.

Thomas S. Smith, s/o Thomas S. and Mary G. Smith, d. 9 Dec. 1881.

Constant M. Eakin b. 2 June 1853 and d. 26 Apr. 1885.

Eleanor Caroline, w/o Rev. Daniel Stratton and d/o Morris and Sarah Hancock, d. 4 Aug. 1886, aged 73-8-5.

Sarah Maria, w/o Quinton Gibbon and d/o Morris and Sarah Hancock, d.26 Feb. 1904, aged 79-11-26.

George B. Rumsey d. 17 Oct. 1914, aged 49 yrs.

Maria H. S. Eakin d. 12 Feb. 1917, at Salem, N. J.

John Browne Bible
Philadelphia

John Browne, s/o Peter and Priscilla Browne, b. 14 Apr 1739.

Mary Arrell, d/o William and Mary Arrell, b. 13 May 1742.

John Browne and Mary Arrell mar 7 Aug 1760.

Their children: John Browne b. 20 Jul 1761; Priscilla Browne b. 30 May 1763, at 4:00 in the morning; William Arrell Browne b. 18 Jan 1766, at 9: at night; Mary Browne b. 8 May 1768, at 12:00 at night; Aquilla A. Browne b. 26 Jan 1770, at 3:00 in the afternoon; Melissa Letty Browne b. 4 May 1772, at 6:00 in the morning; Adelissa Browne b. 6 Jul 1774; Peter Browne b. 15 Aug 1776, in the morning; Peter Browne b. 22 Feb 1778, in the evening; Johanna Browne b. 26 Apr ____, in the morning; Peter Arrell Brown b. 20 Apr 1782, at 8:00 in the evening.

John Browne, s/o John and Mary Browne, b. 20 Jul 1761.

Susanna Browne, w/o John Browne and d/o Benjamin and Elizabeth Akerly, b. 9 Sep 1768.

John Browne and Susanna Akerly mar 15 Oct 1785.

John Arrell Browne, s/o John and Susanna Brown, b. 27 Aug 1796, at night, and d. 28 Jan 1789, at 5:00 in the afternoon.

Susanna Browne, w/o John Browns, d. 16 Dec 1802, at 7:00 in the evening.

John Browne and Sarah Hall mar 28 Mar 1803.

Susanna Akerly Browne, d/o John and Sarah Browne, b. 30 Sep 1804, at 4:00 in the afternoon and d. 14 Aug, 1805.

John Rattone Browne, s/o John and Mary (Sarah?) Browne, b. 6 Jan, 1808, at 7:00 in the morning and d. 5 Aug 1808.

John Brown, s/o Alexander and Elizabeth Brown, b. 10 Jun 1768.

Mary Browne, d/o John and Mary Browne, b.8 May 1768, at midnight.

John Brown and Mary Browne were married by the Rev. James Abercromie, one of the Assistant Ministers of Christ Church and St. Peter's, on 7 Mar 1795.

Mary Arrell Brown, d/o John and Mary Brown, b. 28 Sep 1797 at half past 4:00 in the afternoon in the city of New York, in Chamber Street.
William Walton, s/o George and Rachel Walton, b. 18 Dec 1797.

William Walton and Mary Brown mar 26 Apr ___ by Joseph Walton, Mayor of the city of Philadelphia.
Their children: Henry Pemberton Walton b. 7 Mar 1827 at 2:20 in the morning; William Walton b. 23 Sep 1823.

Henry Durell Walton, s/o Henry and Lydia Walton, b. 1 Jan. 1859, near Moorestown, N. J.

Mary Brown, w/o John Brown, d. 11 May 1830/31?

Henry Pemberton Walton and Lydia Troth Weaver mar. 17 Jan. 1856,by J. Wheaton Smith, in Philadelphia.

William Walton, s/o William and Mary Walton, and Margeret Butterfield mar. 30 Dec. 1886.

Peter Browne, s/o John and Mary Browne, d. 7 Mar ___, at 7:00 in the morning, aged 6 mo, 20 dys.
Peter Browne, s/o John and Mary Browne, d. 5 Aug 1778, at 4:00 in the afternoon, aged 5 mo, 14 dys.
William Arrell Browne, s/o John and Mary Browne, sailed out of the Port of New York, was ship wrecked off Boston and was never heard of more.
Priscilla Hulings, w/o Abraham Hulings, and d/o John Browne, d. 24 Oct 1793 of the Yellow Fever and was bur in the family ground.
Johanna Browne, d/o John and Mary Browne, d. 1803 of the Yellow Fever.
John Browne, s/o John and Mary Browne, d. the 2nd day of the week, 31 Jul 1820 in the city of Baltimore, aged 59 yrs and 11 days. Buried in the Methodist Burial Ground in the back of town and a handsome tomb erected to his memory.
Mary Browne, w/o John Browne N. L. d. 1 Aug 1823, at 18 minutes before 12 morning, aged 81-3-18.
John Browne N. L. d. 20 Jun 1825, abt 4:00 in the morning, in his 85th year.
Mary Arrell Walton, w/o William Walton, d. 7 Oct. 1878.

William Walton, h/o Mary Arrell Walton, d. 27 Aug. 1883.
Henry Pemberton Walton, s/o William and Mary Walton, d. 4 Sep. 1905.
Lydia T. Walton, w/o Henry P. Walton, d. 7 Oct. 1915.
William Walton, s/o William and Mary Walton, d. 11 Mar. 1923.
Margaret Walton, w/o William Walton, d. 21 June 1921.

Isaac Smith Bible
Kimber and Sharpless, Philadelphia

Isaac Smith, s/o Powell and Sarah Smith, b. 3 Apr 1799.
Margaret Smith, d/o Henry and Margaret Earnest, b. 24 Nov 1804.
Isaac Smith and Margaret Earnest mar 4 May 1826.
Their children: Mary Smith b. 28 Oct 1829; Josiah Smith b. 5 Jul 1831; Sarah
    Smith b. 16 Dec 1863(?); Powell Smith b. 8 Dec 1826(?); Sarah _____
    Smith b. 28 Aug 1828(?); Isaac Smith b. 5 Dec 1836; Anna Hillerman
    Smith b. 18 Aug 1840; Margaret Matilda Smith b. 5 Apr 1845.

Mary Earnest d. 28 Dec 1831, aged 57 yrs and 10 mo.
Henry Earnest d. 4 Jul 1834.
Powell Smith d. 9 Sep 1819.
Sarah Smith, w/o Powell Smith, d. 29 mar 1841, aged 77-3-17.

Josiah Smith Bible
John B. Perry, Baltimore, 1856

Isaac Smith, s/o Powell and Sarah Smith, b. 3 Apr 1799.
Margaret Smith, d/o Henry and Mary Earnest, b. 24 Nov 1804.

Josiah Smith, s/o Isaac and Margaret Smith, b. 5 Jul 1831.
Catherine Smith, w/o Josiah Smith and d/o George and Hannah Larrence, b. 19
    Sep 1837.
Josiah Smith and Catherine Larrance mar 1 Mar 1855.
Their children: Hannah Larrance Smith b. 17 Jan 1856; Sara Ambler Smith b. 5
    Oct 1857; Arthur Pease Smith b. 28 Sep 1863.

Children of George and Elizabeth Winfield: Kate Ladan Winfield b. 23 Apr.
    1867; Thomas Elwood Huff Winfield b. 3 Aug. 1869.

Isaac Smith d. 17 Nov. 1868.

George Lawrence b. 8 Apr. 1794 and d. 6 Jan. 1852, aged 57-8-28.

Josiah Smith d. 4 Oct. 1904, aged 73-2-29.

Hannah L. Smith d. 2 Dec. 1919.

Catherine S. Smith, widow of Josiah Smith, d. 31 Aug. 1923, aged 85-11-12.

Harriet Wood Bible
Kimber & Sharpless, Philadelphia, 1824

Benjamin Allen, s/o Benjamin and Patience Allen of Greenwich Twp,
    Gloucester County, State of New Jersey, b. 7 Aug 1755.

Neamiah Richman, s/o Michael and Rebecca Richman of Pittsgrove Twp, Salem
    County, West New Jersey, b. 22 Oct 1755.

Hannah Allen b. 15 May 1765.

William Allen, s/o Benjamin and Hannah Allen, b. 8 Mar 1798.

Hannah Richman b. (no date).

Harriet Richman, d/o Neamiah and Hannah Richman, b. 31 May 1802.

Harriet More Richman, d/o Neamiah and Hannah Richman, b. 31 May 1804

Hannah Allen, d/o William and Harriet Allen, b. 7 Jul __.

William Allen Wood, s/o Charles and Harriet Wood, b. 29 Dec 1828.

William Allen and Harriet Richman mar 25 Sep 1823 (1st Husband)

Charles Wood and Harriet Allen mar 3 Apr 1828. (2nd Husband)

William Allen, s/o Benjamin and Hannah Allen, d. 27 July 1825, aged 27-4-19.

Andrew S. Long Bible

Andrew S. Long b. 2 Jul 1783 in New Jersey.

Lettuce Long b. 27 Apr 1796.

Andrew S. Long and Lettuce ___ (Letitia Dawson) mar 20 Oct 1810. (Both are
bur at Glassboro)

Their children: Samuel Dawson Long b. 25 Oct 1812 and mar Mary Cox b. 8
    Feb 1816; Catherine Harris Long b. 6 Dec 1817; John Long b. 10 Mar 1820
    in Salem Co; Abigail Ann Long b. 17 Jan 1822 in Salem Co; Andrew Long
    b. 19 Apr 1824 in Gloucester Co; Benjamin Duncan Long b. 18 Nov 1826
    in Gloucester Co; William and Elizabeth Long b. 18 Feb 1830 in
    Philadelphia; Sarah Jane Long b. 22 Apr 1834 at Glassborough; Joshua
    Dawson Long b. 30 Jun 1836 at Glassborough and mar Annie F. Carson;

Hannah Ann Dehart Long b. 26 Sep 1839 at Glassborough and mar Samuel Mills.

Eugene P. Long b. 10 Sep. 1858 in Fislerville, now Clayton, N. J. and mar. Annie Gibson, sister of Artimis.
Artimis C. Long b. 29 July 1862 in Clayton, N. J. and mar. John R. Ballinger, Jr.
Albert C. Long b. 11 Sep. 1870 and mar. Henrietta Davis.

Samuel Long and Hannah Fisler mar 24 Dec 1835.
Catherine H. Long and Joel Clark mar 12 Oct 1839.
Abigail Ann Long and George Hewet mar 31 Oct 1840.
Andrew Long and Ann Mariah Morgan mar in Salem Co. 1 Mar 1845.
Elizabeth Long and Charles Young mar in Gloucester Co. 5 Aug 1847.
William Long and Mary Whitacre mar 7 Sep 1850.
Benjamin D. Long and Mary Stanley mar 9 Mar 1851.
Joshua D. Long and Annie R. Corson mar. 3 Aug. 1857, parents of Artimis.

Mary Cox Long d. 8 May 1830.
John Long d. 23 Sep 1838 in Glassboro.
Andrew S. Long d. 15 Sep. 1855 in Fislerville, aged 72-9-12.
Letitia Long d. 17 Mar. 1851 in Fislerville, aged 64-10-20.

Coombs Bible
Mathew Carey, Philadelphia 1812

John Coombs, s/o John and Lydia Coombs, b. Sat., 11 Jun 1774.
Rebecca Clark, d/o David and Rebecca Clark, b. 6 Mar 1782.

John Coombs and Rebecca Clark mar 8 Nov 1798.
Their children: Israel Coombs b. Wed., 21 Aug 1799; David Coombs b. Sat., 21 Feb 1801; Susanna S. Coombs b. Fri., 20 Jan 1804; John Coombs b. Sat., 15 Nov 1806; Isaac Coombs b. Sat., 21 Jan 1809; Rebecca Ann Coombs b. Thurs., 7 Mar 1811; William Giles Coombs b. Sat., 17 Apr 1813; Lydia Reed Coombs b. on Easter Sunday, 26 Mar 1815; Anna Meriat Coombs b. Mon., 21 Apr 1817; Anna Meriat Coombs b. 13 Aug 1819; Elizabeth Coombs b. 8 Jun 1821; Sarah Coombs b. 8 Jan 1824.

Anna Meriat Coombs, d/o John and Rebecca Coombs, d. 25 Aug 1818, aged 1-4-5.
Elizabeth Coombs, d/o John and Rebecca Coombs, d. 4 Sep 1822, aged 1-2-26.

Isaac Coombs, s/o John and Rebecca Coombs, d. 7 Aug 1823, aged 14-6-17.
David Coombs, s/o John and Rebecca Coombs, d. 27 Mar 1834, aged 3/1/6.
Sarah N. Elwell Coombs d. 2 May 1887, in her 69th yr.

Woodruff Bible
John B. Perry, Baltimore, 1854

Generation 5: Jared Woodruff married Rebecca Mulford.
Generation 6: Charles J. Woodruff, b. 24 Apr. 1794, Roadstown, NJ, married 12
    May 1819, Roadstown, NJ, Maria Davis, b. 29 June 1796, Carlltown, N.J.,
    d. 15 Jan 1876, Shiloh, NJ.
Generation 7: Ercurius S. Woodruff, b. 8 Mar. 1822, Bowens Corner, NJ,
    married 28 Feb 1852, Carlltown, NJ, Mary B. Bowen,, b. 5 Oct 1831.
Generation 8: Warren Woodruff, M. D., b. 13 Mar. 1853, Bowen's Corner, d. 5
    June 1931, Carneys Point, N. J. and mar., 21 June 1882, Bridgeton, N. J.,
    Emelie F. Sims, b. 1 Apr. 1857, Camp Grove, Ill.
Generation 9 Mabelle Woodruff Bradway b. 13 May 1885, Hastings, Neb.,
    mar., 8 June 1900, Atlantic City, N. J, Raymond Bradway, b. 13 Oct. 1882,
    Quinton, N. J.

Everett Sims Woodruff b.31 Oct. 1888, Akron, Col., and d. 13 Oct. 1882,
    Quinton, N. J.

Generation 5: Joseph Bowen married Phebe Ayars.
Generation 6: Joseph A. Bowen, b. 1800, Carlltown (Bowens Corner), NJ,
    married Mary Brooks, b. 1798, Carlltown.
Generation 7: Mary B. Bowen mar. Ercurius S. Woodford 28 Feb. 1852,
    Carlltown, N. J.

John McQueen Bible
Mathew Carey, Philadelphia, 1807

John McQueen b. 14 Oct. 1762.
Hannah Foster b. 28 Apr. 1773.
John McQueen and Hannah Foster mar. 6 July 1791.
Their children: William McQueen b. 17 Sept. 1792; Rebecca McQueen b. 9
    May 1795; Ephraim McQueen b. 7 May 1797; Elizabeth McQueen b. 20 Jul
    1799; Sarah McQueen b. 8 Aug. 1801; Hannah McQueen b. 15 Jan. 1806.

Jonathan Swing and Rebecca McQueen mar. 15 July 1818
William McQueen and Mary Mosier married 21 June 1825.
Ephraim McQueen and Margaret Cameron mar. 15 Nov. 1827.
Hannah McQueen and Benjamin Van Meter mar. 26 Nov. 1828.
Elizabeth McQueen and John Garrison mar. 25 Dec. 1834.
Almira C. Garrison and Lewis In. Shimp mar. 12 Apr. 1900.

Mary Vanmeter, d/o of Benjamin Vanmeter and Hannah McQueen, b. 4 Mar.
    1830.
Hannah McQueen Vanmeter b. 15 Aug. 1831.
Erasmus Vanmeter b. 20 Oct. 1832.
John McQueen Vanmeter b. 2 May 1836.
Almira C, Vanmeter b. 10 Sep. 1837.

John McQueen, s/o Ephraim McQueen and Margaret, his wife, b. 27 Sep. 1828.
Jane Ann McQueen b. 14 Apr. 1830.
William McQueen b. 2 Jan. 1832.
Margaret McQueen b. 23 Aug. and d. 24 Aug. 1833.

Margaret McQueen, w/o Ephraim McQueen, d. 24 Aug. 1833, aged 29 yrs.
Elizabeth Leake d. 27 Jan. 1802, aged 76 yrs.
John McQueen d. 21 Sep. 1805, aged 43 yrs.
Mary Vanmeter d. 16 Nov. 1831, aged 1-8-13.
Hannah McQueen Vanmeter d. 9 Jan, 1833, aged 2-4-24.
Ephraim Foster McQueen d. 15 Nov. 1842, aged 44 yrs.
Sarah McQueen d. 19 Feb. 1864, aged 62 yrs.
William McQueen d. 16 Aug. 1863, aged 71 yrs.
Hannah Vanmeter d. 21 Aug. 1865, aged 59 yrs.
Elizabeth Garrison d. 8 May 1875, aged 75 yrs.
John B. Garrison d. 9 July 1883, aged 79 yrs.
Jonathan Swing d. 9 May 1875.
Rebecca McQueen Swing d. 9 Mar. 1878, aged 83 yrs.
Ephraim Foster d. 2 Feb. 1794, aged 55 yrs.
Hannah Foster d. 30 Nov. 1818, aged 77 yrs.
Jonathan, s/o Ephriam and Hannah Foster, d. 28 June 1808, aged 32 yrs.
Ruth Thompson d. 2 Jan. 1825, aged 54 yrs.
Hannah Foster, d/o Davis Foster, d. 10 May 1827.
Esther Osborn d. 7 June 1835, aged 51 yrs.
Phebe Sneethen d. 8 Sep. 1845, aged 76 yrs.
Hannah McQueen d. 13 Dec. 1854, aged 82 yrs.

Samuel Swing Bible 1712
Thomas Newcomb and Henry Hills, Deceased
Printers to the Queens Most Excellent Majesty

Samuel Swing b. 15 Sep. 1729.
Sarah Diament b. 16 Mar. 1830.

Samuel Swings children: Jeremiah Swing b. 31 Dec. 1760; Sarah Swing b. 27
Oct. 1762; Christianna Swing b. 25 Oct. 1764; Samuel Swing b. 4 Nov.
1767; Ruth Swing b. 4 Oct. 1769; Abraham Swing b. 26 Oct. 1771.

Samuel Swing d. 13 Mar. 1801, aged 71 yrs. and 6 mo., an Elder in the
Presbyterian Church, Pittsgrove.
Sarah Swing, widow of said Samuel Swing, d. 7 June 1808, aged 78 yrs.
Jeremiah Swing d. 24 June 1794, aged 34 yrs., 5 mo.
Ruth Lawrence Swing d. 8 Sep. 1793, aged 24 yrs.
Abraham Swing d. 10 Oct. 1832, an honored and respected Elder in the
Presbyterian Church, Pittsgrove.

Abraham b. 26 Oct. 1771.
Hannah Lumis b. 10 Oct. 1773.

Abraham and Hannah mar. 2 Dec. 1794.

Jonathan Luis Swing b. 23 Oct. 1796.
Nathaniel Swing b. 30 Mar. 1798.
Ruth Swing b. 27 Jan. 1800.
Leonard Swing b. 11 Mar. 1802.
Hannah Swing b. 6 May 1804.
Sarah Swing b. 27 Nov. 1806.

Falconar Bible

Joseph Falconar and Elizabeth Shelly mar. 21 July 1720 in Philadelphia.

William Falconar b. 24 Apr. 1721, at half past 8:00 at night.
Benjamin Falconar b. 30 Mar. 1725, at 2:00 in the morning.
Ann Falconar b. 2 Mar. 1727, at 5:00 in the afternoon.
Felix Falconar b. 26 July 1729, at 8:00 in the morning, and d. 26 Oct. 1738.

John Falconar b. 16 Aug. 1731, at half past 1:00 in the afternoon, and d. 20 Oct.
   1755.
Jams Falconar b. 17 Mar. 1734, at 4:00 in the morning.
Daniel Falconar b. 20 July 1736, at 6:00 in the afternoon, and d. 4 Jan. 1758.
b. (no date).
Sarah b. (no date).

Elizabeth Falconar d. 10 Sep. 1771, aged 73 yrs.

James Falconar and Ann Townsend mar. 20 Nov. 1771 by the Rev. Ross, Rector
   of the Hallows Parish, Worcester Co., Md., in the town of Snowhill.

Samuel B. Holton Bible
R. White, Hutchinson and Divier 1836

John Holton b. (No date).
Mary Summerill b. 12 Jan. 1772.
Thomas Summerill b. 14 Aug. 1779.
Elizabeth Borden b. 3 Mar. 1788.
Hannah Summerill, d/o Thomas and Elizabeth Summerill, b. 3 June 1806.
Samuel Holton, s/o John and Mary Holton, b. 12 July 1806.
Harriet Amanda Holton, d/o Samuel and Hannah Holton, b. 6 May. 1834.
Samuel Borden Holton, s/o Samuel and Hannah Holton, b.24 Jan. 1836.
Hannah Jane Holton, d/o Samuel and Hannah Holton, b.22 July 1838.
Ellen Middleton Shimp. d/o George and Ketturah Shimp. b. 6 Jan. 1836.
Hannah Jane Holton b. 10 Jan. 1855.
Ella Kitturah Holton, d/o Samuel B. and Ellen M. Holton, b. 4 Aug. 1857.
Carrie Vanneman Holton, d/o Samuel B. and Ellen M. Holton, b.27 Oct. 1861.
Samuel Borden Holton, s/o Samuel B. and Ellen M. Holton, b. (no date).
Bella May Holton, d/o Samuel B. and Ellen M. Holton, b.21 May 1870.

John Holton d. (no date).
Mary Holton d. (no date).
Elizabeth Summerill, w/o Thomas Summerill, d. 13 Mar. (no yr. given).
Thomas Summerill d. (no date).
Harriet Amanda Holton d. 31 Aug. 1835.
Samuel Holton d. 28 Jan. 1839.
Hannah Jane Holton, d/o Samuel and Hannah Holton, d. 10 Dec. 1842.
Ella Kitturah Holton, d/o Samuel B. and Ellen M. Holton, d. 11 Feb. 1862.
Samuel Borden Holton, s/o Samuel B. and Ellen M. Holton, d. (no date).

Carrie V. Horton Dolbow, d/o Samuel B. and Ellen M. Holton, d. 20 Oct. 1908.
Hannah J. Holton Avos, d/o Samuel B. and Ellen M. Holton, d. Nov. 1924.
Samuel Borden Holton, s/o Samuel and Hannah Holton, d. 18 Sep. 1889.
Ellen M. Horton d. 10 July 1927.
Hannah Summerill, d/o Thomas and Elizabeth Summerill, d. 23 Feb. 1879

Edward Mortimer Mulford Family Record

William Mulford .came from Devonshire, England, to Salem, Mass., and moved
from there to East Hampton, Long Island, about 1645 or 1649, purchasing
land from the Indians. He was the father of Benjamin Mulford who moved
about 1699 to Cape May, N. J. He was the father of Benjamin Mulford, Jr.,
(his wife, Mary Sheppard, was the d/o Thomas and Rachel Sheppard) in
1745 was a resident of Roadstown, Cumberland Co., N. J., and d. there in
1794. He built the brick house, with the date 1770 still plain to be seen on
it, now standing. He was the father of Mason Mulford, b. 20 Apr. 1761 and
d. 2 Sep. 1836. He mar., 1 Jan. 1788, Margaret Teal, b. 14 Oct. 1766 and d.
26 Mar. 1842. Their children:

Phebe b. 20 Apr. 1792, mar. Garrison Maul, and d. 30 Oct. 1860.
John S. b. 10 Sep. 1794 and d. 28 Aug. 1860.
Priscilla b. 10 Oct. 1796, mar. David Minch, and d. 17 Dec. 1841.
Nancy B. b. 1 Mar. 1802 and d. 23 Aug. 1823.
Maria b. 9 Dec. 1807, mar. Jonathan Bowen, and d. 20 Oct. 1886.
Benjamin T. b. 1 Feb. 1804 and d. 15 Aug. 1861. He mar., 11 Apr. 1829, Mary
Ann Fithian, b. 21 July 1809 and d. 5 Oct. 1866, d/o Enoch Fithian and
Sarah Moore, who mar. 28 Dec. 1807.

Children of Benjamin and Mary Ann Mulford:
Julia A. b. 30 Dec. 1833 and mar. Stephen G. Porch of Franklinville.
Benjamin Fithian b. 7 Mar. 1838, unmarried and still living, May 1902.
Enoch Mason b. 11 Mar. 1836 and d. 31 July 1854.
Edward Mortimer b. 15 July 1840 and mar., 7 May 1862, Margaretta B.
Hilliard. b. 29 May 1841.

Children of Edward Mortimer and Margaretta B. Mulford:
Anna Viola b. 14 May 1863 and mar., 30 May 1894, William H. Caley of West
Chester, Pa. Edward Mortimer, Jr., b. 7 Jan. 1865 and mar., 9 Jan. 1890,
Sybilla A. de Leur.
Mary Lydia b. 13 Apr. 1869 and mar., 26 Mar. 1891, J. Rulon Dare, Jr.

Lizzie Elma b. 2 June 1871 and mar., 14 Nov. 1899, Albert T. Leonard.
Clare Hilliard b. 20 Jan. 1879 and mar., 1 Jan. 1900, Bertha Liche.

Children of Edward Mortimer, Jr., and Sybilla A. Mulford:
Marjorie Sybilla.
Edward Mortimer, 3rd.
Nelson Hilliard.

Enoch Matthews Mulford Bible

Enoch Mulford b. 26 July 1773 and d. 9 Dec. 1798. He mar., Temperance
    Mathews b. 8 Dec. 1776 and d. 3 Mar. 1826.
    Their only child, Enoch Mulford, Jr., b. 7 Aug. 1799 and d. 30 May 1867. He
    mar., 26 Dec. 1821, Mary Davis, b. 17 Mar. 1793 and d. 13 Apr. 1879.

Martha Matthews b. 18 Dec. 1774.

Children of Enoch, Jr., and Mary Davis Mulford:
James Lewis Mulford b. 25 June 1822 and mar. Annie Owen.
Richard Mulford b. 1 Mar. 1824 and mar. (1) Ann Elizabeth Shute; mar. (2)
    Eliza Leonard. Among his children - Frank, who lives in Greenwich; a son
    who lives in Greeley, Co.; a son who lives in Jersey City, N. J.
Edward Davis Mulford b. 14 Feb. 1826 and mar. Eliza Chard. No issue.
Mary Jane Mulford b. 15 Mar. 1828 and d. 7 June 1844.
Enoch Matthews Mulford b. 20 Dec. 1829 and mar., 10 June 1857, Emily
    Seeley Hawkins, b. 19 Jan. 1832. Their only child, Samuel M. Mulford, b. 4
    Feb. 1860 and d. 28 Sep. 1884.
 William L. Mulford b. 14 June 1832 and d. 19 Apr. 1833.
Beulah Ann Mulford b. 29 July 1834 and mar. Henry Long.
Harriet Amanda Mulford b. 8 Jan. 1837 and d. 16 Oct. 1838.

Ballinger Records

Samuel Ballinger, s/o Thomas and Elizabeth Ballinger, b. 19th of 5th mo. 1733 -
old stile.
Elizabeth Ballinger, d/o Garret and Sarah Goff, b. 17th of 1st mo.1740 - old stile.
Mary Shin Ballinger, w/o Samuel Ballinger, b. 17th of 6th mo. 1741.

Samuel Ballinger and Elizabeth Goff mar. 10 Jan. 1760.

Samuel Ballinger and Mary Shin mar. 14 May 1788 and had no issue.

Children of Samuel and Elizabeth Ballinger: Henry Ballinger b.3rd of 10th mo.
    1760; Joshua Ballinger b.20 Oct. 1762; William V26th of 12th mo. 1764 and
    d. 18 Aug. 1815; Samuel Ballinger b.25th of 11th mo. 1771 and d. 9 Mar.
    1808; Reuben Ballinger b.12th of 6th mo. 1774;

Isaac Ballinger b. 29th of 7th mo. 1776; John Goff Ballinger b.15th of 7th mo.
    1780; a son b. 26 Feb 1784.

Elizabeth Ballinger d. 20 Oct. 1786.
Samuel Ballinger d. 22 Feb. 1822.
Mary Ballinger d. 17 Dec. 1822.
John G. Ballinger, Sr., d. 14 Jan. 1859.

Reece Edwards b. 12 Apr. 1745.
Sarah Edwards b. 16 June 1750.
Children of Reese and Susannah Edwards: Rebecca Edwards b. 13 May 1773;
    Hannah V14 Oct. 1774; Joseph Edwards b. 7 Jan. 1777.

Children of Reese and Sarah Edwards (2nd marriage): Mary Edwards b. 11 Nov.
    1779 and mar. J. G. Ballinger; William Edwards b. 20 Aug. 1781; Elizabeth
    V17 Aug. 1783; Thomas and Samuel Edwards b. 9 Jan. 1786; Phebe
    Edwards b. 17 Dec. 1787.

Samuel Edwards d. 30 Apr. 1825.
Phebe Edwards d. 8 Nov. 1839.
Elizabeth Edwards d. 11 Apr. 1847.
Mary Edwards Ballinger d. 1 June 1862, aged 83 yrs.
Thomas Edwards d. 23 May 1868, aged 83 yrs.

John G. Ballinger came to Salem County from Evesham, Burlington County, in
    1803.

Mary Edwards, d/o Reese and Sarah Edwards, mar. J. G. Ballinger, Sr.
Children of John G. and Mary Ballinger: William Ballinger b. 12 Oct. 1802 and
    d. 18 Aug. 1815; Samuel Ballinger b. 11 Nov. 1804 and d. 9 Mar. 1808;
    Sarah Ann Ballinger b. 11 Dec. 1806 and d. 9 Mar. 1836; Thomas Ballinger
    b. 25 Jan. and d. 6 Dec. 1810; Thomas E. Ballinger b. 15 Sep. 1811 and d.
    14 Apr. 1830; Mary Jane Ballinger b. 3 July 1813 and d. 28 July 1832;
    Susannah Ballinger b 6 July and d. 15 Aug. 1815; Elizabeth Ballinger b. 10

Jan. 1817; John G. Ballinger b. 8 Jan. 1819 and d. 1 Oct. 1902; Richard
Clark Ballinger b. 15 Jan. 1820 and d. 21 Oct. 1858.

John G. Ballinger, s/o John G. and Mary, d. 14 Jan. 1899.
Mary Ballinger, d/o John G. and Mary, d. 31 May 1862.

Sarah Ann Ballinger mar. William Applegate and had issue: Mary and Amelia.
Elizabeth Ballinger mar. Samuel W. Miller. They were the parents of Richard C.
Miller.

Thomas Edwards was the brother of Mary Ballinger.
Children of Thomas Edwards and his 1st wife, Mary: Benjamin Edwards b. 6
July 1813; Samuel Edwards b. 5 June 1815.
Children of Thomas Edwards and his 2nd wife, Sarah Lippincott: Mary Edwards
b. 15 Jan, 1819 and mar. Samuel Borten; Arron Edwards b. 19 Apr. 1820;
Wm. Edwards b. 17 June 1821; Sarah Edwards b. 5 Dec. 1822; Barkley
Edwards b. 3 Dec. 1824; Ann Edwards b. 18 Nov. 1826; Thomas L.
Edwards b. 31 Mar. 1828.

Thomas Edwards d. 23 May 1868, aged 83 yrs.
Samuel Edwards d. 24 Mar. 1828.
William Edwards d. 10 July 1821.
Sarah L. Edwards d. 30 Apr. 1863.

Mary Edwards Borten d. 5 Feb. 1888, aged 69 yrs. and 2 dys.

Sarah Ann Ballinger, d/o Stephen and Sarah Reeves, b. 13 July 1819.

Children of John G. and Sarah Ann Ballinger: Stephen Reeves Ballinger b. 9
Feb. 1842; Samuel E. Ballinger b. 7 Sep. 1843; Thomas Ballinger b. 21
Nov. 1845; John Groff Ballinger b. 4 Feb. 1848 and d. 28 July 1851;
William P. Ballinger b. 25 Feb.. 1850 and d. 2 Aug. 1851; Mary Ellen
Ballinger b. 19 Dec. 1851 and d. 14 Aug. 1853.

Stephen Reeves Ballinger mar. 18 Mar. 1875, Sarah Richman Dubois, d/o
Garret and Elizabeth Richman Dublis.

John Pierson Bible, 1813

John Pierson and Elizabeth Mulford mar. 23 Nov. 1783.
John High and Mary Pierson mar. 10 Feb. 1803.
Howell Mulford and Ann Pierson mar. 9 Dec. 1804.
Reuben Dare and Sarah Pierson mar. 26 Aug. 1809.
Daniel Pierson and Sarah Garrison mar. 16 Nov. 1910.

Azel Pierson, father of John Pierson, b. 19 Jan. 1739.
Philathea Sayre, w/o Azel Pierson, b. 8 May 1741.
John Pierson b. 30 May 1762.
Elizabeth Mulford b. 4 Oct. 1765.
Mary Pierson b. 4 Sep. 1784.
Ann Pierson b. 17 Sep. 1786.
Daniel Pierson b. 20 Apr. 1789.
Sarah Pierson b. 23 Sep. 1792.
John Pierson b. 12 Jan. 1795.

Philathea Pierson d. 18 Oct. 1794.
Azel Pierson d. 16 Oct. 1798.
Mary High, d/o John and Elizabeth Pierson, d. 5 May 1807.
John Pierson, s/o John and Elizabeth Pierson, d. 17 June 1815.
John Pierson d. 15 Feb. 1826.
Elizabeth Pierson, w/o John Pierson, d. 13 Oct. 1845.
Ann Mulfrod, d/o John and Elizabeth Pierson, d. 18 Oct. 1846.
Sarah Danzenbaker, d/o John and Elizabeth Pierson, d. 28 Oct. 1852.

Peter Dubois Bible

Abraham Richman b. 10 Apr. 1755.
Sarah Richman, his wife, b. 21 Feb. 1755.
Their children: Isaac Richman b. 14 Mar. 1772; Benjamin Richman b. 8 Sep.
    1774; Abraham Richman b. 9 Sep. 1776; Moses Richman b. 8 Aug. 1878;
    Sarah Richman b. 15 Nov. 1780; Joseph and Elizabeth Richman b. 16 Aug.
    1783; John Richman b. 25 Mar. 1785; Whitten Richman b. 31 July 1787;
    Margaret Richman b. 26 Mar. 1789; Sarah Richman b. 14 Mar. 1791;
    Abraham Richman b. 29 Aug. 1794.

Moses Richman mar. (1st), Sep. 1803, Martha Webb.
Moses Richman mar. (2nd), Feb. 1806, Abigail Ewalt.

Moses Richman mar. (3rd), Feb. 1817, Ann Cook, d/o Joseph Cook and Mary Reeves.

Children of Moses Richman: James W. Richman b. 27 Sep. 1802; Martha W. Richman b. 13 Apr. 1805; Jacob E. Richman b. 3 Sep. 1807. Abraham E. Richman b. 3 Dec. 1808; John E. Richman b. 5 Feb. 1811; Ewalt Richman b. 13 Jan. 1813; Abigail E. Richman b. 21 Dec. 1814; Mary C, Richman b. 25 June 1818.

Martha Webb, 1st w/o Moses Richman, d. 15 Apr. 1805.
Abigail Ewalt, 2nd w/o Moses Richman, d. Feb. 1816.
Ann Cook, 3rd w/o Moses Richman, d. 25 Mar. 1849.
Mary C. Richman d. 2 Dec. 1821.
James W. Richman d. 30 Sep. 1862.
Moses Richman d. 8 Apr. 1868.

Peter Dubois Bible, 1838

Peter Dubois and Sarah Ann Newkirk mar. 6 June 1816
Edward Dubois and Amy D. Sparks mar. 19 Aug. 1841.
Charles Dare and Abigail H. Dubois mar. 10 Sep. 1846.
William Avis and Sarah A. Dubois mar. 18 Nov. 1846.
John D. Miracle and Emma M. Avis, d/o Wm. and Sarah A. Avis, mar. 26 Nov. 1878.

Peter Dubois, s/o Thomas and Sarah Dubois, b. 24 July 1789.
Hannah Newkirk, d/o Cornelius and Abigail Newkirk, b. 17 Feb. 1798.
Children of Peter and Hannah Dubois: Edward Dubois b. 10 May. 1817; Abigail Ann Dubois b. 21 May 1819 and d. 3 June 1822; Sarah Ann Dubois b. 30 Sep. 1821; Abigail Hannah Dubois b. 10 Oct. 1824; Matthew A. Dubois b. 17 Feb. 1827; Caroline Matilda Dubois b. 8 July 1829; Joseph Sanford Dubois b. 4 Aug. 1831; George Janvier Dubois b. 4 Feb. 1835; Garret Newkirk Dubois b. 3 June 1837; William Weaver Dubois b. 23 Jan. 1841; Mary Janvier Dubois b. 19 Jan. 1844.

William Avis b. 5 Apr. 1822.
Sarah Ann Dubois b. 30 Sep. 1821.
Levi Janvier Avis b. 16 Sep. 1847 and d. 25 Aug. 1848.
Edward Dubois Avis b. 58 Dec. 1848 and d. 24 Feb. 1864.
Sarah Frances Avis b. 514 Apr. 1851 and d. 20 Mar. 1864.

Neal Dow Avis b. 517 July 1853.

Theodore Cuyler Avis b. 526 Dec. 1855.

Mary Emma Avis b. 520 Jan. 1859 and d. 19 Oct. 1889.

Hannah Louise Avis b. 52 Oct. 1862 and d. 4 Apr. 1864.

Harriet Melvina Avis b. 55 Dec. 1866.

Children of J. D. Miralce and Mary Emma Avis: Isabelle Halford Miracle b. 9 Mar. 1882; Edmonia Marrian Miracle b. 6 Dec. 1884.

Ridgway-Ballinger Bible

Children of Zaccheus and Hope Ballinger: Jacob Ballinger b. 16 Sep. 1775; Joshua Ballinger b. 8 Mar. 1881: Jacob Ballinger b. 8 Mar. 1881; Mary Ballinger b. 1 Sep. 1883; Isaac Ballinger b. 7 Jan. 1886; Naomi Ballinger b. 19 Jan. 178_; Benjamin Ballinger b. 8 Aug. 1892; Josiah Ballinger b. 22 Sep. 1801.

Zaccheus Ballinger, s/o Benjamin and Elizabeth Ballinger, b. 16 Mar. 1817.

Mary Ballinger, d/o Benjamin and Elizabeth Ballinger, b. 19 Dec. 1818.

Levi Ridgway and Mary Ballinger mar. 4 Feb. 1841.

Their children: Theresa Ridgway b. 13 Nov. 1841; Isaac Ridgway b. 16 Apr. 1843; Henry Clay Ridgway b. 10 Nov. 1844; Anne Ridgway b. 24 July 1846; Charles Ridgway b. 1 Sep. 1947; Franklin Ridgway b. 2 May 1849.

Gerrard Sparks Bible
Sumner and Goodwin, Hartford 1846

Robert Sparks b. 25 Sep. 1791 and d. 7 Aug. 1881, aged 89-10-14.

Abigail Sparks b. 18 May 1797.

Jonathan Sparks b. 15 Nov. 1817.

Gerrard Sparks b. 23 Dec. 1818.

Charles H. Sparks b. 5 July 1820.

Richard P. Sparks b. 24 Aug. 1822.

Christian H. Sparks b. 24 Aug. 1824.

Citturah H. Sparks b. 3 Oct. 1826.

Elizabeth Sparks b. 28 Dec. 1828.

Naomi E. Sparks b. 6 July 1832.

Robert Sparks b. 10 Oct. 1834.

Gerard Sparks, s/o Robert and Abigail Sparks, b. 23 Dec. 1818.
Mary Ann Barber, d/o Samuel and Hannah Barber, b. 16 Sep. 1826.

Gerard Sparks and Mary Ann Barber mar. 17 Jan 1846.
Their children: Maurice L. Sparks b. 16 Feb. 1847; Anna Plummer Sparks b. 13
    Dec. 1853; Charlotte Barber Sparks b. 22 Dec. 1855; Lewis Broomall
    Sparks b. 2 Nov. 1857; David Guest Sparks b. 26 Feb. 1860; Harry Barber
    Sparks b. 5 Mar. 1862.

Hannah Borden, d/o John and Susan Borden, b. 22 July 1817.
Gerrard Sparks and Maria Borden mar. 9 July 1871.
Gerrard Sparks mar. (3rd.) Elizabeth _____.

Jefferson Borden b. 10 Sep. 1815.
Maria Borden b. 22 July 1817.
Mary A. Borden b. 16 Feb. 1819.
Lydia Borden b. 4 June 1821.
John B. Borden b. 20 Mar. 1826.
Abigail Jane Sparks b. 11 Apr. 1837.
Harriet Margaret E. Sparks b. 25 Nov. 1840.

John Borden, father, d. 5 May 1859, aged 68 yrs. and 1 dy.
Mary Ann Sparks, w/o Gerrard Sparks, d. 25 May 1870, aged 43-8-1-1.
Charles H. Sparks d. 25 Dec. 1872, aged 52-5-2-6.
Lewis Broomall Sparks d. 27 June 1880, aged 22-7-25.
Mariah Sparks, w/o Gerrard Sparks, d. 21 Aug. 1883, aged 66 yrs., 25 dys.
Harry Barber Sparks, s/o Gerrard and Mary Ann Sparks, d. 26 June 1899, in
    Philadelphia.
Elizabeth P. Sparks d. 31 Dec. 1904, aged 72 yrs.
Thomas Robbins d. 5 Jan. 1863.
Hannah Robbins d. 30 Jan. 1869, aged 74-6-2.

Vanneman Bible

Henry Vanneman, s/o Joseph and Marget Vanneman, b. 16 Nov. 1763.
Philadelphia Vanneman, w/o Joseph Vanneman, b. 28 Sep. 1781
Hannah Vanneman, w/o Joseph Vanneman, b. 19 Jan. 1779.

Children of Joseph and Darcus Vanneman: Israel Vanneman b. 11 Dec. 1772; Pheby Vanneman b. 18 Aug. 1874; Joseph Vanneman b. 18 Nov. 1775; Samuel Vanneman b. 2 Mar. 1778.

Mary Vanneman, d/o Joseph Vanneman, Jr., and Hannah, his wife, b. 3 May 1799.

Elizabeth Vanneman, d/o Joseph Vanneman and Philadelphia, his wife, b. 10 Aug. 1803.

Ovid Vanneman, s/o Joseph Vanneman and Philadelphia, his wife, b. 5 Sep. 1805, in the morning.

Persis Vanneman b. 3 July 1808, abt. 8:00 in the morning.

Henry Vanneman b. 27 Apr. 1810, 3rd s/o Joseph Vanneman and Philadelphia, his wife.

Dorcas Vanneman d. 28 Feb. 1794, aged 45 yrs.

Henry Vanneman d. 21 June 1798.

Hannah Vanneman d. 19 Jan. 180_, aged 22 yrs.

Elizabeth Vanneman d.28 Jan. 1805.

Henry Vanneman d. 22 June 1810.

Persis Vanneman d. 22 Oct. 1810.

Richard Seeley Bible

Richard Seeley b. 4 Nov. 1782.

Elizabeth Seeley b. 17 Aug. 1781.

Richard Seeley and Elizabeth Moore mar. 28 Dec. 1803.

1st child, a son, b. 1 Feb. 1805.

Caroline Seeley b. 27 Mar. 1806.

Mary Seeley b. 21 July 1807.

Harriet Seeley b. 12 Nov. 1809.

Emily Seeley b. 23 Nov. 1814.

Mason Seeley b. 18 Feb. 1821.

1st child d. 3 Feb. 1805.

Caroline Seeley d. 6 June 1806.

Mason Seeley d. 17 May 1821.

Emily Seeley d. 19 Sep. 1823.

Elizabeth Seeley d. 24 Mar. 1821.

Elizabeth Seeley d. 24 Mar. 1821.
Richard Seeley d. 4 Nov. 1846.
Harriet Seeley (Dowdney, Ware, twice married) d. 28 Mar. 1869.

Hancock Bible 1782
R. Aitken, at Pope's Head,
3 doors above the Coffee House, in Market Street

Sarah Hancock, d/o Benjamin and Elizabeth Hancock, b. 1784.

Children of John and Elizabeth Hancock: Ann Hancock b. 18 Sep. 1891;
    Edward Hancock b. 27 June 1793; Mary Hancock b. 18 Jan. 1796; Edward
    Hancock b. 8 Aug. 1798; Robert Moore Hancock b. 15 Sep. 1800;
    Elizabeth Hancock b. 15 Sep. 1802.

Children of Benjamin and Phebe Hancock: Robert Hancock b. 16 Aug. 1806,
    abt. 1:00 in the day; Hannah Hancock b. 18 Apr. 1808, abt. 1:00 at night;
    Daniel P. Hancock b. 26 July 1810, abt. 3:00 in the morning; William
    Hancock b. 26 May 1813, at 10:00 in the morning; Elizabeth Hancock b. 6
    Jan. 1817; Susannah Hancock b. 9 July and d. 13 Aug.1818; Phebe
    Hancock b. 23 Sep. 18199; Gilbert Hancock b. 3 Mar. 1824.

John Nelson's Bible
M. Carey and Son, Philadelphia 1821

Sarah Rambo, b. 30 Oct. 1761, mar. Davis Nelson and had 7 children. After his
    death, she mar. George Mullen and had 8 children by him.

John Nelson and Martha Stetson, both of the Township of Deptford, county of
    Gloucester, mar. 29 Aug. 1810.

Martha Nelson b. 16 Oct. 1788.
John Nelson b. 3 Jan. 1789.
Christina Nelson b. 23 Aug. 1811.
Mary M. Nelson b. 21 May 1814, at half past 7:00 in the evening.
Sarah M. Nelson b. 8 Aug. 1816, at half past 9:00 in the evening.
Isaac D. Nelson b. 10 Aug. 1818, at 7:00 in the evening.
David I. Nelson b. 25 Aug. 1820, at half past 11:00 in the evening.
John R. Nelson b. 5 Oct. 1823, at 45 min. past 3:00 in the afternoon.

Christiann Nelson Miller b. 23 May 1833, d/o Daniel and Mary Miller.
Charles S. Nelson b. 28 Aug. 1824, at 4:00 in the morning.
Ann Y. Nelson b. the same morning, at 5:00. They were twins.
Alice B. Nelson b. 25 Mar. 1828, at half past 11:00 in the evening, at
  Allowaystown.
Martha I. Nelson b. 19 Nov. 1830, at half past 6:00 in the morning, at
  Allowaystown.

Sarah Mullen d. 11 Mar. 1824, at half past 7:00 in the evening, aged 62-4-11,
  leaving 9 children, the youngest past 21 yrs. of age. Bur. in the churchyard
  at Berkley.
Ann Y. Nelson d. 12 Sep. 1824, aged 15 dys.
Charles S. Nelson d. 14 Nov. 1825, at half past 5:00 in the morning, aged 1-2-
  17. Bur. in the churchyard at Berkley.
Christina Nelson d. 22 Apr. 1830, at 15 min. past 5:00 in the morning, aged 18-
  7-29, bur. in the M. E. Churchyard at Allowaystown.
Martha Nelson d. 27 Apr. 1849, abt. 2:00 in the afternoon, aged 60-6-11, and
  left her husband and 7 children. Bur. in the M. E. Churchyard at
  Allowaystown.
John Nelson 10 May 1851, abt. 2:00 in the afternoon, age 27-7-25, and left his
  wife and 1 child, Buley Nelson. Bur. in the M. E. Churchyard at
  Allowaystown.
John Nelson d. 6 Sep. 1872, in his 83rd yr.
Isaac D. Nelson d. 2 Oct. 1863, aged 45 yrs. Interment in M. E. Church Yard at
  Alloway.
Mary M. Miller d. 14 Feb. 1869, aged 55 yrs. Interment at M. E. burying
  ground, Salem.
Sarah Ray d. 24 Mar. 1885, aged 68-7-16. Interment at Pennsgrove M. E.
  Cemetery.

Joseph Foster's Bible
McCarty and Davis, Philadelphia 1830

Joseph Foster b. 24 Dec. 1787.
Jemima Harvey, his wife, b. 28 July 1786 and d. 5 July 1832.
Elizabeth Harvey b. 12 Feb. 1887.
Sarah Shimp b. 23 Oct. 1809 and d. 8 July 1882 or 3.

Joseph Foster and Jemima Harvey mar. 26 Dec. 1807.
Joseph Foster and Elizabeth Harvey mar. 6 Apr. 1833.

Joseph Foster and Sarah Shimp mar. 5 Apr. 1834.

Children of Joseph and Jemima Foster: Mary Foster b. 6 Nov. 1808; Amariah
Foster b. 15 Apr. 1811; John Foster b. 4 July 1813; Joseph Foster b. 11 Feb.
1815; Sarah Foster b. 3 June 1816; Jemima Foster b. 24 Apr. 1818;
Emmaline Foster b. 5 Jan. 1825; Henry Foster b. 15 Aug. 1827.

Job Denn's Bible
William W. Harding, Philadelphia 1875

Ralph Allen, s/o David and Sarah Allen, b. 29 July 1785.
Margaret Hitchner, d/o Andrew and Sarah Hitchner, b. 1 June 1794.
Ralph Allen and Margaret Hitchner mar. 5 Mar. 1813.
Their children: Sarah Allen b. 14 Oct. 1814; William Allen b. 7 Feb. 1819; John
Allen b. 23 July 1821; Benjamin Allen b. 24 Nov. 1823.

Job Denn, s/o James and Mary Denn, b. 22 May 1809.

Job Denn and Sarah A. Allen mar. by the Rev. Mr. Miller of Leaton, 10 Jan.
1838.
Their children: Mary Elizabeth Denn b. 8 Jan. 1845; William Denn b. 8 Oct.
1846; Benjamin A. Denn b. 20 Nov. 1848; John Denn b. 8 Oct. 1850, Job
Denn b. 9 Sep. 1852; Charles W. Denn b. 2 Aug. 1855.

Children of Job and Harriett Denn: Anna M. Denn b. 26 Aug. 1881; Tessie F.
Denn b. 7 Sep. 1888; Norman J. Denn b. 23 Nov. 1891.

Children of Edmund and Anna Turner: Harriett Louise Turner b.17 Aug. 1817
(?); Francis Turner b. 28 July 1901; Russell Turner b. 20 Apr. 1903; Luke
C. Turner b. 27 Aug. 1906; Norman J. Turner b. 9 Dec. 19010; Edna Turner
b. 18 July 1915.

Sallie D. Smith b. 2 May 1867.

J. Fithian Smith and M. Lizzie Denn mar. by J. R. Murphy, Salem Co., 20 Feb.
1866.

Tessie F. Denn, d/o Job and Harriett Denn, d. Sat., 29 Oct. 1896.
Job Denn, s/o Job and Sarah Denn, d. 27 Feb. 1914.
Ralph Allen d. 26 Sep. 1835, aged 49 yrs. and 3 mo.

John, s/o Ralph and Margaret Allen, d. at Baltimore, 7 July 1857, aged 35-11-14.

Joseph Cook Bible

Joseph Cook, s/o William Cooke and his 2nd wife, Lydia Corlis, d/o Joseph Corlies and Margaret Woodmansee. b. 23 Nov. 1761

Mary Reeves, d/o Arthur Reeves, of Deptford, Gloucester Co., N. J., b. 17 Nov. 1864.

Joseph Cook and Mary Reeves mar. 16 Feb. 1785.

Their children: Ann Cook b. 23 Mar. 1786, abt. half past 3:00 in the afternoon; Lydia Cook b. 9 Sep. 1787, abt. 11:00 at night; Elizabeth Cook b. 23 Jan. 1790; Mary Cook b. 1 April ___; William Cook b. 28 Jan. 1794; Joseph Cook b. 4 Feb. 1796 and d. 1801; Arthur Cook b. 11 June 1798; Marmaduke Cook b. 10 Mar. 1801; Joseph Cook b. 14 Sep. 1805 and d. 1829; David R, Cook b. and d. young.

Ann Cook (3rd wife) and Moses Richman mar. Feb. 1817.

Mary Cook mar. Dr. Richard Parker as his 2nd wife; his 1st wife was a Seeley of Cumberland Co.

Marmaduke Cook mar. Mary Gosling. She mar. (2nd) 1929, Stacy French.

William Cook and Eliza Hitchner mar. 21 May 1835. She mar. (2nd), 1842, James Reed.

Lydia Cook d. 7 Jan. 1791, aged 3-3-29.

Joseph Cook d. 27 Aug. 1801, abt. 2:00 in the morning, aged 5-6-23.

Elizabeth Cook d. 19 Nov.1801, aged 11-9-22.

Arthur Cook d. 12 May 1806, killed by a runaway horse and wagon.

Joseph Cook d. 12 Apr. 1824.

Marmaduke Cook d. 8 Nov. 1827; left issue.

Joseph Cook d. 3 Nov. 1829, unmarried, at Louisville, Ky.

William Cook d. 19 Feb. 1839; had one dau. who d. unmarried.

Mary Reeves Cook d. 17 Dec. 1840.

Ann Cook Richman d. 25 Mar. 1849; had issue.

Mary Gosling Cook French d. 25 Apr. 1858.

Mary Cook Parker d. 12 Mar. 1862; had no issue.

Moses Richman d. 16 Apr. 1868, aged 90 yrs.

Dr. Richard Parker, with his 2 sons, was lost at sea in a fishing boat.

Josiah Wood Bible

Jeremiah Wood b. 24 Nov. 1767.
Sarah Wood, his wife, b. 29 Jan. 1772.
Nehemiah Richman b. 22 Oct. 1855.
Josiah B. Wood b. 9 Oct. 1801.
Hannah M. Wood, his wife, b. 31 May 1804.

Josiah B. Wood and Hannah M. Richman mar. 16 Mar. 1825.

Jeremiah Wood d. 27 May 1829, at 20 min. past 3:00 in the evening, aged 61-6-3.
Nehemiah Richman d. 20 Feb. 1826, aged 70-3-28.
Hannah Richman, his wife, d. 29 Jan. 1823, at 20 min. past 10:00 p.m.
Nehemiah Richman, s/o Nehemiah and Hannah Richman, d. 31 Mar. 1816, aged 16-9-16.

Wood Bible

Children of Joseph Wood: Priscilla Wood b. 12 Apr. 1736; Joseph Wood b. 28 Aug. 1738; Robert Wood b. 18 Feb. 1744; Moses Wood b. 19 Sep. 1746.

Elizabeth Miller, d/o John and Margaret Miller, b. 15 Mar. 1749.

Moses Wood and Elizabeth Miller mar. 27 June 1775.
Their children: Thomas Wood b. 11 June 1776; Margaret Wood b. 19 Oct. 1778.

Andrew Hann Bible
Jasper Harding, Philadelphia

Sara Van Meter, d/o Benjamin and Ann his wife, b. 23 Apr. 1793.
Israil, their son, b. 13 Sep. 1795.
William and Nathan, their sons, b. 28 Aug. 1797.
Marmaduke, their son, b. 25 Aug. 1799.

Benjamin Van Meter b. 19 Feb. 1774.
Rachel Moore Van Meter, his wife, b. 5 Sep. 1781.

Benjamin Van Meter and Rachel Moore mar. 25 Aug. 1801.
Their children: Elizabeth Van Meter b. 27 Jan. 1802; Harriet Van Meter b. 1
    June 1803; Ann Van Meter b. 13 Apr. 1805 and mar. Andrew Hann;
    Mariah Van Meter b. 6 Apr. 1807; Benjamin Van Meter b. 27 Mar. 1809;
    Enoch Van Meter b. 31 Dec. 1811.

Andrew Hann b. 15 Oct. 1806.
Ann Van Meter b. 13 Apr. 1805.
John Van Meter b. 31 Jan. 1812.

Andrew Hann and Ann, d/o Benjamin and Rachel M. Van Meter, mar. 12 Feb.
    1842 at Friesburg, Salem Co., N. J. by Rev. John Wilcox.
Their children: Josephine Van Meter (Hann) b. 1 Dec. 1843; Jonathan Hann b.
    12 Oct. 1845; Rachel Moore (Hann) b. 12 May 1847; Ellen Salesatena
    (Hann) b. 19 Aug. 1849.

Jeremiah Foster and Josephine Hann, his 2nd wife, mar. 1 Feb, 1866; no issue by
    either marriage.
John Mowers and Rachel V. M. Hann mar. 17 Mar. 1869.
Jonathan Hann and Hettie C. Ewan mar. 15 Dec. 1875.
George W. Callaway and Ella C. Hann mar. 28 Nov. 1912.

Ella Salesatena Hann, d/o Jonathan and Hettie C. Ewan Hann, b. 7 Sep. 1880
    and d. 1940.
Vesta Hicks, d/o George W. and Ella C. Hann Callaway, b. 7 July 1914,
    Philadelphia.
George Hann, s/o George W. and Ella C. Hann Callaway, b. 18 Sep. 1916,
    Albany, N. Y.

Benjamin Van Meter d. 10 Sep. 1814, aged 40-6-20.
Marmaduke Van Meter d. at Easton, 19 Mar. 1860, aged 60-6-24.
Benjamin Van Meter d. 12 Dec. 1863, aged 54-8-12.
Ann Hann d. 18 May 1879, aged 74-1-2.
Andrew Hann d. 17 Aug. 1887, aged 80-10-2.
Josephine Foster d. 23 May 1924.
Jonathan Hann d. 5 July 1912.
Rachel Mowers d. 1904.
Ellen Hann Walker d. 8 May 1926.
Hettie, w/o Jonathan Hann, d. 12 Aug. 1928.

David Buck Bible
M. Carey, Philadelphia

Property of David Buck and Lydia, his wife, bought 23 Aug. 1804.

Ruth Siffin b. 17 Dec. 1763 and d. 7 Sep. 1828, aged 64-9-17.
Lydia S. Buck b. 12 May 1790.

Children of David and Lydia Buck: Phebe Buck b. Sunday, 11 Mar. 1810; Mary
    Buck b. Friday, 6 Mar. 1812; Ruth S. Buck b. Saturday, 1 Oct. 1814; David
    S. Buck b. Tuesday, 14 Jan. 1817; Priscilla Buck b. Saturday, 12 June 1819;
    Sarah Jane Buck b. 9 Feb. 1822.

Abraham Gilman and Phebe Buck mar. 15 Jan. 1830.
Owen Kelty and Mary S, Buck mar. 3 Mar. 1832.
Andrew Sparks and Sarah Jane Buck mar. 29 July 1844.
Abraham Gilman and Priscilla Buck mar. 24 July 1852.

David Buck, s/o John and Priscilla Buck, d. 7 Sep. 1821.
David S. Buck, s/o David and Lydia Buck, d. 10 June 1846.
Lydia Buck, d/o John and Ruth Siffin, d. 29 Dec. 1861, in her 72nd yr.
Phebe Gilman, d/o David and Lydia Buck, d. 22 Mar. 1852.
Mary Kelty, d/o David and Lydia Buck, d. 20 Nov. 1859.
Priscilla Gilman, d/o David and Lydia Buck, d. 15 Oct. 1872.

James Thompson Bible

Edith and Martha Vannaman b. 17 Sep. 1787.
Hannah Vannaman b. 24 Dec. 1794.

James Thompson and Edith Vannaman mar. 24 Feb. 1806.

Aaron H. Thompson, s/o James and Edith Thompson, b. 18 Dec. 1823
_____ Thompson, d/o James and Edith Thompson, b. 23 Jan. 1826.
John Wesley Thompson b. 1 July 1829.

Maria Thompson d. 22 Oct. 1806, aged 4 yrs.
Martha Thompson d. 26 Jan. 1811, aged 13 dys.
John C. Thompson d. 22 Nov. 1821, aged 2 yrs., 9 mo.
Aaron H. Thompson d. 3 Mar. 1825, aged 1-2-3.

Benjamin Thompson Bible

Elizabeth Ware, d/o Joseph and Elizabeth Ware and w/o Benjamin Thompson, b. 8 Oct. 1722.
Children of Benjamin and Elizabeth Thompson: Milliscent Thompson b. 12 June 1747; Hannah Thompson b. 14 Oct. 174950; John Thompson b. 24 Dec. 1750/51; Elizabeth Thompson b. 12 Aug. 1753; Benjamin Thompson b. 18 Dec. 1756; Sarah Thompson b. 26 Mar. 1769.

Elizabeth Cleaver, d/o Peter and Susannah Cleaver, b. 20 Apr. 1757.

Benjamin Thompson and Elizabeth Cleaver mar. 8 Dec. 1778.
Their children: Isaac Thompson b. 4 Apr. 1779; Sarah Thompson b. 20 June 1783.

Ann Fogg, d/o Daniel and Grace Fogg, b. 25 Nov. 1757.

Benjamin Thompson and Ann Fogg (Moore?) Mar. 2 Dec. 1802.

Benjamin Thompson, Sr., d. 29 June 1775, abt. 10:00 in the afternoon.
Elizabeth Thompson, w/o Benjamin Thompson, d. 2 Oct. 1775, abt. 10:00 in the evening.
Milliscent Thompson, d/o Benjamin and Elizabeth Thompson, d. 29 June 1776, about noonday.
Elizabeth Thompson, w/o Benjamin Thompson, d. 20 May 1802, ant. 15 min. after 10:00 in the evening, aged 45 yrs. and 1 mo.
Isaac Thompson d. 9 Feb. 1804, aged 24-10-5.
Benjamin Thompson d. 19 Sep. 1821, 64-9-1.

John Holme Bible
Mathew Carey, Philadelphia 1806

Samuel Holme, s/o John and Mary Holme, b. 18 Sep. 1761.
John Holme, s/o John and Mary Holme, b. 29 June 1764, abt. 10:00 in the evening
Ezra Holme, s/o John and Mary Holme, b. 15 Nov. 1766.
Ann Holme, d/o John and Mary Holme, b. 6 June 1769.
Smith Oharo, s/o Charles and Elizabeth Oharo, b. 9 Aug. 1816.
Samuel Holme, s/o Ezra and Mary Holme, b. 19 Oct. 1805.
Hannah Ann Holme, d/o Ezra and Mary Holme, b. 4 June 1808.

Ebenezer Holme, s/o Ezra and Mary Holme, b. 9 Aug. 1810.
Mary Sheets, d/o Joseph and Mary Sheets, b. 19 Jan. 1799 or 1800.
Smith Sheets, s/o Joseph and Mary Sheets, b. 5 Jan. 1803.
Ezra Holme, s/o Ezra and Mary Holme, b. 12 Apr. 1813.

John Holmes and Mary Smith mar. 7 Dec. 1781.
Samuel Holme and Mary Wentzell mar. 6 Mar. 1803.
Ezra Holme and Mary Dickinson mar. 8 Aug. 1804.
John Shimp and Mary Sheets mar. 3 Oct. 1818.
Joseph Cake and Elizabeth Shimp mar. 22 Feb. 1840.
Isaac T. Lambert and Mary A. Shimp mar. 1 Jan. 1842.
Jacob House and Sallie Ann Shimp mar. 9 Sep. 1860.
David Shimp, Jr., and Annie H. Crispin mar. 30 Oct. 1860.

John Holme d. 27 Aug. 1792.
Samuel Holme d. 5 July 1805.
Joseph Sheets d. 26 Mar. 1812.
Smith Oharo d. 9 Sep. 1819.
Mary Sheets d. 16 Apr. 1825.
Ann Sheets d. 14 May 1836.
Jacob Sheets d. 25 Nov. 1847, aged 68 yrs.
Mary Sheets d. 16 Oct. 1849, aged 58 yrs.
Barbara Townsend d. 14 Mar. 1855.
Mary Shimp, d/o Smith and Lydia Shimp, d. 19 Feb. 1855, aged 4 yrs.
Smith Sheets d. 13 Nov. 1856, aged 53 yrs.
Annie H. Shimp, w/o David Shimp, d. 20 Mar. 1861, in her 19th yr.
John Shimp d. 2 Apr. 1864, aged 66 yrs.
David Shimp, Jr., eldest s/o John and Mary Shimp, d. 6 Apr. 1866, at 4:00 p.m.,
    aged 43-6-25.
Mary Shimp, widow of John Shimp, d. 12 Aug. 1866 at 6:00 p.m., aged 66-6-
    21.

William Lambert Bible
Isaac Collins, Trenton MDCCXCI

William Lambert, s/o John and Mary Lambert, b. 25 Aug. 1775.
Sarah Lambert, d/o Benjamin and Elizabeth Thompson, b. 19 June 1783.

William Lambert and Sarah Thompson mar. 22 June 1802.

Their children: Elizabeth Thompson Lambert b. 28 Feb. 1805; Mary Lach
    Lambert b. 23 Nov. 1807; Benjamin Thompson Lambert b. 14 Apr. 1810;
    William C. Lambert b. 16 Jan. 1813; Joseph C. Lambert b. 4 July 1815;
    Isaac T. Lambert b. 1 June 1818; Sarah Thompson Lambert b. 14 Aug.
    1820.

John H. Lambert, s/o William and Mary Lambert, b. 16 Dec. 1799.
Margaret B. Sutton, d/o William and Ann Sutton, b. 11 May 1818.

William C. Lambert and Margaret B. Sutton, of Roadstown, Cumberland Co.,
    mar. 22 Feb. 1838.
Their children: Sarah Elizabeth Lambert b. 19 June 1839; William Sutton
    Lambert b. 21 Feb. 1841.

Mary Ann Shimp, d/o John and Mary Shimp, b. 22 Nov. 1824.

Isaac T. Lambert and Mary Ann Shimp, of Upper Alloway Creek, mar. 1 Jan.
    1844 by Ezekiel Sexton.

Isaac Franklin Lambert, s/o Isaac T. and Mary Ann Lambert, b. 1 Aug. 1844.

William Lambert d. 20 May 1824.
Sarah T. Lambert d. 20 Apr. 1857.
Benjamin Thompson Lambert, s/o William and Sarah Lambert, d. 16 July 1828.
Sarah Thompson Lambert, d/o William and Sarah Lambert, d. 15 Jan. 1821,
    aged 5 mo. and 1 dy.

                        Hugh Dunham Bible
                    Isaac Collins, Trenton MDCCXCI
            Hugh Dunhams Book, bought 11 Oct. 1810. Price $3.00.

John Dunham, s/o Ephraim Dunham and Phebe his wife, b. 15 Sep. 1732.
Phebe, his wife, b. 14 Feb. 1751.

Francis Dunham and Amy, his wife, mar. 9 Mar. 1757.
Their children: Elizabeth Dunham b. 30 Jan. 1758; Samuel Dunham b. 1 Feb.
    1760; Zurviah Dunham b. 12 Sep. 1762; Hugh Dunham b. 11 Oct. 1766;
    Hezekiah Dunham b. 8 Aug. 1769; Delily Dunham b. 27 Nov. 1772.

Hugh Dunham b. 11 Oct. 1766.

Barthsheba Dunham, his wife, b. 9 Dec. 1772.

Hugh Dunham and Barthsheba, his wife, mar. 12 Jan. 1790.

Delilah Dunham d. 9 Mar. 1777.
Phebe Dunham, w/o John Dunham, d. 1784.
John Dunham d. 22 Dec. 1819.
Marah Lake d. 9 Dec. 1818, in her 39th yr.
Rachel Wood d. 2 Aug. 1821, in her 44th yr.
Hugh Dunham d. 16 Jan. 1824, in his 58th yr.
Bathsheba Wood, former w/o Hugh Dunham, d. 3 Aug. 1853.
Eadeth Guinn d. 4 Nov. 1882, in her 80th yr.
Sarah Applegate d. 20 July 1823 in her 62nd yr.
Mary Dunham Lake, d/o Christopher and Mary Lake, d. 29 Oct. 1813.

Catherine Brooks Bible
Mathew Carey, Philadelphia 1811

Rebecca Champneys and Joseph Howard mar. 11 Apr. 1783.
Benjamin Champneys and Sarah Potter mar. 18 Apr. 1795.
Phebe Brooks, d/o Almarin Brooks, mar. Hiram Paul (no date).
Catherine Brooks, d/o Almarin Brooks, mar. Christopher Streeper 7 Dec. 1822.
Charles G. Stinson and Phebe Paul mar. 14 Dec. 1835. They went to California.
Clarence M. Streeper mar. Rebecca Dubois 4 Nov. 1847. They went to Kansas.
Children of Almarin and Sarah Brooks: Kitty Brooks b. 10 Mar. 1786; Phebe
    Brooks b. 8 Oct. 1787; Dela Luzon Stuband Brooks b. 28 May and d. 15
    June 1790; Sarah Brooks b. 10 July 1791 and d. 11 Apr. 1794; Phebe
    Brooks b. 22 Feb. 1794; Sarah Champneys Brooks b. 9 May 1796 and d. 27
    May 1797.

Joseph Champneys b. 8 Feb. 1740.
Benjamin Champneys b. 2 Feb. 1744.
Almarin Brooks b. Feb. 1756.
Elizabeth Champneys b. 10 Apr. 1762.
John Champneys b. 2 Apr. 1765.
Sarah Champneys b. 12 Aug. 1767.
Joseph Champneys b. 24 Aug. 1770.
Benjamin Champneys b. 17 Aug. 1773.
Hiram Paul b. 13 Aug. 1792.
Almarin Brooks Paul b. 13 Sep. 1823.

Clarence Mulford Streeper b. 3 June 1824.
Christopher Streeper d. 15 June 1825, aged 30- yrs., 11 mo.
Mary Streeper b. 1 Apr. 1825.
Sarah Champneys Paul b. 17 Apr. 1826.
Rollins Foster Streeper b. 27 Aug. 1848.
Alinda Louise Streeper b. 29 Apr. 1850.
Almarin Brooks Streeper b. 30 Sep. 1852.

Joseph Champneys d. 25 July 1773, at 5:00 and 50 min. in the morning, aged
    33-5-17.
Rebecca Champneys d. 20 Jan. (no year), at 3:00 in the morning.
John Champneys d.24 June 1781, aged 16-2-22.
Joseph Champneys, Jr., d. 27 June 1781, aged 10-9-17.
Benjamin Champneys d. 16 July 1814 at 9:00 in the morning.
Almarin Brooks d. 25 Jan. 1824.
Christopher Streeper d. 13 June 1825.
Hiram Paul d. 26 Mar. 1828.
Catherine Streeper, d/o Almarin and Sarah Brooks, d. 13 June 1835, at quarter
    past 4:00 in the afternoon.
Sarah Brooks, consort of the late Major Almarin Brooks, d. 19 Nov. 1835, in
    her 68th yr.
Sarah Champneys Higgins, d/o Hiram and Phebe Paul, d. 27 June 1847.
Almarin Brooks Streeper d. 4 Feb. 1853 at 3:00 in the morning, aged 5 wks. and
    1 dy.

Harding Bible
C. Alexander, Philadelphia 1839

Thomas Harding b. 26 July 1772 and d. 12 Aug. 1851, aged 77 yrs.
Lydia Harding b. 8 Feb. 1776 and d. 14 June 1850, aged 74 yrs.
Sarah Harding b. 6 Sep. 1801.
Thomas Harding b. 6 Dec. 1808.
Moses Burt Harding stillborn 21 Jan. 1841.
Emily Harding b. 18 June 1842.
Samuel Johnson Dubois b. 17 July 1842 and d. 14 June 1921.
G. W. Janvier, aged 74 yrs. in Jan. 1858.

Thomas Harding, 2nd, and Lydia Richman mar. 20 Oct. 1795.
Thomas Harding, Jr., and Sarah Burt mar. 6 June 1833.
Samuel Johnson Dubois and Emily Harding mar. 18 Mar. 1867.

Thomas Harding, 1ˢᵗ, d. 24 Apr. 1798, aged 63 yrs. and 2 mo.
Catherine Harding d. 20 Oct. 1809, aged 80 yrs.
Thomas Harding, 3rd, d. 19 Sep. 1858.
Sarah Burt Harding d. 6 Sep. 1880.
Emily Harding Dubois d. 25 Oct. 1910.

John Richman Bible

John Richman b. 1 Jan. 1737.
Rebecca Elwell Richman b. 7 Feb. 1741.
Their children: William Richman b. 9 Feb. 1863; Catherine Richman b. 5 Mar.
    1764; Rachel Richman b. 27 Sep. 1765; David Richman b. 12 Feb. 1767;
    Rhoda Richman b. 3 Dec. 1768; Henry Richman b. 7 Nov. 1770; Sarah
    Richman b. 29 Jan. 1772; Liddia Richman b. 1774; Rebeka Richman b.
    1776.

Children of John Richman and Sarah VanMeter: Rebecca bapt. 1 May 1743;
    Isaac, bapt. 17 Nov. 1745; Abraham b. 10 Apr. and bapt. 21 May 1749;
    Benjamin d. 17 June 1859, aged 6 yrs.

Richman/Coleman Bible
7 July 1817, Rachel Richman. Steal not this book.

Rachel Richman, d/o Isaac and Rebecca Garrison, b. 25 May 1774.

Children of Benjamin and Rachel Richman: Elizabeth Richman b. 27 Oct.
    1797; Josiah Richman b. 28 Mar. 1800; Ann Richman b. 6 June 1803 at
    5:00 in the morning; Rebecca Richman b. 13 Sep. 1806 at 2:00 in the
    afternoon; Isaac Richman b. 27 May 1809; Jacob Richman b. 15 Sep. 1812.

Moses Coleman, s/o John and Elizabeth Coleman, b. 2 Nov. 1818.
Joel Coleman 11 Feb. 1821. (born?)
Rachel Coleman b. 21 June 1824.
Jay Coleman b. 6 Sep. 1826.
John Coleman b. 8 Oct. 1829.
Rebecca Coleman, d/o John and Elizabeth Coleman, b. Sep. 1832.
Josiah Coleman, s/o John and Elizabeth Coleman, b.2 Mar. 1836.

Jeremiah Wood Records

Jeremiah Wood b. 24 Nov. 1767 and d. 27 May 1829, aged 61-6-3.
Sarah Wood b. 29 Jan. 1772 and d. 1 July 1846, aged 74-5-1.
Jeremiah Wood and Sarah Richman mar. 15 Nov. 1792.
Their children: Rachel Wood b. 8 Oct. 1793; Thomas B. Wood b. 1 July 1795;
    Isaiah Wood b. 25 July 1797; Charles Wood b. 17 Jan. 1799 d. 8 Oct. 1877;
    Maria R. and Josiah B. Wood b. 9 Oct. 1801; Wood b. 9 Oct. 1801; Eliza,
    Ephraim and Esther Wood b. 29 July 1803; Jeremiah Wood b. 5 Feb. 1805;
    Sarah Wood b. 25 July 1807; Rebecca and John Wood b. 4 Apr. 1809;
    Elizabeth Wood b. 3 July 1813.

Rachel Wood d. 6 July 1856.
Thomas B. Wood d. 5 May 1857, aged 61-10-4.
Isaiah Wood d. Mar. 1886, aged 88 yrs.
Charles Wood d. 8 Oct. 1877.
Maria R. Wood d. 1 Mar. 1844.
Josiah B. Wood d. 24 Aug. 1832.
Eliza Wood d. 9 Aug. 1803.
Ephraim Wood d. 21 Aug. 1803.
Esther Wood d. 22 Aug. 1803.
Jeremiah Wood d. 20 Jan. 1806.
Sarah Wood d. 2 Apr. 1866.
Rebecca Wood d. 29 Jan. 1884.
John Wood d. 16 Feb. 1888, aged 78-9-22.

William Cook Bible

William Cook b. 28 Jan. 1794.
Eliza Cook b. 10 Dec. 1813.
James M. Reed b. 10 July 1816.
Mary P. Cook b. 14 Nov. 1838.
Ann R. Cook b. 17 June 1837.
Evaline D. Reed b. 19 Oct. 1842.
Victory L. W. Reed b. 2 Jan. 1844.
Elizabeth C. Reed b.10 Jan. 1846.
Georgianna Reed b. 5 Dec. 1848 and d. young.
R. Matlock Reed b.8 July 1851.
Aubrey Reed b.26 Mar. 1855.
Ralph L. Kelsay b. 16 June 1865.

Harry T. Kelsay b. 5 Jan. 1868.
Mary C. Levy b. 29 Aug. 1869.
Blanch L. Reed b. 28 Mar. 1882.
Mary Reed b. 2 Nov. 1883.
Matlock R. Reed b. 6 Nov. 1885.
Ethel K. Reed b. 17 Jan. 1888.
Maude Eliza Matlock b. (no date).
James Aubrey Reed b. Sept. (no date).

William Cook and Eliza Hitchner mar. 21 May 1835.
James M. Reed and Eliza Cook mar. 12 Jan. 1842.
Rufus B. Kelsay and Evaline D. Reed mar. 5 May 1863.
Joseph R. Matlack and Louisa W. Reed mar. 11 Apr. 1868.
Thomas Levy and Elizabeth C. Reed mar. 20 Sep. 1868.
Aubrey C. Reed and Caroline Henry mar. 23 Aug. 1881.

William Cook d. 19 Feb. 1839.
Ann R. Cook d. 15 Feb. 1838.
Mary P. Cook d. 30 Jan. 1862.
Mary C. Levy d. 8 Aug. 1870.
R. Matlock Reed d. 2 Feb. 1879.
James M. Reed d. 7 May 1887.
Elizabeth C. Reed d. 26 Oct. 1890.
Caroline H. Reed d. 17 Jan. 1890.
Eliza Reed d. 21 Jan. 1901, aged 87 yrs.

Gerrard Sparks Bible
Isaac Collins, Trenton 1741

Gerrard Sparks b. 28 Aug. 1760.
Elizabeth Sparks, his wife, b. 5 Feb. 1768.
Gerrard Sparks mar. Elizabeth Pitman mar. 1 Jan. 1782.
Their children: William Sparks b. 2 Aug. 1783; John Sparks b. 2 Dec. 1784;
    Ann Sparks b. 19 Mar. 1786; Elizabeth Sparks b. 10 Jan. 1788; Susannah
    Sparks b. 12 Jan. 1790; Robert Sparks b. 25 Sep. 1791; Gerrard Sparks b.
    15 Aug. 1793; Ebenezer Sparks b. 18 Sep. 1795; Edward Sparks b. 13 Oct.
    1797; Edith Sparks b. 13 Nov. 1799; Cathrine Sparks b. 15 Feb. 1802;
    Gerrard Sparks b. 26 Apr. 1804; Samuel Sparks b. 2 Jan. 1806; Marion
    Sparks b. 2 June 1809.

Ebenezer Sparks b. 18 Sep. 1795.
Maria Sparks b. 25 Dec. 1797;

Ebenezer Sparks and Maria Pedrick mar. 14 Sep. 1818.
Their children: Joshua P. Sparks b. 7 Dec. 1819; George P. Sparks b. 31 Jan.
1822; Maria Sparks b. 19 Feb. 1826; Thomas Sparks b. 9 June 1829; Elmer
Sparks b. 22 Aug. 1831; Mary Ann Sparks b. 4 Jan. 1833; Ann Elizabeth
Sparks b. 18 Jan. 1836.

Elizabeth Sparks d. 8 July 1822, aged 54-5-3.
Joshua P. Sparks, s/o Ebenezer and Maria Sparks, d. 27 May 1832.
Mary Ann S. Tidmarsh, their dau., d. 5 Aug. 1832, aged 23-2-3.
Gerrard Sparks d. 10 Dec. 1843, aged 83-3-12.
Elizabeth Robinson d. 4 Aug. 1855, aged 39-2-12.
Ebenezer Sparks d. 22 Sep. 1855, aged 60 yrs., and 4 dys.
Maria Sparks, his wife, d. 19 Mar. 1858, aged 61-2-17.
Elizabeth Peterson d. 16 Aug. 1860, aged 72 yrs.
Robert Sparks d. 7 Aug. 1881, in his 90th yr.

Thomas Summerill Bible
Alexander Kinkaid, Edinburgh 1784
His Majesty's Printer

John Summerill b. 23 Jan. 1746.
Naomi Summerill b. 22 Sep. 1750.
Mary Summerill b. 12 Jan. 1772.
Hannah Summerill b. 20 July 1774.
Rebecca Summerill b. 23 Mar. 1778.
Elizabeth Summerill b. 3 Mar. 1788.
Hannah Summerill b. 3 June 1806.
Joseph Summerill b. 9 July 1808.
Samuel Summerill b. 20 Aug. 1810.
Thomas Summerill b. 3 Sep. 1812.
Paul Summerill b. 14 Oct. 1814.
Jonathan Summerill b. 28 Oct. 1816.
Furman Summerill b. 16 Oct. 1818.
Hannah Jane b. 22 July 1838.

Naomi Summerill d. 13 Mar. 1803(?).
Joseph Summerill d. (no date).

Thomas Summerill b. 14 Aug. 1779.
William Summerill b. __ June 178_.
Joseph Summerill b. _5 Apr. 1784.
Thomas Halton, s/o John and Mary Halton, b. 21 Jan. 1804.

John C. Gaventa b. 27 May 1868.
Jacob Gaventa b. 9 Feb. 1870.
Albert Gaventa b. 4 Aug. 1873.
Edward Gaventa b. 4 Aug. 1873.
Emma Gaventa b. 1 Jan. 1876.
Harvey Gaventa b. 22 May 1879.

Edward Gaventa d. 9 Aug. 1873.
Albert Gaventa d. 9 Jan. 1874.
Anna Gaventa Bouvier d. 19 Apr. 1918.
Kate Gaventa d.3 Aug. 1919.
Frank J. Gaventa d.29 May 1928.
George H. Gaventa d.13 Feb. 1932.
Louisa S. Gaventa d.2 Apr. 1937.

Hannah H. Fogg Bible
J. B. Lippincott, Philadelphia 1856

Aaron Fogg, s/o Charles and Sarah Fogg, b. 12 Mar. 1762.
Hannah Allen, d/o David and Rebecca Allen, b. 5 Mar. 1767.
Elisha Fogg b. 12 Jan. 1786.
David Fogg b. 30 Sep. 1789.
Samuel Fogg b. 14 Sep. 1791.
Rebecca Fogg b. 7 Dec. 1792.
Ebenezer Fogg b. 13 May 1795.
Sarah Fogg b. 5 June 1797.
Aaron Fogg b. 3 Sep. 1799.
Thomas Fogg b. 12 June 1802.
Samuel Fogg b. 20 Feb. 1805.

Aaron Fogg, father of the above, d. 11 Nov. 1804, aged 42 yrs.
Hannah Bradway, mother of the above, d. 30 Mar. 1833, aged 66 yrs. and 25
    dys.

David Fogg, s/o Aaron and Hannah Fogg, b. 30 Sep. 1789.
Hannah Fogg, d/o Jonathan and Joanna Hildreth, b. 16 May 1791.

David Fogg and Hannah Hildreth mar. 25 Mar. 1813.
Their children: Lydia H. Fogg b. Aug. 1814; Joseph H. Fogg b. Apr. 1817;
    Aaron A. Fogg b. 4 Mar. 1820; Joanna M. Fogg b. 29 June 1822; David A.
    Fogg b.29 Oct. 1825; Hannah H. Fogg b.11 Nov. 1827.

Jonathan B. Grier and Lydia H. Fogg mar. 28 Nov. 1833.
Joseph H. Fogg and Rachel Allen mar. 3 Nov. 1842.
Aaron A. Fogg and Mary Sheppard mar. 22 Mar. 1843.
David A. Fogg and Sarah Jane Chispen mar. 6 Mar. 1856.

Joanna M. Fogg, d/o David and Hannah Fogg, d. 25 July 1823, aged 1 yr. and
    25 dys.
Joanna H. Fogg, d/o David and Hannah Fogg, d. 10 Sep. 1851, aged 23 yrs. and
    10 mo.
Hannah H. Fogg, d/o David and Hannah Fogg, d. 17 July 1908, aged 80-8-6.
    (Twin to Joanna H. Fogg)
Joanna M. Fogg, d/o Joseph H. and Rachel Fogg, d. 7 Sep. 1855, aged 3-3-22.
David Fogg, s/o Aaron and Hannah Fogg, d. 28 Nov. 1874, aged 85 yrs. and 28
    dys.
Hannah H. Fogg, d/o Jonathan and Joanna Hildreth, d. 19 July 1883, aged 92
    yrs. and 3 mo.

Grier Bible
Mathew Carey, Philadelphia 1802

George Grier b. 3 Nov. 1748.
Rebekah Grier b. (no date).
George and Rebekah Grier mar. 15 Feb. 1779.
Their children: Mary Grier b. 17 Nov. 1781; Richard Grier b. 22 Fb. 1784;
    David Grier b. 3 Apr. 1788.

Ruth Butcher, d/o Jonathan and Rachel Butcher, b. 9 Sep. 1792.

George Grier and Ruth Butcher mar. 18 Oct. 1808.
Their children: Richard Butcher Grier b. 14 Oct. 1809; Jonathan Grier b. 8 Dec.
    1811; David Grier b. 21 Aug. 1814; Rachel Grier b. 4 Sep. 1816; Robert

Grier b. 23 Feb. 1819; James Grier b. 31 Oct. 1821; David Grier b. 7 Aug. 1827; Charles Grier b. 24 Sep. 1831.

Mary Grier d. 26 Apr. 1784.
Richard Grier, s/o George and Rebekah Grier, d. 4 Sep. 1808, aged 24 yrs.
Rebekah Grier d. 18 Nov. 1807, in her 49th yr.
George Grier d. 13 Sep. 1808, aged 59 yrs.
David Grier, s/o George and Ruth Grier, d. 18 Oct. 1823, aged 1-11-18.
David Grier, s/o George and Rebekah Grier, d. 6 Jan. 1828, aged 41-9-27.
David Grier, s/o George and Ruth Grier, d. 21 July 1830, aged 2-11-13.
Richard Grier, s/o George and Ruth Grier, d. 10 Aug. 1830, aged 20-9-26.
George Grier d. 23 Feb. 1849, aged 60-10-20.
Charles Grier, s/o George and Ruth Grier, d. 29 Aug. 1854.
Ruth Grier, w/o George Grier, d. 8 Dec. 1864, aged 72 yrs.

Hancock Bible
Isaac Collins, Trenton 1791

Children of Edward and Mary Hancock: John Hancock b. 25 Feb. 1759; Benjamin Hancock b. 23 Nov. 1760 and d. 1 Aug. 1803; Edward Hancock b. 1 Feb. 1764 and d. 16 Jan. 1790; David Hancock b. 31 Aug. 1768 and d. 9 Oct. 1771.

Mary Hancock, w/o Edward and mother of the 4 sons, d. 5 Jan 1773.

Children of Edward and Rebekah Hancock: Mary Hancock b. 28 Oct. 1776; William Hancock b. 29 Dec. 1779 and d. 11 Oct. 1798.

Abigail Hancock, d/o Edward Hancock, Jr., b. 5 Mar. 1783.
Rebekah Cyrll, d/o Jesse and Mary Cyrll, b. 10 Sep. 1797.

Children of Edward and Clarissa Hancock: Elizabeth Ann Hancock b. 9 Mar. 1824 and d. 7 Oct. 1826; Ann Hancock b. 21 Fe. 1828; Richard Hancock b. 3 Nov. 1830; Joseph Hancock b. 30 Nov. 1834 and d. 15 Aug. 1835; Clarissa Hancock b. 11 July and d. 3 Sep. 1836, aged 1 mo. and 23 dys.

Rebekah Hancock, w/o Edward Hancock, d. 15 July 1784.
Edward Hancock, Jr., d. 16 Jan. 1790.
Hannah Hancock, Sr., d. 12 Apr. 1803, aged 70 yrs.
Elizabeth Hancock, w/o John Hancock, d. 23 Aug. 1810.

Elizabeth Hancock, w/o John Hancock, d.10 Sep. 1819, aged 50 yrs.
John Hancock d. 20 Mar. 1820, aged 61 yrs.
Rebecca Finlaw, w/o John Finlaw, d. 20 July 1830, aged 64 yrs.
Ann Hancock, d/o Edward Hancock, d. 20 May 1831, aged 3 yrs. and 3 mo.

Hancock Bible
R. Aitkin, Philadelphia 1782

Children of John and Elizabeth Hancock: Benjamin Hancock b. 1784; Ann
Hancock b. 18 Sep. 1791; Edward Hancock b. 27 June 1793; Mary
Hancock b. 12 Feb. 1796; Edward Hancock b. 8 Aug. 1798; Robert M.
Hancock b. 15 Sep. 1800; Elizabeth Hancock b. 15 Sep. 1802.

Children of Benjamin and Phebe Hancock: Robert Hancock b. 16 Aug. 1806;
Hannah Hancock b. 10 Apr. 1808; Daniel P. Hancock b. 26 July 1810;
William Hancock b. 26 May 1813; Elisabeth Hancock b. 6 Jan. 1817;
Susannah Hancock b. 9 July 1818; Phebe Hancock b. 23 Sep. 1819; Gilbert
Hancock b. 3 Mar. 1824.

Carl Williams Bible
George Grierson, London
Printer to the Kings Most Excellent Majesty

Mary Paget, d/o Moses and Rachel Paget, b. 1 Mar. 1787.
Aaron Paget, s/o Moses and Rachel Paget, b. 7 Feb. 1789.

Anna Bradway, w/o Edward Bradway, d. 29 May 1811.

Isaac Fogg Bible
Matthew Carey, Philadelphia 1811

Martha Fogg, d/o of Isaac and Rebeckah Fogg, b. 9 Nov. 1778 at 1:00 in the
morning.

Children of Isaac and Martha Fogg: David Fogg b. 23 Oct. 1782 at 2:00 in the
afternoon; Joseph Fogg b. 11 Oct. 1784 at 7:00 in the evening; Rebecca
Fogg b. 7 Nov. 1786 at 6:00 in the morning; Benjamin Fogg b. 25 Oct.
1788 at 6:00 in the morning; Thomas Fogg b. 30 Oct. 1790 at 3:00 in the

morning; Isaac Fogg b. 9 Apr. 1793 at 5:00 in the morning; William Fogg
b. 21 Mar. 1798 at 5:00 in the evening; Sarah Fogg b. 18 July 1800;
Hannah Fogg b. 3 Aug. 1803 at 11:00 in the evening.

Children of David and Mary Fogg: Martha Ann Fogg b. 29 Nov. 1808;
Elizabeth Fogg b. 19 May 1810; James Fogg b. 20 Sep. 1813; Isaac Fogg b.
29 Nov. 1815; Rebeckah Fogg b. 18 Jan. 1818; Firman Fogg b. 27 Dec.
1819.

Isaac Fogg, s/o Joseph and Elizabeth Fogg, b. (no date).
Martha Wallace, d/o Benjamin Wallace, b. (no date).

Children of Isaac and Mary Fogg: Joseph D. Fogg b. 29 Feb. 1844; Martha D.
Fogg b. 31 July 1846; David H. Fogg b. 10 May 1851; Elizabeth B. Fogg b.
3 Dec. 1853; James Clifford Fogg b. 25 Mar. 1857.

Isaac Fogg, s/o Joseph D. and Emily Fogg, b. 19 Nov. 1885.

David and Mary Fogg mar. 18 Jan. 1808.
Joseph D. Fogg and Emily S. Powers mar. 24 Mar. 1884.

Isaac Fogg, s/o Isaac and Martha Fogg, d. 4 June 1794, aged 1-2-5.

Isaac Fogg, s/o Joseph and Elizabeth Fogg, d. 26 Apr. 1814.
Isaac Fogg, s/o Isaac and Martha Fogg, d. 25 Apr. 1814, aged 17-7-15.
Thomas Fogg, s/o Isaac and Martha Fogg, d. 25 Jan. 1816, aged 22-2-26.
Hannah Fogg, d/o Isaac and Martha Fogg, d. 25 Aug. 1819, aged 16 yrs. and 22
dys.
Martha Fogg, widow of Isaac Fogg, d. 9 Sep. 1819.
Rebecca Fogg, d/o David and Mary Fogg, d. 27 Sep. 1821, aged 2-7-26.
Martha Ann Dunn, w/o Thackara Dunn and d/o David and Mary Fogg, d. 9 Apr.
1846, aged 37-4-10.
Mary Fogg, w/o David Fogg, d. 17 Feb. 1856, aged 71 yrs.
Thomas Fogg, s/o David and Mary Fogg, d. 29 May 1860, aged 41-5-2.
David Fogg d. 18 May 1870 at abt. 7:00, aged 87 yrs. and 7 mo.

Cunningham Bible
H. and E. Phinney, Cooperstown, N. Y.

John Cunningham b. 24 Apr. 1791.

Rachel B. Cunningham b. 12 Feb. 1797.

Children of John and Rachel E. Cunningham: James S. Cunningham b. 24 Apr. 1825; Mark Cunningham b. 15 Feb. 1827.

Rebecca Cunningham b. 30 Dec. 1810.

Children of John and Rebecca Cunningham: John W. Cunningham b. 6 Dec. 1835; Charles T. Cunningham b. 26 Nov. 1836; Hannah Elizabeth Cunningham b. 27 July 1839; Jerome Cunningham b. 14 June 1842; Martha Ann Cunningham b. 30 Mar. 1846; Theodore Cunningham b. 20 Mar. 1847; Alfred M. Cunningham b. 15 Oct. 1849; Jehiel Cunningham b. 22 Feb. 1853.

Rachel B. Cunningham d. 12 Feb. 1832, aged 35 yrs.

John Cunningham d. 13 Jan. 1860, aged 68-8-19.

Mark D. Cunningham d. 2 Nov. 1875, aged 48-8-17.

Martha Ann Cunningham d. 6 Nov. 1877, aged 32-7-7.

Jerome Cunningham d. 8 Dec. 1887, aged 45-5-24.

Rebecca Cunningham d. 25 Sep. 1888, aged 77-8-30.

Charles Cunningham d. 12 Jan. 1890, aged 53 yrs. and 2 mo.

Jehiel A. Cunningham d. 14 Sep. 1854, aged 1-6-21.

Alfred M. Cunningham d. 24 Sep. 1854, aged 4-11-9.

John W. Cunningham d. 11 Nov. 1855, aged 19-11-5.

Theodore Cunningham d. 23 Feb. 1865, aged 18-11-3.

Mitchell Bible
M. Carey and Son, Philadelphia 1818

Apacarius Pouner b. 22 Oct. 1771.

Mary Mitchell, d/o Asher and Hippicary Pouner, b. 20 Jan. 1795.

John Mitchell, s/o George and Anny Mitchell, b. 28 Mar. 1790.

Asher Pouner Mitchell, s/o John and Mary Mitchell, b.22 dec. 1815.

Sarah S. Mitchell, d/o Providence and Mary Sheppard, b. 26 Aug. 1814.

Mary Sheppard Mitchell, d/o Asher and Sarah Mitchell, b. 12 Apr. 1849.

James Butcher's Bible
Kimber and Sharpless, Philadelphia 1824

James Butcher b. 7 Mar. 1783.
Hannah Sayre b. 21 July 1781.
James Butcher and Hannah Sayre mar. 17 Apr. 1806.
Their Children: Elizabeth Butcher b. 16 July 1807; Job E. Butcher b. 18 Nov.
    1809; Ann Butcher b. 9 Jan.. 1812; Hannah Butcher b. 7 May 1813; James
    Butcher b. 10 Dec. 1816;
Robert Butcher b. 20 Dec. 1819; Lydia Ann b. 20 Mar. 1823.

John H. Lambert and Elizabeth Butcher mar. 25 Mar. 1826.
John Linzey and Hannah Butcher mar. 7 Apr. 1832.
James Butcher, Jr., and Barbara Carlle mar. 25 Feb. 1841.
Robert Butcher and Mary Ann Patrick mar. 14 Apr. 1842.
James Butcher and Mary B. Shimp mar. 26 Apr. 1848.
Mary Butcher, d/o James and Mary Butcher, b. 13 Apr. 1849.

Ann Butcher d. 11 Sep. 1812.
Job E. Butcher d. 12 Sep. 1813.
James Butcher, Jr. d. 14 May 1845, aged 28-5-4.
Robert Butcher d. 28 July 1881, aged 62-7-8.
Elizabeth Lambert d. 29 Apr. 1880, aged 73 yrs.
John H. Lambert d. 30 Aug. 1867, aged 68 yrs.
Hannah Butcher d. 25 Dec. 1843, aged 62-5-5.
James Butcher d. 24 Jan. 1851, aged 67-10-17.
Mary Ann Butcher d. 25 May 1864, aged 39-1-18.

Butcher Bible
Adrien Watkins, Edinburgh 1756
His Majesty's Printer

Jonathan Butcher, s/o Aaron and Mary Butcher, b. 29 Dec. 1762.
Rachel Butcher, w/o Jonathan Butcher and d/o James and Elizabeth Stretch, b. 2
    Mar. 1768.
Their children: Hannah Butcher b. 10 Apr. 1789; John Butcher b. 9 May 1791;
    Ruth Butcher b. 9 Sep. 1892; Jonathan 20 June 1795.

Sarahann Butcher, d/o Jonathan and Prudence Butcher, b. 12 Feb. 1802.
Jervis Butcher, s/o Jonathan and Prudence Butcher, b. 29 July 1804.

Jonathan Butcher, s/o Jervis and Rachel Butcher, b. 15 Sep. 1829.
Jonathan Butcher, s/o Jonathan and Ann Butcher, b. 29 Jan. 1809.

Jonathan Butcher b. 28 Dec. 1762.
Elizabeth Butcher b. 17 Dec. 1764.
Thomas Butcher b. 10 Apr. 1869.
Aaron Butcher b. 30 Oct. 1780.
James Butcher b. 7 Mar. 1783.
Phebe Butcher b. 11 Mar. 1785.

Aaron Butcher d. 19 Feb. 1786.
Rachel Butcher d. 2 Aug. 1795, in her 28th yr.
Jonathan Butcher, s/o Jonathan and Rachel Butcher, d. 12 Sep. 1795.
Jonathan Butcher d. 10 Dec. 1816.

Samuel Fish Bible
James Blow, Belfast 1751

Samuel Fish, s/o Benjamin and Sarah Fish, b. 1 Nov. 1737.

Joannah Fish, d/o Samuel and Hannah Fish, b. 27 Nov. 1767 at 11:00.
Jonathan Fish b. 19 Mar. 1770.
Sarah Fish, d/o Samuel and Hannah Fish, b. 20 Dec. 1772.

Samuel Fish d. 30 Apr. 1772.

Nieukirk-Foster Bible
Matthew Carey, Philadelphia 1803

Matthew Nieukirk b. 28 Feb. 1763.
Catherine, his wife, b. 21 Nov. 1767.
Matthew Nieukirk and Catherine, his wife, mar. 18 Dec. 1785.
Their children: Rachel Nieukirk b. 4 Mar. 1787; Hannah Nieukirk b. 22 Sep.
1789; Christiana Nieukirk b. 17 Sep. 1791; Benjamin Nieukirk b. 18 Dec.
1794; Matthew and Mary Nieukirk b. 29 July 1799; Matthew Nieukirk, the
younger, b. 26 Aug. 1801.

Samuel Niewkirk and Rachel, his wife, mar. 30 May 1809.

Their children: Ethan Nieukirk b. 5 Mar. 1810; George W. In. Nieukirk b. 11 Nov. 1801; Elizabeth Nieukirk b. 4 Mar. 1813; Christiana Nieukirk b. 29 Dec. 1814; Charles H. Nieukirk b. 2 Mar. 1816; Constant W. Nieukirk b. 27 Dec. 1818; Samuel Nieukirk b. 17 Apr. 1820.

Judah Foster b. 29 Mar. 1788.
Judah Foster and Christiana, his wife, mar. 17 Mar. 1812.
Christiannah Foster, their dau. b. 4 Apr. 1813.

Judah Foster and Hannah, his wife, mar. 4 Apr. 1814.
Their children: Catherine Foster b. 15 May 1815; Matthew N. Foster b. 1 June 1817; Rolins L. Foster b. 27 Aug. 1817; Hannah Foster b. 4 Apr,. 1821; Ira Foster b. 6 June 1823.

Judah Foster and Saloma, his wife, mar. 4 Mar. 1830.
Their children: Jane Foster b. 3 Dec. 1830; Harriet C. Foster b. 11 Apr. 1832.

Judah Foster and Barbary, his wife, mar. 1 Oct. 1833.

Benjamin Nieukirk and Rebecca, his wife, mar. 1 Jan. 1814.
Their children: Harrison Nieukirk b. 18 Apr. 1811; Cyrus Nieukirk b. 4 Apr. 1814; John Cyrus Nieukirk b. 24 May 1815; Margaret Cyrus Nieukirk b. 29 Aug. 1820.

Matthew the older, s/o Matthew and Catherine Nieukirk, d. 29 July 1799.
Mary, their dau. d. 4 July 1800.
Matthew the younger, their son, d. Oct. 1802.
Christiana Foster d. 8 Apr. 1813.
Margaret, d/o Benjamin and Rebecca Nieukirk, d. 2 June 1821.
Rachel, d/o Matthew and Catherine Nieukirk, d. 4 Sep. 1823.
Ethan, s.o Samuel and Rachel Nieukirk, d. 19 Aug. 1811.
Benjamin, s/o Matthew and Catherine Nieukirk, d. 18 Jan. 1824.
Catherine Nieukirk d. 28 Apr. 1828.
Hannah Foster, w/o Judah Foster, d. 24 Nov. 1828.
Saloma, w/o Judah Foster, d. 16 Feb. 1833.
Barbara Foster, w/o Judah Foster, d. 31 May 1857.
Hannah Avis, d/o Judah Foster, d. June 1853.
Ira Foster, s/o Judah Foster, d. 4 Feb. 1857.
Christianna Foster, d/o Judah and Christianna Foster, d. 28 Apr. 1813.
Matthew N. Foster, s/o Judah Foster, d. 2 Mar. 1882.
Judah Foster d. 10 Aug. 1871.

Jane Zebley d. 27 Apr. 1904.
Jane F. Zebley d. 4 April 1904.

Paullin Bible
Charles Bill, London 1698
Printer to the Kings Most Excellent Majesty

Henry Paullin b. 2 May 1715.
Whitlock Paullin b. June 1722.
Elizabeth Paullin b. 14 Dec. 1724.
Joseph Paullin b. 9 June 1727.
Easter Paullin b. 30 Sep. 1729.
David Paullin b. 6 Feb. 1732.
Grace Paullin b. 6 Feb. 1735.
Jacob Paullin b. 19 June 1738.
Sarah Paullin b. 8 June 1742.
Ann Paullin b. 23 Aug. 1753.
Joseph Paullin b. 2 Nov. 1755.
William Paullin b. 4 Nov. 1757.
David Paullin b. 14 Oct. 1759.
Whitlock Paullin b. 20 Oct. 1761.
Uriah Paullin b. 21 Oct. 1763.
Temperance b. 27 Apr. 1766.
Joseph Paullin, 2nd., 27 Jan. 1769.
Joel Paullin b. 1771.
Ann Paullin b. 13 Oct. 1786.
Marget Paullin b. 10 Jan. 1789.
Joseph Paullin b. 29 May 1791.
David Paullin b. 14 Nov. 1793.
Ann Paullin b. 12 Aug. 1791.
William Paullin b. 30 Aug. 1793.
Charlot Paullin b. (no date)
Mariah Paullin b. 27 Dec. 1797.
Elizabeth Paullin b. 10 Sep. 1800.
Isaac H. Paullin b. 16 Nov. 1804.
Sarah Wood Paullin b. 24 Jan. 1806.
Joseph B. Paullin b. 17 June 1808.

Morgan Bible
H. C. Carey and I. Lea, Philadelphia 1823

Joseph Morgan b. 18 Nov. 1797.
Alice C. Locke b. 10 Jan. 1796.
Samuel Morgan, s/o Joseph and Alice C. Morgan, b. 14 Dec. 1825.
Thomas Locke Morgan b. 30 Jan. 1827.
Samuel Richman Morgan b. 1 Feb. 1829.
Joseph Morgan b. 15 May 1831 and mar. Mary Sithens, d/o Champney and
    Salome Sithens.
Charles Morgan b. 3 Aug. 1833.
Israel Lock Morgan b. 24 May 1836 and mar. Talitha Conover, d/o Allen and
    Mary Conover.

Charles Morgan, s/o Joseph and Alice C. Morgan, d. 28 Sep. 1836.
Thomas Locke Morgan d. 5 Oct. 1842.
Samuel Morgan d. 6 Apr. 1824.
Joseph Morgan d. 10 Mar. 1868, aged 71 yrs.
Alice Morgan d. 26 Aug. 1870, aged 74 yrs.

Children of Samuel S. and Mary E. Miller: James M. Miller b. 9 June 1855;
    Allan W. Miller b. 1 Mar. 1858; Theodore Richman Miller b. 27 Aug.
    1862.

Warner Miller b. 6 Nov. 1824 and d. 24 Mar. 1897, aged 73 yrs.
Mary E. Miller, w/o Samuel S. Miller, b. 8 Oct. 1825 and d. 23 Feb. 1891, aged
    66 yrs.
Ann Elizabeth Miller b. (no date).
Anna M. Miller Richard, w/o Allen W. Miller, b. 28 Feb. 1862.
William Henry Miller, s/o Samuel C. and Ella E. Miller, b. 26 Feb. 1870.

Riley S. Miller, s/o Samuel S. and Mary E. Miller, d. 13 Dec. 1882, aged 30-4-
    5.
Mary E. Miller, w/o Samuel S. Miller, d. 23 Feb. 1891, aged 55-4-15.

Charles M. Miller, s/o Samuel S. and Mary E. Miller, d. 27 Apr. 1893, aged 48-
    9-2.
Samuel S. Miller d. 14 June 1898, aged 77-6-11.
Samuel C. Miller d. 22 June 1905, aged 57-3-26.
Elizabeth Miller, w/o Charles M. Miller, d. 12 Apr. 1920.

Anna M. Miller Richard, w/o Allen W. Miller, d. 18 Aug. 1923, aged 61-6-18.
Mar. 42 yrs., 5 mo. and 8 dys.
James M. Miller d. 23 June 1921, aged 66 yrs. and 14 dys.
Sarah Ann Miller, w/o Charles M. Snitcher, d. Sunday, 1 Feb. 1925 at 7:00 a.m.,
aged 75 yrs. and 18 dys.

Reuben Woolman Bible
M. Carey, Philadelphia 1814

Reuben Woolman, s/o Abraham and Elizabeth Woolman, b. 14 Feb. 1780.
Mary Mason, d/o James and Mary Mason, b. 16 Feb. 1785.
Their children: James Woolman b. 11 Sep. 1804; Abraham Woolman b. 8 Feb.
1807; Abigail Woolman b. 15 Mar. 1809; Charles Woolman b. 17 Apr.
1811; Mary Woolman b. 18 Oct. 1812; Elizabeth Woolman b. 28 Dec.
1815; Keziah Woolman b. 1 May 1818; Alice Ann Woolman b. 19 June
1820; John and Jane Woolman b. 2 Jan. 1823.

Charles Woolman d. 31 May 1811.
Keziah Woolman d. 25 Sep. 1822.
Reuben Woolman, the father, d. 28 Feb. 1830.
Mary Woolman, Sr., d. 3 Mar. 1830.
Jane Woolman d. 25 Oct. 1842.
John Woolman d. 7 Jan. 1864.
Mary Woolman Fogg d. 16 Jan. 1879.
James Woolman d. 15 May 1879.
Abraham Woolman d. 3 Oct. 1883.
Abigail Woolman d. 10 July 1885.
Elizabeth Woolman Clark d. Sep. 1892.
Alice Ann Woolman Tyler d. 28 Sep. 1896.

Wentzell Bible
H. C. Carey and I. Lea, Philadelphia 1823

acob Wentzell, s/o Charles and Catherine Wentzell, d. 17 Sep. 1778.
Susannah Wentzell, d/o Aaron and Ann Hewitt, b. 10 Jan. 1785.
Their children: Harriett Wentzell b. 16 Feb. 1807; Eli Wentzell b. 11 Aug. 1808;
James Wentzell b. 17 Dec. 1809; Charles Wentzell b. 2 June 1812; Robert
Wentzell b. 26 Sep. 1813; Firman Wentzell b. 12 May 1815; Rebecca Ann
Wentzell b. 28 Jan. 1817; Catherine Wentzell b. 6 Aug. 1818; Clarissa

Wentzell b. 11 Nov. 1820; William Wentzell b. 27 Aug. 1822; Aaron
Wentzell b. 12 July 1824; Hannah Wentzell b. 11 Apr. 1827.

Harriett Wentzell d. 9 Oct. 1814.
Rebecca Ann and Catherine Wentzell d. 28 Aug. 1821.
James Wentzell, s/o Jacob and Susannah Wentzell, d. 15 Sep. 1821.
Hannah Wentzell, d/o Jacob and Susannah Wentzell, d. 21 Sep. 1827.

Johnson Family Records

John Johnson b. 1731 and d. 1802. He mar., in Ireland, Jane Sauyberry, b. Nov.
1732 and d. 28 June 1825.
Their son, Isaac Johnson, b. 21 July 1772 and mar., 24 June 1795, Mary Elwell,
b. 23 May 1778, d/o Samuel and Amelia Morgan Elwell.

Children of Isaac and Mary Johnson: Harriet b. 23 Oct. 1796; Elizabeth b. 18
Apr. 1798; Isaac b. 1 Oct. 1799; Amelia b. 26 Oct. 1801; Mary b. 15 Mar,.
1804; Sarah b. 18 Sep. 1805; John b. 5 Mar. 1810; Samuel b. 19 May 1812;
Emma Ann b. 29 Sep. 1814; William b. 5 Jan. 1817; Benjamin b. 15 June
1818; James b. 7 Feb. 1820.

Isaac Johnson, s/o Isaac Johnson and Mary Elwell, mar. 17 Mar. 1823, Rachel
DuBois, d/o Isaac and Elizabeth Burroughs DuBois.
Their children: Joseph b. 16 Apr. 1824; Rebecca b. 27 July 1825; Elizabeth b.
14 Apr. 1827; Mary E. b. 7 Oct. 1829; Isaac b. 30 Dec. 1830; Emma Ann b.
16 June 1832; Esther b. 26 Oct. 1833; Christianna b. 27 Mar. 1835; Adaline
b. 5 Feb. 1837; Thomas b. 27 Oct. 1839; Matilda b. 31 July 1842; Martha b.
2 Jan. 1845.

Ray Family Records

Samuel Ray and Mary Moore mar. Nov. 1769.
Their children: Zaccheus Ray b. 1780; Benjamin Ray b. 11 Apr. 1790.

Benjamin Ray and Mary Johnson, b. 18 Jan. 17__, mar. 5 Mar. 1815.
Their children: William b. 21 July 1817; Johnson b. 26 Mar. 1819; Benjamin b.
15 Feb. 1821.

Catherine Pierpont, d/o Joshua Pierpont and Caroline Hewes, b. 10 July 1827
and d. 14 Aug. 1887.

Johnson Ray and Catherine Pierpont mar. 29 June 1844.

Burroughs Records

Benjamin Burroughs b. in Morris Co., N. J., 1742 and d. 1803. He mar. in
Trenton, June 1763, Mary Van Horn, who d. 1810.
Their children:
Benjamin b. 20 July 1864 and mar. Judith Lumas.
Elizabeth b. 1765, mar. Isaac DuBois. and d. 1803.
Joseph b. (no date).
Cornelius b. 26 Nov. 1767.
Catherine b. 26 Nov. 1767 and mar. Matthew Newkirk.
John b. (no date).
Hannah b. (no date) and mar. William Rose.

Dilks Bible

Elisha Dilks b. 12 Aug. 1792.
Sarah Vendegrift b. 16 Oct. 1796.
Elisha Dilks and Sarah Vendegrift mar. 24 Dec. 1818 by Gideon Ferrel, Pastor
of the Baptist Church at Welsh Tract, Delaware.
Children of Elisha Dilks and Sarah Vendegrift: Elizabeth b. 23 May 1820;
Rebecca b. 29 July 1822; James b. 24 July 1824; Mary Jane b. 19 Oct.
1826; Calvin b. 26 June 1828; Margaret Remster b. 28 Feb. 1830; George
Shimp b. 10 Jan. 1832; Sarah b. 22 Sep. 1833; Susannah Pennington b. 19
Feb. 1835; Joanna Heioer b. 27 Mar. 1837; Infant dau. b. and d. 18 Jan.
1839.

Susanna Vandergrift d. 28 Aug. 1841, in her 85th yr.

Elwell Records

Samuel Elwell b. 1688 and mar. his 1st cousin, Tamson Elwell.
Their son, Jacob Elwell, b. 1714 and d. 26 Sep. 1773.
Catherine Dubois b. 10 Sep. 1716 and d. 1798.

Jacob Elwell and Catherine Dubois mar., in England.
Their son, Samuel Elwell, b. 1745 and d. 10 July 1822, mar. Amelia Morgan, d.
    8 Mar. 1800.
Their children:
Samuel mar. Mary Johnson.
Mary mar. Isaac Johnson, brother of Mary Johnson.
Sarah.
Amelia mar. Andrew Urion.
Sarah mar, 2nd, Charles Chambers.

Evans Bible
John D. Berry, Philadelphia 1848

Isaac Evans b. 30 Sep. 1821, s/o Thomas and Lydia.

Children of Isaac and Elizabeth Evans:
Sarah A. b. 13 June 1847.
George R. b. 13 Feb. 1849.
Daniel S. b. 28 Mar. 1851.
Mary A. b. 9 May 1853.
Lydia S. b. 4 Oct. 1854.
Walter S. b. 1 Nov. 1855.
Eva L. b. 27 Sep. 1858.
Howard L. 9 Aug. 1860.
Isaac Newton b. 4 Jan. 1866.
Lizzie Emma b. 22 Oct. 1868.
Martha Blanche b. 1 Nov. 1870.

Lydia S. Evans d. 19 Dec. 1854.
Isaac Newton Evans d. 12 July 1864.
Thomas Evans d. at Cohansey, Cumberland Co., 30 Apr. 1877.

Remster Bible
Collins and Co., New York 1814

Margaret Remster b. 3 Oct. 1780.
Susanna Remster b. 27 Jan. 1782.
Barbara Remster b. 31 ___ 1786.

Mary Shimp b. 4 Nov. 1787.
Elizabeth Shimp b. 2 Aug. 1788.
George Remster b. 4 Nov. 1788.
Andrew Remster b. 6 Sep. 1791.
Phillip Remster b. 3 May 1793.
Benjamin Remster b. 31 May 1797.
Sarah Remster b. 7 Sep. 1801.
Joseph Remster b. 15 Jan. 1814.
Mary Remster b. 31 May 1816.
Juliannah Remster b. 5 Mar. 1817.
Daniel Remster b. 10 Aug. 1819.
George Remster, Jr., b. 28 Sep. 1822.
Smith Remster b. 5 Mar. 1825.
Elizabeth Remster b. 18 Dec. 1927.
Theophilus Remster b. 24 Sep. 1831.
Sarah Remster, d/o Benjamin and Sarah, b. 18 Jan. 1821.

George Remster and Mary Shimp mar. 16 Mar. 1830.
Benjamin Remster and Sarah Shimp mar. 7 Mar. 1820.
Joseph Remster and Susan Johnson mar. 19 Mar. 1839.

Juliannah Remster d. 6 Oct. 1804.
Barbara Remster d. 5 Sep. 1805.
Mary Shimp, w/o George, d. 6 June 1806.
Elizabeth Remster d. 3 Mar. 1809.
Mary Remster, d/o George and Mary, d. 9 Apr. 1816.
Sarah Remster, w/o Benjamin, d. 6 Feb. 1821.
Frederick Remster d. 28 Jan. 1823, aged 71 yrs.
George Shimp d. 22 Jan. 1833.
Daniel Remster, s/o George and Mary, d. 14 Feb. 1834.
Daniel Shimp d. 20 July 1837.
Juliannah Elwell, d/o George and Mary Elwell, d. 13 Nov. 1850.

William W. and Meraba England Bible

William W. England b. 6 Apr. 1783.
Meraba Barber b. 1 Sep. 1783.
Their children: Daniel England b. 30 Sep. 1805; Elias England b. 26 Nov. 1808;
    Rebecca England b. 27 June 1810; Aquilla England b. 7 Oct. 1812; Mary

England b. 15 Nov. 1814; William England b. 2 Nov. 1816; Sarah
Anderson England b. 24 Oct. 1818; Elizabeth England b. 27 July 1826.

Mary England, w/o William W. England, d. 9 Sep. 1806.
Daniel England, s/o William W. and Mary England, d. 16 July 1824.
Meraba, d/o William W. and Meraba, d. 16 Sep. 1824.
Elizabeth England, d/o William W. and Meraba England, d. 19 May 1884.
Meraba England, w/o William W. England, d. 17 July 1847, aged 63-10-17.
William W. England d. 1 Jan. 1856, aged 72-8-26.
Elias England, s/o William W. and Meraba England, d. 20 May 1876.

Barber Bible

Lydia Barber, d/o Aquilla and Meriba Barber, b. 13 July 1795.
Daniel Barber, s/o Samuel and Sally Barber, b. 2 Dec. 1801.

Aquilla Barbar d. 4 Dec. 1794.
Meriba Smith d. 19 Aug. 1808.

Holme Bible
Printed London, 1738

Benjamin Holme b. 22 Oct. 1685 at 2:00 in the morning.
Ebenezer Holme, s/o the above named Benjamin Holme and Hannah his wife, b.
    10 Sep. 1716. Elizabeth Holme, d/o the first above named, b. 6 Dec. (no
    year) at 10:00 at night.
Benjamin Holme, s/o Benjamin and Hannah Holme, b. 14 May 1723 at 11:00 at
    night.
John Holme, s/o Benjamin and his latter wife Rachel, b. 25 Oct. 1726 at 5:00 at
    night.
Benjamin Holme, s/o Benjamin and his latter wife Rachel, b. 28 Feb. 1727/8 at
    9:00 at night.
Hannah Holme, d/o Benjamin and his latter wife Rachel, b. 22 Aug. 1830 at
    6:00 at night.

Jane Smith, d/o Daniel and Sarah Smith, b. 10 Oct. 1729 at 10:00 at night.

Benjamin Holme, Jr., and Jane Smith mar. 29 Dec. 1750.

John Holme, s/o Benjamin Holme, Jr., and Jane his wife, b. 19 Dec. 1751 at
1:00 in the afternoon and d. 26 Sep. (no year) at 6:00 in the afternoon, aged
8 mo. and 27 dys.
Benjamin Holme d. 7 Mar. 1756 at abt. 5:00 in the morning, aged 71-4-5.

Benjamin Holme, s/o John and Ann Holme, b. 17 Mar. 1756 at 9:00 or a little
past in the afternoon.

In memory of Jane Holme, w/o Benjamin Hole, who d. 8 Oct. 1776 abt 8:00 in
the evening, being well and harty about an hour before, but her sister Ruth,
getting into a chare drawn by a wicked horse, said Jane's ususl care of her
sister seized said wicked horse by the bridle, who ran away with her, bore
her down, dragged the chare over her, as was Jane, and it kicked her so that
she died in less than an hour as was thought by those present. Said Jane was
47 years, lacking 2 days and 2 hours. Said Jane was a loving wife to said
Benjamin Holme 25 years, 9 months and 6 days.

Benjamin Holme and Esther Gibbon mar. 28 Oct. 1778 by the Rev. William
Holinshead.
Their children: John Gibbon Holme b. 8 Nov. 1780 at 45 after 2:00 in the
morning; Jane Smith Holme b. 11 Oct. 1873 at 9:00 in the morning.

Benjamin Holme d. 14 July 1794 at half after eight in the morning, aged 64-4-
14.
Jane S. Harris, d/o Benjamin and Esther Holme, d. 27 Aug. 1809.
Esther Holme, widow of Benjamin Holme, d. 22 Jan. 1814, aged 72 yrs.
John G. Holme d. 6 Oct. 1821.

Benjamin Seeley Holme, s/o John and Margaret Holme, b. 26 Sep. 1811 and d.
2 Feb. 1867.

Morris Bible
Charles Bill, London 1696
Printer to the Kings Most Excellent Majesty

Joseph Morris b. 6 Aug. 1692 and d. 23 Mar. 1742/3.
Prudence Brathweit b. 16th day of 9th mo. 1703 at half past one in the afternoon,
the 1st day of the week, and d. ___ Nov. 1748.
Their children: Margret Morris b. 13 Jan. 1722 at 7:00 in the morning, the 1st
day of the week; Marcy Morris b. 9 Nov. 1724 at two of the clock in the

afternoon on the 2nd day of the week, and d. 1 Dec. at two of the clock in the afternoon, in the same year; Sarah Morris b. 31 Mar. 1728 about 9:00 in the morning, upon the 1st day of the week and d. in the 1st mo., 1754; Rothra Morris b. 31 Mar. 1728 upon the 1st day of the week and d. the same day.

Margret Hall d. 21 Sep. 1785, aged 61 yrs. and near 7 mo.

Hall Records

Jael Lewis aged 50 yrs. on the 9th of the 4th mo. called June, 1710.

John Lewis aged 45 the 1st day of May, 1750.

Margaret Hall, d/o Clement and Margaret Hall, b. 18th of the 1st mo., 1765 at 12:oo in the day on the 6th day of the week and d. 14th of the 10th mo., in the same yr.

Clement Hall and Margaret Morris mar. 13 Feb. 1745/6.

Margaret Hall d. 25 Sep. 1786 , aged 61 yrs. and near 7 mo.

Clement Hall d. 14th of the 1st mo., 1769, aged 44 yrs.

Prudence Hall b. 29 Nov. 1746 about 2:00 in the afternoon, on the 7th day of the week.

Elizabeth Hall b. 29 Jan. 1748/9 at 8 min. after 11:00 in the morning, on the 1st day of the week, and d. 12 Oct. 1749.

Morris Hall b. 26 Nov. 1750 at ___ of the clock in the morning, on the 2nd day of the week, and d. 5th Jan. of the same yr.

_____n Hall b. 20 Apr. 1752 at 7 min. before ___ o'clock in the afternoon, on the 2nd day of the week, and d. 20 Sep. on the same yr.

Clement Hall b. 13 Nov. 1753 at 2:00 in the morning, on the 3rd day of the week.

Sarah Hall b. 14 Apr. 1755 at 7:00 in the morning, on the 2nd day of the week, and d. 23 Mar. 1793, aged 38 yrs., all but 22 dys.

Joseph Hall b. 5th of the 2nd mo. 1757 at 4:00 in the morning, on the 2nd day of the week, and d. ___ of the same mo.

Joseph Hall b. 10th of the 5th mo., 1757 at 2:00 in the afternoon, on the 5th day of the week.

John Hall b. 19 of the 11th mo., 1760 at 3:00 in the afternoon, on the 4th day of the week.

Morris Hall, 11th of the 10th mo., 1762 at 10:00.

Hall Bible
Griffith and Simon, Philadelphia 1846

Clement Hall and Margaret Morris mar. 13 Feb. 1745.

Children of Clement and Margaret Hall: Prudence Hall b. 29 Nov. 1746;
Clement Hall b. 13 Nov. 1753; Sarah Hall b. 14 Apr. 1755; Joseph Hall b.
19 Nov. 1759.
John Hall b. 19 Nov. 1760.
Morris Hall b. 11 Oct. 1762.

Clement Hall and Rebecca Kay mar. 11th mo., 1777.

Ann Hall, d/o Clement and Rebecca Hall, b. 30 May 1780.
Margert M. Hall b. 14 June 1786.
Morris Hall b. 11 Oct. 1788.
Prudence Hall b. 1 June 1790.
Sarah Hall b. 1 July 1792.
Deborah Kay Hall b. 27 Feb. 1796.
Rebecca Kay Hall b. 30 June 1798.

John G. Holme and Margaret H. Hall mar. 27 Nov. 1810.
Benjamin Seeley Hall, s/o John G. and Margaret Holme, b. 28 Sep. 1811.
Jane Smith Holme b. 15 June 1813.
Caroline Morris Holme b. 1816 and d. 1830.

Benjamin S. Hall and Elizabeth Dennis mar. 28 Oct. 1837.
John Hall and Jane S. Hall mar. 3 Dec. 1839

Robert Turner Bible
3 April 1796

Margaret Gregory, d/o William and Martha Gregory, b. 19 July 1788.

David Sparks and Martha his wife mar. 18 Sep. 1801.

Katherine Gregory Bible

Matthew Carey, Philadelphia 1803Catherine Gregory d. 5 Mar. 1841, aged 71 (or 4) yrs.

Children of Peter and Ann Sparks: Acy Sparks b. 18 Aug. 1804; Elijah Sparks b. 1 Nov. 1805; Samuel Sparks b. 25 Mar. 1808; Elizabeth Sparks b. 5 Sep. 1810; Ledy Sparks b. 10 Jan. 1812.

Mary G. Elwell Records

David Paulin b. 14 Nov. 1793 and d. 25 Apr. 1850, aged 56-6-10.
Abigail Turner b. 15 Oct. 1795 and d. 31 Aug. 1852, aged 56-10-16.
Their children:
Joseph T. Paulin b. 24 May 1816.
Catherine Paulin b. 28 May 1818 and d. 11 May 1898 - 4 children.
Margaret Paulin b. 22 Feb. 1820 and mar. John Ramsey - no issue.
Martha Ann Paulin b. 27 Apr. 1822, mar. Robert Hewitt of Woodstown, N. J., and d. 22 Jan. 1870.
Sarah Paulin b. 5 Apr. 1825 and d. 10 June 1831.
David Paulin b. 17 Oct. 1827.
Jeremiah Paulin b. 10 Oct. 1830.
Elizabeth Paulin b. 21 Apr. 1836 and never married.

Morris R. Elwell and Catherine Paulin, d/o David and Abigail Paulin, mar. 19 July 1851.
Their children: Joseph B. Elwell b. 24 May 1852; David P. Elwell b. 4 July 1854; Abigail Elwell b. 25 Aug. 1856; Margaret R. Elwell b. 15 July 1859.

Joseph B. Elwell and Carrie Mitchell mar. 4 June 1873.
Their dau. - Mary Gregory Elwell.

1st generation - Isaac Elwell - had children.
2nd generation - Wharton Elwell - had children.
3rd generation - John Elwell b. 5 Sep. 1776 and mar. Ann Hutchinson.
Joseph Elwell b. 9 Jan. 1778.
Thomas Elwell b. 10 May 1780.
Isaac Elwell b. 27 Feb. 1782 and mar. Elizabeth Rose.

Children of Isaac Elwell and Elizabeth Rose: Joseph Brick Elwell b. 1811;
Morris Rose Elwell b. 1814.

Joseph Brick Elwell's 1st wife was Mary W. Cleaver. He d. 14 Dec. 1885, aged
74yrs, at Shiloh, N. J.
Their children: William C.; Mary Elizabeth; Mary Watkins.

His 2nd wife was Ann Fagan.
Their children:
Adelaide b. 13 May 1845 and mar. Asa Randolph.
Morris b. (no date).
Isaac b. 5 Apr. 1846 and mar. Ducetta Carll.
Margaret b. (no date.
Sarah b. 7 Feb. 1865 and mar. Lambert Newkirk.

John and Catherine Mower mar. Mar. 1783.
John and Lydia Mower mar. Aug. 1786.
John and Ester Mower mar. 29 Nov. 1808.
George and Rebecah Mower mar. 13 Sep. 1804.
Jacob and Mary Fox mar. 4 Dec. 1804.
James and Margaret Megill mar. Jan. 1806.
Elisha and Catherine Derrickson mar. Feb. 1810.
James and Elizabeth Powell mar. 19 Sep. 1812.
William and Ann Mower mar. 26 Feb. 1817.
John and Rebecah Powell mar. 17 Nov. 1821.
William and Hannah Shepard mar. 7 Aug. 1822.
David and Lydia Hannah mar. 17 Feb. 1825.
Samuel and Ann Kerlin mar. 17 Nov. 1825.
Diah and Margret Garison mar. 23 July 1848.
John and Ruth Willis mar. 4 Oct. 1849.
Michal and Ann Vanlier mar. 19 Jan. 1850.
George Watson and Elen Mower mar. 7 Oct. 1854.
Absalom and Clarissa A. Mower mar. 24 Oct. 1866.

Ruth Cox b. 23 June 1817.
John Lloyd b. 23 Nov. 1847.

John Lloyd d. 2 Jan. 1871.
Lydia White d. 30 Aug. 1876.
Ruth Willis d. 10 May 1876.
John Willis d. 7 May 1876.

John Mower b. Nov. 1760.
Lydia Mower b. 30 Sep. 1765.
George Mower b. 25 Aug. 1783.
Mary Mower b. 4 Dec. 1786.
Margret Mower b. 21 Sep. 1788.
Catherine Mower b. 8 May 1790.
William Mower b. 28 May 1792.
Elizabeth Mower b. 24 July 1794.
Rebecca Mower b. 15 Mar. 1797.
Lydia Mower b. 18 Jan. 1800.
Hannah Mower b. 12 Apr. 1802.
Ann Mower b. 30 June 1804.
Esther Ayrs b. 3 Apr. 1777.

John Mower d. 10 Nov. 1822, aged 62 yrs.
Lydia Mower d. 12 July 1807, aged 41-12-9.
Margret Garison d. 29 Sep. 1849, aged 24 yrs.
Mary Earley d. 23 Sep. 1867, aged 80-9-19.
Margret Megill d. 2 Sep. 1824, aged 36 yrs.
Catherine Derveon d. 12 June 1811, aged 21-1-4.
William Mowers d. 9 July 1860, aged 68-1-11.
Elizabeth Megill d. 10 Mar. 1872.
Rebecca Powell d. 5 May 1869, aged 72-1-20.
Lydia Hanners d. 15 Mar. 1859, aged 59-1-25.
Hannah Sheppard d. 20 July 1869, aged 67-3-8.
Ester Robins d. Oct. 1831, aged 54 yrs. and 6 mo.
Joseph Powell d. 26 June 1848.
John Mowers d. 16 Oct. 1851.
Ann Megill d. 2 Aug. 1852.
Margret Freas d. 11 Dec. 1866.
Elizabeth Megill d. 1 Feb. 1869.

William Krewson Bible
Kimber and Sharpless, Philadelphia 1824

William Krewson, S/O John and Dianna Krewson, b. 7 Sep. 1774 in the state of
    New Jersey.
Sarah Krewson, late Johnson, (or more properly) d/o Abraham and Elizabeth
    Johnson, b. 1 June 1782.
Henry Shephard b. 15 Mar. 1779.

Sarah Krewson b. 13 Aug. 1819.

Griffith L. Shephard b. 11 Nov. 1819.

Henry Shephard b. 8 Apr. 1854.

Lydia Jane Shephard b. 11 June 1856.

Charles Finney Shephard b. 6 Mar. 1857.

George McKinney Shephard b. 13 Sep. 1858.

Amos Tomlinson Shephard b. 24 May 1861.

William Krewson and Sarah T. Johnson mar. in Newtown, Bucks Co., Pa., 30
    Nov. 1774.

Griffe L. Sheppard and Sarah Krewson mar. 7 Jan. 1852.

Lydia Egbert b. 18 June 1778.

Isaac Kroesen b. 31 Aug. 1783.

Isaac and Lydia Kroesen mar. 29 Aug. 1804

Diana Kroesen b. 17 June 1805.

Mary Kroesen b. 6 Sep. 1806.

John Kroesen b. 17 May 1808.

Lydia Ann Kroesen b. 5 Jan. 1812.

Louisa Kroesen b. 18 Jan. 1815.

William E. Kroesen b. 21 Sep. 1817.

Sarah Kroesen b. 13 Aug. 1819.

Sarah Krewson, w/o William Krewson, d. 21 Jan. 1843.

Louisa Kroesen d. 3 July 1816.

William Krewson, of the borough of Newtown, Bucks Co., Pa., d. 23 Mar. 1851
    and was bur. on Tues. morning following in the Newtown Presbyterian
    Church Yard.

Henry Shephard d.21 June 1854.

Lydia Krewson d. 22 Oct. 1854.

Charles Finney Shephard d. 7 June 1857.

Henry Shephard d. 2 Apr. 1860.

Amos Tomlinson Shephard d. 4 June 1864.

Isaac Krewson d. 4 Apr. 1865.

Sarah K. Shephard d. 4 May 1888, in her 69th yr.

G. Lewis Shephard d. 4 Feb. 1894, in his 75th yr.

Sarah K. Shephard d. 4 May 1888.

In Newtown on the 22nd ult., Mrs Jane Krewson, in her 72nd yr.

Barns Bible
Jasper Harding, Philadelphia 1849

Jacob Barns, s/o Robert and Rachel Barns, b. 23 Feb. 1786.
Mary Barns, his wife, b. 21 May 1787.
Their children: Sarah Ann Barns b. 25 Oct. 1809; Nathaniel B. Barns 7 Nov.
    1811; Rachel Barns b. 28 Apr. 1814; Susanna B. Barns b. 17 Sep. 1816;
    Mary Barns b. 9 Dec. 1818; Ashbel W. Barns b. 29 Apr. 1821; Franklin
    Barns b. 25 May 1823.

George L. Yerkes, s/o Jonathan and Mary Yerkes, b. 4 May 1821.
Susanna B. Barns, his wife, b. 17 Sep. 1816
Their children: Winifred S. Yerkes b. 12 July 1849; Israel Yerkes b. 15 June
    1851; Howard K. Yerkes b. 8 Sep. 1853; Lewellin W. Yerkes b. 12 July
    1856; Harriet K. Yerkes b. 22 Sep. 58.

Jacob Barns d. 10 Nov. 1824.
Mary Barns d. 18 Oct. 1829.
Nathaniel B. Barns d. 25 Sep. 1844.
Mary H. Barns d. 12 Feb. 1850.
Mary C. Barns d. 3 Dec. 1857.
Franklin Barns d. 22 Dec. 1859.
Franklin Barns d. 28 Mar. 1861.

Sarah Hancock Bible

Thomas Yorke and Margaret Robinson, his 2nd wife, were intermarried by the
    Rev. Mr. Ross of Oxford, Pa., County of Philadelphia, by whom he had
    issue: Thomas Yorke, now of London, and Andrew his brother.

Andrew Yorke intermarried with Eleanor Cox by the Rev. Mr. Wrangel of
    Wicacoa, by whom he had issue:
Christian b. 17 May 1767 and d. July 1769.
Lewis b. 19 Feb. 1770 at Alloway Creek, Salem County.
Marget b. 26 Apr. 1772 and d. Mar. 1773.
Eleanor b. 20 Feb. 1774 and d. 21 Oct. 1840
Martha b. 7 Jan. 1778 and d. 22 Dec. 1815.
Andrew b. 5 Sep. 1779.
Mary b. 4 Dec. 1781 and d. 1784.
Thomas b. 1 Oct. 1785.

Andrew Yorke Bible

Andrew Yorke d. 23 Mar. 1794 in his 50th yr. and was bur. the churchyard in the
town of Salem, N. J.
Elinor Yorke, widow of Andrew York, d. 24 Jan. 1802 in her 56th yr. and was
bur. in the churchyard in the town of Salem, N. J.
Thomas Yorke d. 28 June 1820, aged 34-8-27.
Andrew Yorke, s/o Andrew and Elinor Yorke, d. 12 Oct. 1806 in his 27th yr. and
was bur. the churchyard at Salem.
Thomas Y. Hancock d. 7 July 1778, in his 82nd yr.
Rachel N. Hancock d. 1 Dec. 1882, aged 79 yrs.
Children of Thomas Y and Rachel Hancock: Elizabeth N. Hancock b. 24 Jan.
1827; Ellen Maria Hancock b.23 Aug. 1829; William N. Hancock b.2 Feb.
1832; Cornelia Hancock b.8 Feb. 1840; Thomas Y. Hancock b. 23 Nov.
1842.

CUMBERLAND COUNTY

Bible of Jehile Westcott, 1st
Thomas Newcomb and Henry Hills
Printers to the Queen's Most Excellent Majesty
MDCCXLI

Jehile Westcott, s/o Ebenezer and Phebe, b. 31 Oct 1764.
Mary Sheppard, d/o b. 2 Dec 1770.
Jehile Westcott and Mary Sheppard were mar 25 Dec 1787.
Abraham Westcott b. 26 Sep 1789.
Lydia Westcott b. 3 Dec 1792 and d. 22 Jun 1795.
Ann Sheppard d. 1 Dec 1795.
Elias Westcott b. 4 May and d. 13 May 1798.
Jehile Westcott b. 14 Aug 1800.
Jane Westcott b. 5 May 1802.
Elias Westcott b. 30 May 1804 and d. 9 Oct 1805.
John Bunyon Westcott b. 30 Jul 1805.
Mary Westcott b. 14 Jan 1810 and d. 9 Jan 1811.
Susannah Westcott b. 21 Jan 1812.

Lydia Westcott d. 22 Jun 1795.
Susannah M. Westcott d. Aug 1812.

Jehile Westcott d. 9 Mar 1812, in his 49th year

Bible of Samuel Westcott, 2nd
Mathew Cary, Philadelphia, 1812
Samuel Westcott's Book, May 5, 1812

Samuel Westcott b. 26 Jan 1757.
Mary, w/o Samuel Westcott, b. 2 Jun 1762.

Samuel Westcott, s/o Samuel Westcott and Mary Shaw, and Mary Buck, d/o
    John Buck, Esq. and Lorana Whitekar, mar 22 Apr 1778.
Children of Samuel and Mary Westcott: Ruth Westcott b. 13 Jul 1780; Lydia
    Westcott b. 13 Jun 1782; Hannah Westcott b. 18 Jul 1784; Lorany Westcott
    b. 6 Jan 1787; Rebeka Westcott b. 10 Feb 1789; Eunice Westcott b. 31 Jan
    1791; Osborn Westcott b. 13 Nov 1793; Samuel Buck Westcott (twin) b. 13
    Nov 1793; Mary Westcott b. 28 May 1797; Henrietta Westcott b. 6 Sep
    1798; George Burgin Westcott b. 10 Feb 1801; Ann Westcott b. 28 Aug
    1803; Mary Westcott b. 22 Mar 1806.

Marriages of the sons and daughters of Samuel and Mary Westcott:
Samuel B. Westcott, s/o Samuel and Mary Westcott, and Charlotta Godfrey, d/o
    Nickols and Sarah Godfrey, mar 5 Jun 1812.
Henrietta Westcott, d/o Samuel and Mary Westcott, and John Long mar 15 Mar
    1817.
Ann Westcott and Thomas Erricson mar 4 Jul 1830.
Ruth Westcott and Curtis Trenchard, son of John Trenchard, mar (no date).
Lydia Westcott and Thomas Bateman, s/o John and Mary Bateman, mar (no
    date but 1799 is penciled in).
Hannah Westcott and Aaron , s/o Jedediah and Rheuma Seeley, mar 16 May
    1804 (Church Record of "Father Osborn" [the Rev. Ethan Osborn] gives
    the marriage date as 16 May 1803).
Rebekah Westcott and William Whitekar, s/o Jeremiah and Sarah Whitakar, mar
    23 Dec 180_ .
Samuel Westcott mar Ruth Harris 23 Dec 1816, Samuel Westcott being in his
    59th year and Ruth being in her 52nd year.

Deaths of the children of Samuel and Mary Westcott:
Lorany Westcott d. 13 Jul 1793.
Mary Westcott d. 21 Aug 1797.
Osborn Westcott d. 19 Nov 1793

Mary Westcott d. 15 Jul 1806.

Samuel Westcott d. 13 Mar 1834.
Capt. Samuel Westcott d. 11 Mar 1792, in his 63rd year.
Hannah, w/o said Samuel Westcott, d. 21 Aug 1802, in her 68th
year.
Mary Lumas d. 8 Oct 1824, in her 86th year. Sister to my mother.
Ammon Shaw was b. 29 Sep 1764 and d. 27 Sep 1794.
Henrietta, w/o John Lang, d. 3 May 1833, in her 55th year. Lived together 36
yrs, 2 mos.
Lydia Bateman, w/o Thomas Bateman, d. 6 May 1854.

William Taylor Bible

William Taylor b. 5 Oct 1791.
Ann (Nancy) Sheppard Westcott b. 1795.

William Taylor and Ann (Nancy) Sheppard Westcott mar 15 Jul 1815.
David Westcott and Ann (Nancy) Sheppard mar. 13 Feb. 1844.

Mary Taylor b. 16 Apr 1816.
Harriet Taylor b. 29 Jan 1818.
William Henry Harrison and Isaac Henry Williamson b. 31 Jan 1820.
Henry Sheppard Taylor b. 11 Mar 1822.
Benjamin Franklin Taylor b. 11 Mar 1824.
Enos Taylor b. 16 Feb 1826.
Ethan Taylor b. 26 Sep 1827.
John Newton Taylor b. 16 Feb 1828 (?).
Nancy Jane Taylor b. 30 Jan 1833.
Caroline Taylor b. 2 Mar 1835.
Rhoda Westcott Taylor b. 24 Jan 1839.

William Taylor d. 27 Jan 1843.
William Henry Harrison Taylor d. 10 Jul 1820.

Enos Taylor d. 22 Mar 1826.
Isaac Henry Williamson Taylor d. 13 Jan 1838.
Mary S. Taylor d. 20 May 1844.
Rhoda W. Taylor d. 29 Sep 1844.
Benjamin Franklin Taylor d. 22 Mar 1850.

Ann (Nancy) Sheppard d.1865.
Caroline Taylor Husted d. 5 Nov. 1858.
Henry S. Taylor d. ....
John Newton d. 2 Nov. 1882 at Laurence, Kansas.
Harriett Taylor Westcott d. ....
Nancy Jane Taylor Kurtz d. ....
Mary Husted d. 11 Mar. 1858.

Benjamin F. Taylor Bible
Edward W. Miller, Philadelphia, 1847

Richard Powell b. 20 May 1782.
Abigail S. Roary b. 3 Jan 1790.
Richard Powell and Abigail Roary mar 18 Jan 1804.
Their children: Abigail Powell b. 10 Nov 1804; Richard Powell b. 17 May 1809;
    Daniel R. Powell b. 23 Sep 1812; David Powell b. 22 Feb 1817; William
    Powell b. 4 Sep 1817.

Benjamin F. Taylor b. 11 Mar 1824.
Mary Bishop b. 30 May 1825.
Benjamin F. Taylor and Mary Bishop mar 17 Sep 1884.
Benjamin F. Taylor d. 22 Mar 1850, aged 25 yrs, 11 dys.
Harriet L. Taylor d. 1 Jul __, aged 1-8-8.
Richard Powell d. 8 Nov 1822.
Abigail Powell d. 8 Jul 1823.
Abigail Stein d. 5 Mar 1846.
Harriet L. Cossabon d. 5 Jun 1850.

Benjamin Stratton Bible
Griggs & Co. Printers, Philadelphia 1816

Levi Preston of the town of Salem, New England, b. 22 Nov 1662.His children:
    Levi Preston b. 22 Nov 1697; Martha Preston b. 7 Apr 1799; John Preston
    b. 26 Feb 1701; Mary Preston b. 14 Aug 1703; Abagail Preston b. 3 Feb
    1705; Isaac Preston b. 10 Sep 1707; Freelove Preston b. 29 Jun 1714.

Benjamin Stratton, s/o Benjamin Stratton of Long Island, b. 19 Sep 1701.

Benjamin Stratton and Abagail Preston mar 28 Nov 1723.

Their children: Levi Stratton b. 27 Sep 1724 and d. 28 Mar 1728; Abagail
Stratton b. 25 Feb 1726 and d. 4 Apr 1759, aged 33 yrs; Jonathan Stratton
b. 28 Dec 1828 and d. 4 Apr 1759, aged 30 yrs; Benjamin Stratton b. 21
Mar 1730 and d. 3 Feb 1759, aged 28 yrs; Freelove Stratton b. 26 Feb 1732
and d. 1765, aged 33 yrs; Thomazine Stratton b. 20 Jun 1735 and d. 1785,
aged 50 yrs; Elizabeth Stratton b. 28 Oct 1737 and d. 14 Jun 1759, aged 21
yrs; Preston Stratton b. 1 Jan 1740 and d. 1740; Preston Stratton b. 8 Aug
1741 and d. 1759, aged 18 yrs; Levi Stratton b. 21 Mar 1743 and d. 1792,
in his 49th yr.; John Stratton b. 10 Nov 1747; Eleanor Leake b. 18 Sep
1751.

John Stratton and Eleanor Leake mar 5 Apr 1775.
Their children: Elizabeth Stratton b. 24 Apr 1776; John Stratton b. 23 Feb 1778;
Gilbert Stratton b. 6 Feb 1781; Nathan Stratton b. 31 Jan 1786; Levi
Stratton b. 29 May 1791.

Hannah Buck b. 25 Oct 1791.

Nathan L. Stratton and Hannah Buck mar 11 Mar 1815.
Their children: Joseph Buck Stratton b. 25 Dec 1815; Alexander Stratton b. 11
Dec 1817; Eleanor Leake Stratton b. 18 Jan 1820; Nathan Stratton b. 23
Apr 1822; George Stratton b. 11 Jan 1824; John Stratton b. 13 Feb 1826;
Charles Preston Stratton b. 18 Jun 1828; Edgar - Robert - Henry were b. 1
Aug 1833; Sophia Neal Stratton b. 14 Jun 1835.

Joseph Buck b. 1 May 1758.
Ruth Seeley b. 15 Nov 1763.

Joseph Buck and Ruth Seeley mar 19 Mar 1783.
Their children: John Buck b. 1 Apr 1784; Maria Buck b. 25 Sep 1785; Sarah
Buck b. 11 Aug 1787; Jane Buck b. 4 Oct 1789; Hannah Buck b. 25 Oct
1791; Naomi Seeley Buck b. 13 Sep 1793; Ephraim Buck b. 23 Feb 1795;
Joseph Buck b. 23 Dec 1796; Jeremiah Buck b. 8 Sep 1803

Benjamin Stratton, 2nd, d. 24 Jul 1751, aged 50 yrs.
Abagail his wife d. 7 Apr 1782, aged 77 yrs.
Joseph Buck b. 15 May 1803.
Naomi Seeley Buck d. 26 Sep 1798.
Ruth Ogden d. 24 Mar 1827, aged 64 yrs.
John Buck d. 6 Feb 1842, aged 57 yrs and 10 mo.
Jane Stratton, w/o Daniel P. Stratton, d. 29 Feb 1816, aged 26 yrs and 4 mo.

Benjamin Stratton d. 20 Jul 1751, aged 50 yrs.
Abigail his wife d. 7 Apr 1782, aged 77 yrs.
John Stratton d. 11 Feb 1814, aged 66 yrs.
Eleanor his wife d. 9 Mar 1814, aged 62 yrs and 5 mo.

David Westcott Bible

David Westcott b. 6 Dec 1787.
Lydia Taylor b. 3 Oct 1788.

David Waistcoat and Lydia Taylor mar 4 May 1813.

Rebecca Ann Westcott b. 25 May 1817.
John Westcott b. 24 Aug 1819.
David Westcott b. 16 Dec 1823.
Hannah Sheppard Westcott b. 16 Jan 1826.
Daniel Taylor Westcott b. 1 Apr 1828.

Caroline Bateman b. 30 Mar 1819.
Rebecca Jane Westcott, d/o John and Caroline Westcott, b. 7 Jan 1842.

John Westcott and Caroline Batemen mar 4 Mar 1840.
Henry Buck and Rebecca Jane Westcott mar. 27 Dec. 1865.
Enoch P. Allen and Adele Ross Buck mar. 12 Sep. 1916.

Rebecca Ann Westcott d. 17 May 1821.
Lydia Westcott d. 19 Nov 1836.

Charles Bateman Bible

Charles Bateman b. 13 Nov 1793.
Phoebe H. Bateman b. 20 Dec 1799.
Charles Bateman and Phoebe H. Marts mar 23 Apr 1818 by Rev. Michael
    Swing.
Caroline Bateman b. 30 Mar 1819.
Elwood S. Bateman b. 20 Feb 1822.
Mary Bateman b. 29 Nov 1824.
Edwin F. Bateman b. 12 Nov 1840.

Mary Bateman d. 23 Jan 1845.
Edwin F. Bateman d. 28 July 1856.
Charles Bateman d. 24 June 1864.
Elwood Bateman d. 13 Dec. 1875.
Malona Bateman d. 6 Jan. 1876.
Alice W. Bateman d. 1 July 1878.
Pheobe Bateman d. 10 Nov. 1887, in her 88th yr.
Jane Bateman d. 13 May 1882, aged 59 yrs.

David Jaggers Bible
Isaac Moss, Philadelphia (No date)

David Jaggers b. 15 Aug 1740.
Mary Jaggers b. 8 Mar 1738.

Lot Fithian b. 2 Oct 1740.
Deborah Elmer b. 22 Aug 1780.

Lot Fithian and Deborah Elmer mar 3 Jan 1770.

Benjamin Jaggers b. 5 Jul 1780.
Violetta E. Fithian b. 29 Jan 1789.

Benjamin Jaggers and Viollette E. Fithian mar 31 Dec 1805.

Deborah Ann Jaggers b. 3 Dec 1806.
Mary B. Jaggers b. 3 Mar 1809.
Lucy Ann Jaggers b. 17 May 1811.
Martha Jaggers b. 28 Aug 1813.
Artillia Jaggers b. 23 Feb 1816.
Benjamin Jaggers b. 2 Sep 1821.
Violetta Jaggers b. 16 Mar 1825 or 1818.
Joseph Jaggers b. 29 Mar 1818
Jane Clark b. 23 Mar 1819.

Joseph F. Jaggers and Jane Clark mar 5 Mar 1842.
John Holmes and Mary Clark mar 25 Mar 1828.
Lucy A. Jaggers and Elmer Bennett mar 20 Sep 1832.
Mary B. Jaggers and Ephraim Westcott mar Nov 1832.
Deborah A. Jaggers and Robert Westcott mar 25 Jul 1838.

Attillia Jaggers and Ephraim Westcott mar 16 Oct 1847.
Benjamin Jaggers and Hannah O. Campbell mar 21 Mar 1850.
Albert B. Williams and Mary W. Jaggers mar. 24 Sep. 1868.
Frank Burch and Martha Bush Jaggers mar. 14 Mar. 1889 in Philadelphia.
John Trenchard Whiticar and Louisa Burch Jaggers mar. 28 Nov. 1888 by B. L.
    Agnew in Philadelphia.
David Jaggers and Mary Buck mar. 30 Apr. 1872.

Mary Westcott Jaggers b. 12 Feb 1843 and bapt. (?) _nd Dec 1843 by Rev. E.
    Osborn.
Martha Bush Jaggers b. 10 Nov 1844 and bapt. 3 Dec 1845 by Rev. B. B.
    Hotchkiss.
Louisa Bush Jaggers b. 1 Jun 1848 and bapt. Apr 1849 by Rev. Ethan Osborn.

Mary Potter Clark, d/o David and Mary Clark, b. 11 Aug 1805.
Mary Clark Holmes, d/o John and Mary P. Holmes, b. 31 Oct 1830.
Lewis Bush Holmes, s/o John and Mary Potter Holmes, b. 20 Oct 1834.
Hannah Potter Holmes, d/o John and Mary P. Holmes, b. 23 Jan 1840.

Children of Albert and Mary W. Williams: Louisa Gertrude b. 9 July 1869 and
    d. 16 Feb. 1871; Sarah Hall b. 16 Feb. 1871; Abraham Lincoln b. 11 Apr.
    1874 and d. 31 July 1875; Martha Jaggers b. 8 Jan. 1778 and d. 3 July
    1880; Alexander Reed b. 7 Jan. 1879 and d. 19 June 1882.

John Holmes b, 31 Oct. 1880.

David Jaggers d. 15 Nov 1784, aged 44 yrs.
Mary Jaggers d. 8 Jan 1813, aged 75 yrs.
Lot Fithian d. 12 Apr 1810, aged 70 yrs.
Deborah Fithian d. 31 Dec 1824, aged 75 yrs.
Benjamin Jaggers d. 16 Apr 1834, aged 54 yrs.
Joseph Fithian d. 17 May 1837.
Mary Buck Westcott d. 16 Aug 1846, aged 37-5-13.
David Clark d. 17 Jan. 1853, aged 77 yrs.
Mary Potter, w/o David Clark, d. 24 Mar.(no year given), in her 81st yr.
Ruth Clark, w/o Rev. Abijah Davis, d. 10 Nov. 1859.
Joseph F. Jaggers d. 21 Feb. 1896, in his 78th yr.
Jane Clark Jaggers d. 9 Nov. 1899, in her 81stbyr.
Sallie E. Tullis d. 20 Sep. 1863.
Ephrain Fithian d. 5 Mar. 1855.
Ebenezer Fithian d. 1857.

Susan Marts Bible

William Whitekar b. 11 Jul 1787.
Rebecca Westcott, w/o William Whitekar, b. 10 Feb 1789.
William Whitekar and Rebecca Westcott mar 23 Dec 1807.
Their children: Dayton B. Whitekar b. 4 Oct 1808; Susan Whitekar b. 28 Nov
    1810; Nathaniel Whitekar b. 7 Jun 1812; Eunice Whitekar b. 20 Jun 1814;
    William H. Whitekar b. 13 Nov 1816; Rebecca A. Whitekar b. 22 Apr
    1821; Joseph S. Whitekar b. 4 Aug 1826; Mary Maria Whitekar b. 2 Nov
    1828.

Elijah B. Marts b. 26 Dec 1807.
Susan Whitekar, w/o Elijah B. Marts, b. 28 Nov 1810.

Susan Whitekar and Elijah B Marts mar 3 May 1832.
Their children: Mary Jane Marts b. 12 Jun 1834; Rebecca W. Marts b. 11 Apr
    183;6; John Bowen Marts and William Whitekar Marts (twins) b. 27 Jul
    1838; Henry W. Marts b. 6 Jul 1841.

Dayton B. Whitekar d. 22 Jun 1811, aged 2-8-18.
Nathaniel Whitekar d. 8 Jun 1812, aged 6 dys.
Joseph T. Whitekar d. 10 Aug 1826, aged 6 dys.
William Whitekar d. 13 Apr 1829, in his 42nd yr. A sermon was delivered by
    Rev. E. Osborn.
Rebecca Whitekar, widow of William, d. 24 Oct 1830, in her 42nd yr. A sermon
    was delivered by Rev. Mr. Swing.
William H. Whitekar d. 18 May 1846. A sermon was preached by Rev. Mr.
    Hotckin.
Jeremiah Whitekar d. 18 Jun 1814, in his 60th yr. A sermon by Rev. E. Osborn.
John Whitekar d. 11 Jul 1828, in his 46th yr. A sermon was delivered by the
    Rev. E. Osborn.
Marriah Whitekar d. 19 Oct ____, in her 27th yr. A sermon was delivered by
    Rev. E. Osborn.
Sarah Taylor d. 25 Sep 1831, in her 46th yr.
Sarah Whitekar d. 8 Jan 1833, in her 76th yr.

Rebecca W. Marts d. 25 Aug 1837.
Joseph Marts d. 24 Jun 1843.
Jonathan B. Marts d. 21 Aug 1848.
Elizabeth W. Marts d. 13 May 1854.
Elijah B. Marts d. 16 Oct. 1872.

Note: There were some duplicate entries of the births of children of Elijah B. Marts and his wife. They also had a son, David, now (1912) in the U. S. Lighthouse Service at Ready island, in the Delaware River, but his birth is not entered in her bible.

*David died the last week of Feb., 1913.

**On a loose sheet pasted into Susan Mart's bible, in which her son, Henry, says is her handwriting:

Jeremiah Whitekar b. 1 Sep 1754 and Sarah Keen b. 17 Jun 1757. They mar. 19 Feb. 1778.
Persilla Whitekar b. 10 Jan 1779.
Jeremiah Whitekar and Sarah Keen mar 19 Feb 1780.
John Whitekar b. 30 Mar 1783.
Henry and Sarah Whitekar, twins, b. 13 Mar 1785.
William Whitekar 11 Jul 1787.
David Whitekar b. 17 Jan 1790.
Hannah Whitekar b. 8 Apr 1794.
Lydia Whitekar b. 12 Sep 1797.
Thomas Whitekar b. 5 Jun 1800.
Mariah Whitekar b. 2 Mar 1803.

Barber Bible

Gideon Barber b. Saturday, 3 Jul 1779.
Rebecca Barber b. 21 Oct 1779.

Gideon Barber mar 23 Oct 1803.

Amy Barber b. Saturday, 7 Jul 1804.
Mercy Barber b. Sunday, 4 Jan 1807.
David H. James Ball Wager Barber b. Wednesday, 12 Feb 1812.

Rebecca Barber d. 21 Mar 1812, aged 32 yrs, 5 mo.

Priscilla Taylor b. Sunday, 10 May 1778 and mar to G. Barber 31 Dec 1812.

Solomon Taylor Barber b. Wednesday, 10 Nov 1813.

Gideon G. Barber b. Sunday, 18 Jun 1815.

Mary M. Barber b. Monday, 7 Apr 1817.

Hester Julette Barber b. Wednesday, 17 Mar and d. 11 Nov , 1819.

Priscilla Ann Barber b. Thursday, 23 Nov 1820.

Solomon Taylor Barber d. 5 Feb 1824, aged 10-2-26.

Sister Phebe Barber d. 25 Nov 1834.

Gideon G. Barber d. 10 Feb 1846, aged 30-7-23.

Priscilla Barber d. 1 Oct 1846, aged 68- 5-20.

Mercy Turner d. 9 Jun 1848, aged 41-5-5.

Priscilla Ann T...... d. 17 Mar. 1852, aged 31-3-23.

Gideon Barber d. 20 May 1854, aged 74-10-17.

John Smith Brognard's Family Bible
Philadelphia, 1813

First cover page bears the inscription: Presented by him to his son Ferdinand
Francis Brognard on 1 Oct 1838, with the request that at Ferdinand's
decease it shall become the property of his son John Smith Brognard.

John Smith Brognard, s/o Dr. John Brognard and Sarah his wife, b. 28 Oct 1784
at the City of Burlington, NJ.

Sarah Brognard, w/o John S. Brognard and d/o Hudson Burr, b. 6 Mar 1788 in
the township of Northampton, Burlington County, NJ.

John Smith Brognard and Sarah Burr, 2nd d/o Hudson Burr of the Township of
Northampton, County of Burlington & State of New Jersey, were married
on Sunday, 1 Jan 1809 by Joseph Budd, Esq.

Their children: Ferdinand Francis Brognard b. 20 Nov 1809 at Whitehill, NJ;
Sophia Wilhelmina Brognard b. 19 Mar 1812 at Whitehill, NJ; Maria
Louisa Brognard b. 14 Oct 1814 at Whitehill; Joseph Richard Brognard b.
28 Jun 1817 at Whitehill; Margaret Dumphy(?) Brognard b. 25 Oct 1819 at
Philadelphia; Sophia Maria Brognard b. 21 May 1822 in LeRoy, Jefferson
County, NY; Mary Burr Brognard b. 30 Dec 1824 at Evans Mills, Town of
LeRoy, Jefferson Co., NY; Sarah Louisa Brognard b. 1 Jan 1828 at Evans
Mills; Josephine Marian Brognard b. 25 Oct 1830 at LeRoy, Jefferson Co.,
NY.

Amanda Malvina Pierce, d/o Joseph and Lucinda Pierce, b. 7 Jun 1809.

F. F. Brognard and Amanda Malvina Pierce, 1st d/o Joseph and Lucinda Pierce
    of the town of Dummerston, State of Vermont, were married on Sunday, 20
    Jun 1830, by the Rev. Mr. Warner, Esquire.
Their children: Charlotte Malvina Brognard b. 27 Feb 1831; John Smith
    Brognard b. 15 Feb 1834; Joseph Pierce Brognard b. 23 Apr 1837; Sarah
    Burr Brognard b. 17 Dec 1839 at LeRoy, Jefferson Co., NY.

Martha Elizabeth Brognard, 2nd w/o F. F. Brognard and d/o Elijah and Lucretia
    Carman, was b. 14 Mar 1829 in Delanies Valllie, Baltimore County,
    Maryland.

Ferdinand F. Brognard and Martha Elizabeth Carmen, 1st d/o Elijah and
    Lucretia Carman, were married 28 Aug 1851 in Baltimore City, by the Rev.
    Henry Slicer.
Their children: Mary Tappington Brognard b. 15 Jun 1852; Frank Carman
    Brognard b. 17 Aug 1853.

Hiram Wilkie b. 28 Sep 1829, at Evans Mills, Jefferson County, New York.
Hiram Wilkie and Charlotte M. Brognard mar 30 Oct 1855 by Rev. Elder
    Decker.
Cora Mirian Wilkie, d/o Hiram and Charlotte M. Wilkie, grand daughter of F. F.
    Amanda Melvina Brognard, b. 18 July 1858 at Evans Mills, Jefferson
    County, New York.

Margaret D. Brognard and Samuel G. Wright, of Monmouth, NJ, mar 23 Jan
    1849.
Son b. to Margaret B. Wright on 6 Nov 1849 (Edward B. Wright)
Son b. to Margaret B. Wright on 25 Jan 1851. (Joseph B. Wright)

Sarah L. Brognard and John Cass Truefitt, of Philadelphia, mar 13 Feb 1850.

Sophia Wilhelmina Brognard, d/o John S. and Sarah Brognard, d. 22 May 1815,
    aged 3 yrs and 3 dys.
Maria Louisa Brognard, d/o John S. and Sarah Brognard, d. 27 Aug 1817, aged
    2-10-13.
Joseph Pierce Brognard, s/o F. F. and Amanda M. Brognard, d. 30 May 1838,
    aged 1-1-7.
Sarah Burr Brognard, d/o F. F. and Amanda Malvina Brognard, d. 14 May
    1841, aged 1-4-28.

Amanda Malvina Brognard, w/o F. F. Brognard, d. 3 Mar 1850, aged 40-8-26, in Baltimore County, Maryland and was bur at the Fork Meeting House.
Mary Tappington Brognard, d/o F. F. and Martha Elizabeth, d. 22 July 1852, aged 1mo., 7 dys. Buried at Fork Meeting House.
Frank Carman Brognard, s/o F. F. and Martha Elizabeth, d. 9 Sep. 1862, aged 9 yrs, 22 dys. Buried at Fork Meeting House, Baltimore County, Maryland.
Martha Elizabeth, w/o F. F. Brognard and d/o Elijah and Lucretia Carman,, d. 6 June 1870 at 2:00 in the evening, aged 41-2-23. Buried at Fork Meeting House, Baltimore County, Maryland.

Heirs to the Estate of the Patentees of the Town of New Harlem, Incorporated

David C. Bosworth, b. Brooklyn, New York, 7 Mar. 1866, son of -
William Post Bosworth, b. 6 Feb. 1841, (mar. 19 May 1860, Emma Jane Tompkins) son of -
Catherine Post, b. 24 Apr. 1820, (mar. 26 July 1837, Enos Bosworth) dau. of -
Leah Lent, b. 2 Jan. 1782, (mar. 9 July 1798, Jacob Post) dau. of -
Hendricks Lent, b. abt. 1750, (mar. abt. 1775, Margaret Montrose) son of -
Abraham Lent, b. 15 Jan. 17717, (mar. bef. 1750, Mary Waldron, b. 1730) Mary was dau. of -
Resolved Waldron, b. 6 May 1702, (mar. May 1729, Mattie Quackenbush) son of -
Johannes Waldron, b. New Harlem, 12 Sep. 1665, (mar. 25 Apr. 1690, Anna Van Dalsen) son of -Resolved Waldron, b. 10 May 1610, (mar. May 1654, Tanneke Nagle) a patentee of the Town of New Harlem.

Henry Brooks Bible

Henry Brooks was b. 1739 and d. 19 Sep 1774. Bathsheba Harris, 8th child of Thomas and Sarah Daton Harris, was b. Jan 1747 and d. 6 Jul 1814.

Henry Brooks, s/o Henry Brooks and Bathsheba Harris, was b. 6 Jun 1765, was married 5 Jun 1786, d. 9 Oct 1829. He and his wife were buried at the old Stone Church, Cumberland, below Fairton.

The 1st above named Henry Brooks was the grandson of Henry Brooks, whose will was made 18 Feb 1749 and proven Mar 1750.

He was the great-grandson of Josiah and Lucy Brooks. Josiah was b. 23 Aug 1681, in Swansee, Mass., and d. 1732. In 1687 he settled in West Jersey.

He was also the great-great-grandson of Timothy and Mahitable Brooks, his 2nd wife, d/o Henry Maury (or Money, or Monry) of Providence and widow of Eldad Kingsley of Bellerica, Mass.

He was the great-great-great-grandson of Henry Brooks, a Welshman, b. 1592. A clothier by trade who came with his family to Massachusetts and lived in Coburn in 1639. The name of his wife is unknown. He married 3 times but all of his children were by his 1st wife. He d. 12 Apr 1683, in his 90th year.

Amy Pierson Brooks, d/o Capt. David Brooks and Hannah Lawrence, was b. 13 Mar 1769, mar Henry Brooks of Jones Island, 5 Jun 1786, and d. 9 May 1834. Capt. David Brooks was b. 5 Sep 1741, mar Hannah Lawrence 30 May 1768, and d. 10 May 1813. Hannah Lawrence was b. 7 Dec 1746.

She was also the granddaughter of Henry and Hannah Pierson. Henry Pierson was b. 1704 and d. 1776. He was an Elder in the Old Stone Church in 1755 and 1759. He owned the grist mill in Cedarville from 10 Mar 1753 until the beginning of the Revolutionary War.

She was the great-granddaughter of Henry Pierson, b. Southampton, 17 Apr 1678, d. in Cohansy, NJ, 1749. He mar Abigail Ludlam 11 Jun 1702 who d. 27 Mar 1721, after whose death he moved to Cohansy, taking 6 of his 8 children. His will was dated 10 Jul 1747.

She was the great-great-granddaughter of Lieut. Joseph Pierson and Amy Barnes who mar 17 Nov 1675. They had 6 children and his wife d. 3 Oct 1682. He was a prominent man in the community of Southampton, was elected overseer of the town and assessor in 1700. He was Lieut. of the 3rd Co. of Southampton troops and d. 1 Apr 16__ (so written).

She was the great-great-great-granddaughter of Henry Pierson, an Englishman who settled in Southampton about 1640. He was elected town clerk or registrar 6 Oct 1650 and held the position for 30 years. His wife was Admin. of his estate 15 Nov 1681. His wife was Mary Cooper, d/o John and Wilbroe Cooper, was b. in England 1622. John Cooper was b. in England in 1594. He came in the Hopewell from Onley, in Bucks, to Lynn, Mass., with 4 children. He was a Freeman in Boston 8 Dec. 16__ and an Elder in the church at Lynn when it was organized in 16__. He d. in Southampton, L. I., in 1622

Pierson Harris b. 18 Apr 1764 and d. 4 Apr 1803, aged 38 yrs.
Judith Nixon, his wife, b. 14 Jun 1764.

Gilbert Harris b. 6 Nov 1787.
Hannah Jones Harris b. 29 Oct 1789.
Ephraim Harris b. 27 Mar and d. 10 Apr 1792.
Ephraim Harris b. 15 Dec 1793 and d. 5 Sep 1849, aged 55 yrs.
Isaac Harris b. 21 Mar 1796.

Ephraim Harris mar Hannah Davis 31 Nov 1816.

Hannah Jones Harris Ogden d. 14 Jan 1849, aged 58. Her husband was Jedediah
    Ogden. Both went west and died.

Thomas & Abigail Brooks Bible
Printed MDCCXIV

Thomas Brooks b. 24 Sep 1762.
Abigail Conner b. 31 Aug 1764.
Thomas Brooks and Abigail Conner mar 9 Nov 1789.
Sheppard Brooks b. 14 Jan 1791.
Abraham Brooks b. 10 Mar 1793 and d. the next day.
Hannah Brooks b. 10 Apr 1794 and d. 7 Nov 1795.
Sarah Brooks b. 19 Apr 1796.
Elizabeth Brooks b. 16 May 1798.
Lydia Brooks b. 22 Jun 1800.
Rachel Brooks b. 16 Oct 1802.
Hannah Brooks b. 1804, mar. Henry Husted and d. 1874.
Mary Brooks b. 17 Dec 1806.
Henry W. Brooks b. 2 Jun 1810.

Lydia Brooks d. 26 May 1814.
Thomas Brooks d. 16 Sep 1829.

Sheppard Brooks Bible
Printed 1811

Sheppard Brooks b. 14 Jan 1791.
Hannah Keen b. 5 Nov 1793.

Sheppard Brooks and Hannah Keen mar 6 Jan 1813.

Charlette Brooks b. 5 Nov 1813.
Thomas Brooks b. 30 Jul 1816 and d. 10 Jun 1817.
Lydia W. Brooks b. 15 Jun 1820.
Naomi Brooks b. 19 May1827.
Sheppard Brooks, Jr, b. 11 Nov 1835.

Hannah Brooks d. 1851 while on a visit to Delaware and "is bur in that old
    church yard in New Castle."

Edson Family Records

Thomas mar Juliana Bustard, b. at Adderbury, England, about 1480.
Richard mar Agnes _____. Died at Adderbury, England, 1558.
Thomas mar Ellen _____. Died 1578.
Thomas mar Elizabeth Copson – Baptized Tillingby, England, 7 Sep 1572.
Samuel mar Susanna Orcott 1637. Baptized Tillingby 5 Sep 1613. Came to
    Salem, Mass. 1639, then went to Bridgewater.
Joseph mar Mary Turner. Born at Salem, Mass. abt 1649, d. 1712.
Timothy mar Mary Alden, 1719. She was b. at Bridgewater, g-g-dau. of John
    and Priscilla Alden and , d/o Joseph and Hannah. She d. 1775.
Jonathan, born at Bridgewater 1728, died at W_ately, Mass., 1805, mar
    Mehetable Lilly, 1749, Stafford, CT.
Samuel, b. abt 1770, d. 31 Jul 1802, mar 1794, Mariam Edson, d/o Peter and
    Huldah Edson.

Samuel Lilley, b. 6 Jan 1800 at East Randolph, VT, mar (1) 1825, Sarah
    Bordwell b. 30 Aug 1805. Mar(2) 1842, Miranda Reed.

Miranda Reed, d/o Elija and Sally Reed, b. 15 Feb 1822 and d.11 Mar. 1880 at
    Vineland, New Jersey.

Issue: Sylvanus b. 1826 and mar Elvira Streeter; Miriam b. 1828 and mar (1)
    _____ Watson, (2) _____ Cadogan; Joseph b. 1831; Polly b. 1833 and mar
    Henry Spalding; Huldah b. 1837 and mar Josiah Wicks; Sarah b. 1843 and
    mar Ozro Myers; Lydia b. 1846 and mar (1) W. W. Wicks, (2) Isaac D.
    Huff; Medora b. 1849; Daniel Samuel b. 1852 and mar Annie Williams.

Hudson-Huff Bibles
Adrian Watkins, Edinburgh, 1752

Maria Huff b. 13 Nov 1799.
Isaac Huff b. 4 Jan 1804.
Isaac and Maria Huff mar 12 Feb 1824.
Sarahann Huff b. 30 Dec 1825.
Elizabeth Jane Huff b. 29 Sep 1829.
Isaac Doty Huff b. 14 May 1833.

Edson Bible
Silas Andrus, Hartford 1832

Samuel Edson and Sally Bordwell mar 28 Sep 1825.

Silvanus b. 28 Jun 1826.
Miriam b. 12 Jun 1828.
Joseph b. 23 May 1831.
Polly b. 27 Jun 1833.
Huldah b. 28 Jul 1837.

Sally b. 30 Aug 1806 and d. 10 Feb 1841, aged 35 yrs.

Samuel Edson and Miranda Reed mar 20 Sep 1842.

Sarah Edson b. 6 Aug 1843.
Joseph d. (?)17 Mar 1846.
Lydia Edson b. 18 Aug 1848.

Samuel Edson was of Darien, Genesee County, New York.

Eickle Records

Abraham Eickle and Salome Kuntzman mar 1785.
John Jacob Eickle b. 25 Feb and bapt. 20 May, 1787.
John Ludwig Eickle b. __ Aug and bapt. 12 Sep, 1788.
John Christopher Eickle b. 13 Nov and bapt. 12 Dec 1790.
Maria Sarah Eickle b. 30 Apr and bapt __ May 1792.
Maria Catherina Eickle b. and bapt 1794.

Philip Eickle b. __ Aug and bapt. 20 Sep 1795.
Abraham Eickle b. 22 ___ and bapt. 27 Dec 1797.
Maria Eickle b. 20 ___ and bapt. 10 Mar 1799.
Mary Eickle b. __ Apr 1803 and bapt. 24 Apr 1803.
Elizabeth Eickle b. __ Aug and bapt. 26 Aug ___.
Joseph Eickle b. 15 Jul and bapt. 10 Aug 1806.
Benjamin Eickle b. 20 Aug and bapt. 27 Sep ____.
Maria Barbara Eickle b. 24 Sep and bapt. 15 Dec 1808.

Garrison Bible
Aaron Leake, Edinburgh 1793

Front board cover: Sarah Garrison, April 9, A. D. 1835.

Jonathan Garrison b. 8 Sep 1746.

Charles Garrison b. 28 Mar 1771.
Lewis Garrison b. 7 Sep 1777.
Samuel L. Garrison b. 3 Apr 1783.

Samuel Garrison and Sarah his wife were mar 16 Apr 1806

Mary Garrison, w/o Jonathan Garrison, d. 17 Oct 1805.
Doctor Lewis Garrison d. 17 Oct 1806.
Samuel Garrison d. 9 Aug 1807.
Lydia Garrison, w/o Charles Garrison, d. 7 Oct 1834.

Ruth Thackery b. 1 Nov 1812.

Cassell Bible

Arnold Cassell d. 1737.
Lydia Cassel later mar William Cathcart.
Lydia had 3 Cassel children: James, 11; Israel, 9; Arnold, 7 (at the time of his
    death).
They resided on ___ Street, Philadelphia, where he owned 2 houses – 1 brick, 1
    wooden. Fronts were 20 feet depth, 130 ft with 5 ft alley.

Harwood Bible

Simeon Harwood b. 2 Mar 1769.
Lydia Harwood b. 24 Mar 1775.

Simeon Harwood and Lydia Hicks mar 15 Mar 1803.

Silas Harwood b. 29 Feb 1804.
Diantha Harwood b. 5 May 1810

Silas Harwood and Mary Haas mar May 1830
Diantha Harwood and Eathan Holden mar 11 Oct 1855.

Simeon Harwood d. 25 Nov 1851
Lydia Harwood d. 14 Nov 1844.

Harris – Barrett Bible
Isaac Collins, Trenton, NJ 1791

Amariah Harris was the s/o Capt. Thomas Harris.

Lidia Harris's son Datten Harris, b. 15 Nov 1771.

Amariah Harris and Mary Lawrence mar 7 Nov 1776 at Dr. Pearson's.

Account of the ages of their children: Lydia Harris b. 7 Oct 1777; James Harris
    b. 16 Mar 1780; George Harris b. 25 Oct 1784; Mary Harris b. 16 Feb
    1787; Violetta Harris b. 27 Feb 1790; Bathsheba Harris b. 21 Sep 1793.

Amariah Harris d. 28 Mar 1793.
Mary McKnight d. 22 Mar 1815.
James Harris was drowned 15 Dec 1805.
Violetta Harris, w/o Ebenezer Westcote, d. 19 Sep 1813.
Mary Harris, w/o Isaac Alderman, d. 6 Sep 1818.
George Harris was drowned 20 Nov 1835.
James Harris, s/o George Harris, was drowned 20 Aug 1837.
Lydia Sheppard, widow of Jonathan Sheppard, d. 4 May1848.
Mary Ann Daton, w/o Joseph Daton and d/o James Harris, d. 25 Aug. 1660 at
    Jacksonville, Ill., aged 55 yrs, 6 mo.
Bathsheba Harris d. 25 Jan. 1882.

William D. Barrett Bible

William D. Barrett's mother was Mary Van Dyke

William D. Barrett b. 12 Feb 1791.

Bathsheba H. Barrett b. 21 Sep 1793.

William D. Barrett, s/o William Barrett, Jr, of Shiloh, Cumberland Co., NJ, mar Bathsheba Harris, d/o Amariah Harris of Fairfield, said county, 15 Mar 1815.

Their children: Mary Barrett b. 3 Jan 1816; James H. Barrett b. 26 Nov 1820; Lydia Barrett b. 13 Jan 1824.

William D. Barrett d. 10 Apr. 1897, aged 76 yrs., 2 mo.

Lydia B. Lawrence, d/o William D. and Bathsheba Barrett, d. at Tuckerton, Burlington Co., New Jersey, 21 July 186, aged 40 yrs. and 6 mo. Buried in the Old Stone Churchyard.

James H. Barrett d. at Bridgeton, New Jersey, 13 Sep. 1895. Buried in the Old Stone Churchyard.

Mary Barrett Trenchard d. at Bridgeton, New Jersey, 5 Mar. 1900. Buried in the Old Stone Churchyard.

Jacob Benner Bible

Jacob Benner b. 8 May 1757, at 3:00 o'clock in the afternoon.

Catherena Fetter, d/o Caspar Fetter, b. 15 Jul 1761.

Jacob Benner was married unto Catherena Fetter 11 Aug 1782.

Jacob Benner . 30 Aug 1785, at 10:00 o'clock at night.

Mary Benner b. 7 Jun 1786, at 3:00 o'clock in the morning.

George Benner b. 19 Oct 1787, at 8:00 o'clock In the morning.

Rachel Benner b. 26 Jul 1789, at 3:00 o'clock in the afternoon.

Michel Benner b. 4 Aug 1791, at 4:00 o'clock in the afternoon.

Samuel Benner b. 23 Jul 1793, at 4:00 o'clock in the morning.

Elizabeth Benner b. 6 Sep 1795, at 10:00 o'clock in the morning.

Martin Benner b. 16 Jun 1797, at 8:00 o'clock in the morning.

Margaret Benner b. 14 Jan 1802, at 7:00 at night.

William Benner b. 4 Dec 1800, at 11:00 o'clock at night.

De___ Benner b. 20 Dec 1804.

LeVick Benner b. 11 Dec 1805, at 6:00 o'clock in the morning.

Children of Lewis and Rachel Heaton: Jacob Heaton b. 8 Aug 1827; Mary
   Heaton b. 4 Jan 1829; _____ Heaton b. __ Jul 1831.

Elizabeth Benner d. 30 Aug 1798.

Rachel Fetter d. 30 Jan 1813.

Jacob Benner, Jr, d. 5 Feb 1822, at 3:00 o'clock in the morning, aged 36 yrs and
   5 mo.

Catherine Benner, w/o Jacob Benner, d. 24 Jan 1824, aged 62-6-9.

Jacob Benner d. 7 Dec 1825, aged 68-7-1.

Levick Fox d. 23 Jun 1826, aged 3 score and 10 yrs.

Martin Benner d. 23 Sep 1829.

George Benner d. 18 Jul 1830, aged 43 yrs.

Lewis Heaton d. 25 Dec 1831.

William Benner d. 20 Apr 1834, aged 32-3-4.

Mary M., w/o John M., d. 9 Feb 1837.

LeVick Benner d. 3 Nov 1839, aged 32-9-22.

Michael Benner d. 26 Jan 1844, aged 52-5-22.

Hilyard-Wallin Bible

Henry Hilyard, Jr, and Dorcas Wallen, both of Cumberland Co., NJ, mar 1 Aug
   1838.

John Wallen and Hannah Ann Abbot mar 4 Oct 1840.

George A. Harris and Rachel S. Hilyard, both of Cumberland County, mar.13
   Apr. 1867.

Charles C. Hilyard of Hopewell Tp. tp Miss Anna T. Mattison of Stow Creek,
   New Jersey, mar. 10 Sep. 1879.

C. C, Hilyard and Mrs. Mary D. Woodruff, both of Cumberland County, mar.
   31 Dec. 1879 by T. L. Gardner.

John Wallen b. 22 Mar 1815.

Hannah Ann Abbot, d/o William G. Abbot, b. 27 Feb 1821.

John Hilyard b. 8 Feb 1840, in Gloucester County.

William H. H. Hilyard b. 19 Mar 1842, in Cumberland County.

Francis B. Hilyard b. 4 Jan 1844, in Mannington, Salem County.

Rachel S. Hilyard b. 2 Aug 1846, in Salem County.

Charles C. Hilyard b. 10 Jan 1857, in Cumberland County.

E. C. Hilyard b. 13 Feb 1820.

E. A. Hilyard b. 2 Oct 1822.

Henry Hilyard, Sr, b. 14 Feb 1777.

Rachel Hilyard, his wife, b. 1790.

Jacob Hilyard b. 17 Jul 1805.

Mary Ann Hilyard b. 18 Feb 1813.

Henry Hilyard, Jr, b. 8 Jan 1815.

David W. Hilyard b. 1 Apr 1827.

John Wallin b. 3 May 1782.

Mary, his wife, b. 12 Feb 1782.

Mary Wallin, his dau, b. 31 Aug 1804.

Lydia Wallin b. 7 Nov 1807.

Sallie Wallin b. 3 Nov 1810.

Dorcas Wallin b. 15 Jun 1813.

Francis Garton b. 15 Sep 1821.

Ann Garton b. 4 Mar 1823.

Caroline Garton b. 11 Apr 1828.

Lester F. Hilyard b. at Shiloh, New Jersey, 26 Dec. 1894.

Anna T. Mattison b. at Bridgeton, New Jersey, 6 June 1857.

Adella Hilyard b. 9 Mar. 1880.

Florence Hilyard b. 8 Apr. 1882. (The above were the children of C. C. and
 Anna T. Hilyard)

Mary D. Tomlinson b. at Marlboro, Stow Creek Tp., New Jersey, 27 Oct. 1852.

William H. Hilyard b. at Marlboro, New Jersey, 4 Jan. 1887.

Warren T. Hilyard b. at Shiloh, New Jersey,

Eva M. Hilyard b. at Marlboro.

John Wallin, Sr, d. 1 Apr 1817, aged 35 yrs.

Hannah Ann Wallin d. 2 Apr 1843, age 22 yrs.

Rachel Hilyard d. 11 Feb 1847, aged 58 yrs.

Henry Hilyard, Sr., d. 6 Mar. 1853, aged 76 yrs.

Mary D. Minch d. 23 May 18555, aged 22 yrs.

Mary Wallin, w/o John Wallin, d. 7 Sep. 1859, aged 77 and ½ yrs.

Jacob Hilyard d. 20 Aug. 1863, aged 58 yrs.

Ruth P. Wallin d. 4 Apr. 1866.

Anna T. Hilyard, w/o C. C. Hilyard, d. 13 Mar. 1884, aged 26-9-7.

Henry Hilyard, Jr., d. 6 Jan. 1893, aged 80 yrs.

Dorcas Wallin, his wife, d. 8 Feb. 1896, in her 83rd yr.

Warren T. Hilyard, s/o C. C. and Mary D. Hilyard, d. 5 Jan. 1896, of Dyptheria,
 aged 6 yrs., ans 10 mo.

Huff-Howell Bible

Nostrandt – Jacob Jansen came to Albany, New York, from Nostrandt, Holland in 1638.

Van Nostrandt - Jacob Jacobse, d. 1702/3, mar Annalyze Croesvelt 1688.
>   Jacob, b. 1691-d. 1791, mar Annalyze Steinmetz.
>   John, b. 1730, mar Maria Brokaw. He served in the Revolutionary War.

Huff –Isaac, b. 1777-d. 1850, mar Maria Van Nostrand, b. 1781-d.1883.
>   Isaac, b. 1804-d.1875, mar Maria Doty, b. 1799-d.1873, Alden, New York.
>   Isaac Doty, b. 1833, Rochester, N. Y., . 1919, mar 1872, Lydia Edam, b. 1846, Darien, N. Y., d. 1929. Both bur. at Vineland.
>   Bertha Marie mar. 1900 Elmer Stanley Gundy(?)

Howell - Sara Ann, b. 1825, d. 1906, mar.1862 William W. Howell, who d. 1897.

Irick Family Bible Notes

Job Irick, brother of General Irick, of Vincentown, NJ, mar Matilda, d/o Hudson and Hannah (Wooston) Burr.
Mary, w/o John Irick, bur at Mt. Holly, 16 Jan 1771, as reg. St. Mary Church, Burlington.

Polyglott Bible
Brattleboro, VT 1842

Joel Constantine b. 23 Feb 1788, Ashburnham, MA., d. 13 Jan 1859, aged 69 yrs.
Asenath Grimes b. 4/14? Apr 1782, Hubbardstown, MA., 7 Oct. 1861.

Alfred A. b. 5 May 1812, 10:00 p.m., d. 9 July 1902.
Austin b. 9 May 1827, 3:00 a.m., at midnight, 15 Feb. 1905.
George b. 25 Sep 1816 and d. 10 Aug. 1852.
Eliza b. 3/5? Feb 1814 and d. 3 Sep. 1815.

A. A. Constantine b. 5 May 1812, Ashburnham, MA.

Mary Fales b. 21 Sep 1807, Spencer, MA.
Alfred Alexander Constantine b. 5 May 1812 and d. 9 June 1902.

Austin A. Constantine and Mary Fales mar 2 Jul 1840, Mt. Holly, Vt.

Eliza Constantine, d/o Austin A. and Mary F. Constantine, b. 16 Aug 1843,
    Wallingford, VT.

UJ Jennie b. 22 Aug/Sep. 1850, d. 1874.
George A. b. 11:45 p.m., 10 July 1855 and d. 21 Aug/Sep.1898.
Pearl T. b. 6:49 p.m., 21 Feb. 1860.
Urania A. Thompson b. 2 Jan. 1827 and d. 21 Apr. 1860.
Mary S. b. .....
Encie Louise b. 10:00 p.m., 3 June 1873.

(Above records copied as written)

Goodwine- Capp Bible

Aaron P. Goodwine b. 19 Sep 1798 at Moultonborough, New Hampshire and d.
    13 Apr 1870 at Hinedale, New York. Aaron P. Goodwine was a member of
    the New Hampshire Legislature for two terms.
Nancy W. Capp b. 30 Aug 1806 at Warren, New Hampshire and d. 29 Feb 1872
    at Olean, New York.
Aaron P. Goodwine and Nancy W. Capp mar 20 Dec 1825, by Abel Morrill,
    Esq.
Their children: Miriam Goodwine b. 8 Apr 1827 and d. 23 Aug 1829; Miriam
    Augusta b. 25 Feb. 1829; William Capp b. 2 Sep. 1830; George
    Washington b. 1 Mar. 1832; Augustus Capp b. 19 Mar. 1834; Joshua Capp
    b.27 Feb. 1836; Nelson Stephen b. 7 Jan. 1839; Ellan Francis b. 24 Jan.
    1845.

Mirian Augusta mar. Asa Burton Nelson 2 July 1847, by Abram Ward, Esq.
Children of A. B. and Miriam A. Nelson: Mary Frances b. 23 Aug 1850 and d.
    29 July 1851; George E. b. 8 June 1852 and d. 17 Oct. 1877; Charles
    Eugene b. 24 Feb. 1860 and d. 6 Jan. 1929

William Capp Goodwine and Anna S. Morse mar. 28 Apr. 1850, by Rev.
    Phineas Bond.

Children of W. C. and A. S. Goodwine: William Oscar b. 24 Aug. 1860; Anna Mary b. 1 Apr. 1870.

George W. Goodwine mar. Catherine Raub 9 July 1853, by H. Card, Esq. William Augustus, only child of G. W. and C. R. Goodwine, b. 1856 and d. 1933.

Augustus Capp Goodwine mar. Susan Lewis 28 Feb. 1855, by Phillip Lewis, Esq.
Children of A. C. and S. L. Goodwine: Eugene; Frances, Albert, Anna, Nellie and Aaron (birth dates not recorded)

Joshua Capp Goodwine never married and d. July 1897.

Nelson Stephen Goodwine and Agnes Gardiner 14 July 1861, by Rev. Cole. Their children: An infant son b. and d. 20 May 1863; Anna S. b. 29 Sep. 1864 and d. 28 Dec. 1933;

Ellen Frances Goodwine mar. John C. Conrad 25 Aug. 1863, by Rev. King. Children of E. F. and J. C. Conrad: Mary Augusta b. 21 Mar. 1865 and d. Jan. 1870; Daniel D. b. 31 Oct. 1866 and d. 28 Jan. 1870; Lizzie A. b. 21 July 1868 and d. 22 Feb. 1900; Mary Estella b. 10 Jan. 1879 and d. 15 Nov. 1925; Nancy Goodwine b. 8 Feb. 1872.

William Castro, his Bible
6 August 1752

William Castro b. 10 ___ 1717.
Purthenia Castro d. 6 Jan 1752.

Elizabeth Castro, d/o William and Purthenia Castro, b. 9 Dec 1746.
Abel Castro b. 24 Jul 1748.
Azariah Castro b. 1 May 1750.
Lidea Castro b. 29 Aug 1752.
Sarah Castro b. 18 Apr 1736 (56?).
John Castro b. 24 Sep 1759.
Andrew Castro b. 14 Jan 1761.
David Castro b. 16 May 1762.
Jonathan Castro b. 23 May 1764.
Jeremiah Castro b. 3 Jul 1767.

William Castro b. 9 Jul 176.
Jacob Castro b. 11 Feb 1772.
Thomas Castro b. 25 Mar 1776.
Abijah Castro b. 28 May 1777.

William Castro, Jr, s/o John Castro, b. 9 Mar 1794 in Fairfield Township, Cumberland County, West New Jersey, 7 miles from Cohansey Bridge. "Wrote in Maysville, Mason County, Kentucky, 26 Feb 1816."

Thomas Castro Bible

Nancy Heritage b. 23 Oct 1780.
Thomas Castro and Nancy Heritage mar 11 Nov 1800.

Abijah Castro b. 31 Aug 1801 and d. 4 Jan 1803.
Firman Castro b. 1 Mar 1805.
Emilia Castro b. 1/11? Aug 1811.

Firman Castro and Emilia Cast (?) mar 7 Oct 1824.

Jonathan Castro, s/o Firman and Emilia Castro, b. Friday, 27 Jan, 1827.
Thomas Johnson Castro b. 3 May 1828.
William Castro b. Tuesday, 15 Jun, 1830 and d. 6 Jan 1835.
Aquilla Castro b. and d. 13 Feb 1832.
Druzilla Castro b. Wednesday, 18 Mar, 1833 and d. 22 Aug 1834.
James Madison Castro b. Wednesday, 15 Apr, and d. 18 Sep 1835
Nancy Jane Castro b. Tuesday, 21 Sep 1836.
Francis Marion Castro b. Wednesday, 19 Dec 1838.
George Washington Castro b. Wednesday, 19 Dec 1838.
Mary Elizabeth Castro b. Wednesday, 10 Mar 1841.
Sarah Ellenor Castro b. Monday, 14 Jun 1842.
Hannah Ann Castro b. Monday, 11 Mar 1845.
Saybreath Caroline Castro b. Sabbath, 7 Mar 1847 and d. Monday, 26 Nov 1849, at 7:00 p.m.
Cynthia Julia Emilia Castro b. 20 Sep 1849.
Ann Castro d. (no date given).

Clayton Bible
Daniel D. Smith, 1821

Joseph Clayton d. 10 Jan. 1864/9?
Susanna Clayton d. 6 Mar. 1864, aged 24 yrs,
Mary Clayton, w/o Joseph Clayton, d. 13 Apr. 1867.
Enoch Lard and Mary his wife mar 15 Jul 1807.
Richard and Nancy his wife mar 10 Jul 1819.
Levi Brown and Martha Jane Brown mar. 1 July 1862(?).
Joab and Sarah Clayton mar. 9 Sep. 1848.
Joab and Phebe Clayton mar. 2 Sep. 1866..
Enoch Lard b. 18 Aug. 1789.
Mary Lard b. 17 Aug. 1887.
Absolum Barret b. 23 Nov 1794.
Lecrecasa Barret b. 9 Feb 1797.
Jesse Barret b. 6? Jan 1800.
David Barret b. 17 Aug 1802.
Enoch L. Barret b. 12 Oct 1832/3?
Joab Clayton b. 9 Jul 1821.
Phebe Clayton, w/o Joab, b. 3 Dec 1833
Sarah Clayton b. 10 Sep 1827.
Martha Jane Clayton b. 24 Apr 1842.
Rejoyse Dtilton (?) b. 18 Jun 1847.
Daniel J. Clayton b. 23 Jul 1849.
Mary Clayton b. 15 Jan 1852.
Nichless Clayton b. 12 Sep 1854.
Richard Clayton b. 15 Jan 1857.
Enoch Barret b. 16 Aug 1861.
Hanah M. Clayton b. 6 Mar 1863.
Enoch Lard b. 18 Aug 1789.
Mary Lard b. 17 Aug 1787.
Phebe Barret d. 12 Apr 1812.
Enoch Barret d. 2 May 1814, aged 53-18-14.
Mary Clayton, w/o Joab Clayton, d. 14 Jan 1847.
ReJoyse De Deset d. 1 Mar 1852.
Mary Clayton, d/o Joab and Sarah Clayton, d. 21 Oct. 1854.
Lucretia Kendel d. 21 Mar. 1857, aged 59-1-12.
Richard Barrett d. 18 May 1859.
Mary Lard, d/o Enoch and Phebe Barrit, d. 5 Jan. 1861, 71-4-18..
Enoch Lard d. 25 Dec. 1863, aged 74-4-7.
Sarah Clayton, w/o Joab Clayton, d. 27 Mar. 1866.

Nicholas Clayton d. 6 Aug. 1871.
Aunt Lib d. 18 July 1887.
Martha Jane Brown b. 10 Jan. 1888.
Phebe J. Clayton d. 6 Mar. 1903/4?
Joab Clayton d. 9 May 1906, aged 84 yrs., 10 mo.

Cook Bible

Uriah Bacon Cook, s/o David and Mary Cook, b. 19 Jul 1796.
Sarah B. Cook b. 22 Oct 1798.
Deborah Cook b. 2 Nov 1800.
Mary B. Cook b. 2 Feb 1803.
David Cook b. 28 Mar 1805.
Joseph B. Cook b. 9 Apr 1807.
James B. Cook b. 30 Jun 1809.
Phebe Cook b. 24 Jan 1812.
Hannah B. Cook b. 28 May 1814.
William Loree Cook b. 4 Dec 1816.
Rachel Cook b. 18 Mar 1844

Hannah B. Cook d. 14 Oct 1844.

McPherson Bible
Printed 1814

Rachel Russell, d/o William and Phebe Russell, b. 29 Jul 1740.
Ashbery Maul b. 21 Jan 1765.
Lydia Mall b. 22 May 1771.
Thomas Waithman, s/o John and Lydia Waithman, b. 4 Feb 1788.
Rachel Waithman, d/o John and Lydia Waithman, b. 26 Nov 1791. Her dau
    Lydia was b. 20 Feb 1814.

Ruth McPherson, d/o Job and Rachel McPherson, b. 9 Oct 1816.
Elizabeth Watson McPherson b. 17 Mar 1818.
Mara W. Wildin, d/o Jeremiah and Lydia Wildin, b. 19 Jan 1835.

Job Mc Pherson and Rachel Waithman mar 18 Sep 1815.
Jeremiah Wildin and Lydia Y. Waithman mar 8 May 1834.

Lydia Waithman d. 3 Nov 1795.
Rachel Morgan d. 10 Feb 1824.
John Waithman d. 4 Mar 1825.
Thomas Waithman d. 16 Jul 1825.

Moore Family Notes
T. Wright & W. Gill, Oxford 1779

Hannah Moore b. Sept 1778, in Staten. A full cousin of James Moore of Woodbridge, NJ, who migrated to Herkimer Co, NY, in 1803.

William G. Moore, s/o James Moore , b. Woodbridge, NJ, 11 Aug 1801.

Manning Bible, 1836

Richard Manning b. 22 May 1791.
Sarah Shotwell b. 16 Oct 1802.
Richard Manning and Sarah Shotwell mar 13 Nov 1823
Anna Manning b. 18 Oct 1824.
Betsey S. Manning b. 5 Oct 1826.
Mary L. Manning b. 3 Aug 1832.
Emma Bethiah Manning b. 4 Aug 1840.

John V. Hulick b. 23 May ____.

Anna Manning mar John V. Hulick 5 Feb 1857.

Henry V. Line b. 23 May 1833.

Mary L. Manning mar Henry V. Line 9 Jan 1856.

Ralph Shotwell b. 6 Nov 1773.
Betsey Marsh b. 24 Aug 1776.

William Marsh Shotwell b. 20 Aug 1800.
Sarah Shotwell b. 16 Oct 1802.
Jacob Shotwell b. 2 Nov 1804.
Bathsheba Shotwell b. 14 Jul 1807.
William Marsh Shotwell b. 24 Jul 1809.

Mary Shotwell b. 18 Aug 1810.
John T. Shotwell b. 17 Aug 1813.
Betsey Shotwell b. 19 Sep 1815.
Ann Shotwell b. 4 Oct 1818.
David Shotwell b. 20 Nov 1820.

Hosea Tingley b. 25 Aug 1788.

Sarah Shotwell mar Richard Manning 13 Nov 1823.
Jacob Shotwell mar Dorcas Drake 29 Dec 1825.
Bathsheba Shotwell mar Isaac Line 10 Aug 1828.
Mary Shotwell mar Smith Line 25 Aug 1832.
Ralph Shotwell mar Hosea Tingley 14 Oct 1812.
Betsey Shotwell mar James M. Bulman 20 Apr 1836.
Ann Shotwell mar Alfred Berry.
David Shotwell mar Permelia Clark.

William Marsh Shotwell d. 6 Aug 1805.
William Marsh Shotwell d. 22 Nov 1809.
Betsey Shotwell d. May 1812.
Ralph Shotwell d. 4 Sep 1826.
Mary Line d. 31 Mar 1838.
Bathsheba Shotwell d. 2 July 1857.
Richard Manning d. 29 June 1860.
Sarah Shotwell d. 29 Apr. 1883.
Betsey S. Manning d. 12 Nov. 1899.
Emma B. Manning d. 23 Aug. 1912.

Powell Records

Obadiah Powell (g-grandfather) b. 16 May 1839 and d. 1839.
Obadiah Powell (grandfather) b. 18 Nov 1791 and d. 3 Jul 1850.
Moses Powell (father) b. 25 Aug 1812 and d.14 Dec. 1894.
Louisa M. Sweet (mother) b. 22 Feb 1816 and d. 24 Dec. 1894.
Phillip J. Powell (uncle) b. 14 Apr 1822 and d. 1861.
Ardon K. Powell (brother) b. 8 Aug 1841 and d. 22 Dec. 1926.
Adoniram J. Powell (brother) b.7 Dec 1845 and d. 29 Feb. 1894.

Adoniram J. Powell mar. Josie W. Monroe 25 May 1875.
Louisa M. Powell mar. Chas. H. Leassler.

J. C. Powell mar. M. E. Van Buren 16 May 1883, at Grinwoldville, Jones Co.,
    Ga.
J. C. Powell mar. Isabell Theall 28 Aug. 1895, Newburgh, N. Y.

Josie W. Monroe d. 20 May 1883.

Everett Judson Powell, s/o A. J. and J. W. Powell, b. 8 June 1882.
Marion W. Powell b. 12 June 1891.
Louisa M. Powell, d/o A. J. and J. W. Powell, b. 13 Mar. 1876.
James Correggio Powell b. 2 Jun 1849, Stillwater, Saratoga Co, NY.
Mary Elizabeth Van Buren b. 11 Feb 1853, Stillwater, Saratoga Co, NY.

Lebbeus Sweet b. 28 Feb 1808.
Catherin Sweet b. 25 Jun 1812.
Elvira Sweet b. 16 Apr 1814.
Louisa Maria Sweet b. 22 Feb 1816.
Jno. M. Sweet b. 26 Jan 1822.
Delia Sweet b. 15 Apr. 1852.
Libbie Van Buren Powell d. 24 Nov. 1888, aged 35-9-13.

Pierson Bible

In a chest discovered in the former Pierson Property in Erma, now the property
    of Frank Dickinson, an old commentary of the New Testament was found,
    the text being the work of Matthew Henry, whose principle work was done
    in 1710. He died in 1714. At the end of St. Matthew's Gospel a
    genealogical record of great value is written on an unfinished page.

Stephen Pierson, Sr, b. 1 Jan 1746.
Mary Pierson, his wife, b. 3 Mar 1746.

Ruth Pierson , d/o Stephen and Mary Pierson, b. 13 Apr 1765 and d. 10 Dec
    1776.
Ludlam Pierson b. 13 Jun 1767 and d. 1 Feb 1781.
Henry Pierson b. 1 Jan 1770.
William Pierson b. 16 Apr 1773.
Mary Pierson b. 14 Feb 1775.
Stephen Pierson, Jr, b. 2 Sep 1777.
Thomas Pierson b. 21 Nov 1779.
Nancy Pierson b. 7 Sep 1782.

John Bowen Pierson b. 25 Feb and d. 4 Sep 1784.
Ann Pierson b. 30 Aug 1786.

Smith Bible
Matthew Carey, Philadelphia, 1806

Hannah Smith presented this Bible to Samuel Smith on 13 Dec 1826.

Seth Smith, s/o Solomon and Sarah Smith, b. 5 May 1768.
Benjamin Smith b. 25 Aug 1770.
Sarah Smith b. 11 Nov 1772.
Elizabeth Smith b. 20 Oct 1774.
Charity Smith b. 13 Aug 1777.
Solomon Smith b. 3 Mar 1780.
Margaret Smith b. 13 Oct 1782.
William Smith b. 3 Mar 1785.
Abel Smith b. 21 May 1788.

Hannah Acton b. 17 May 1785.

William Smith and Hannah Acton mar 21 Mar 1807 at Salem, NJ, by John Firth,
     Justice of Peace.
Their children: Benjamin Smith b. 18 Dec 1807; Edward Smith b. 3 Mar 1811;
     Samuel Smith b. 15 Dec 1813.

Hannah Smith d. 15 Dec 1826.
William Smith d. 30 May 1825.

Stretch Bible

Front cover – "Samuel Stretch. Jonathan Bradway"
On the margin of a leaf (Exodus, 9-10) - "Luke Stretch 1783 Finis 1783 March
     ye 14 day".

Title page to New Testament - "1769, Edinburgh".
On its reverse – "Samuel Stretch departs this life the last (an F marked over the
     1) of month 1773".
Below is – "Samuel Stretch departed this life the first of the month 1773".

Title page for the Psalms of David in metre. On it's reverse – "Luke Stretch, his
   bible". "Luke Stretch, his book May ye 14 day ---- 1781". "Luke Stretch
   1783".

On back cover page – "Luke Stretch, his hand and pen 1781". "Sus Bradway".
   "Lyd".

Smith Bible
West & Richardson, Boston, 1818

Elijah Smith b. 7 Aug 1783.
Olive Deming b. 19 Oct 1786.
Married 20 Nov 1808.
Mary B. Smith b. 17 May 1811.
Eunice D. Smith b. 30 Mar 1813.
Emily M. Smith b. 1 Jun 1816.
Jane E. Smith b. 22 Apr 1818.
Wm. Elijah Smith b. 11 Dec 1822.
Alfred N. Smith b. 28 Sep 1825.

Samuel Bancroft b. 5 Jun 1810.

Samuel Bancroft and Mary B. Smith mar 15 May 1834.

Samuel Bancroft, Jr, b. 5 Feb 1835.

Buckley P. Heath and Eunice D. Smith mar 11 Feb 1838.

Jane E. Smith d. 17 Feb 1823.
Alfred N. Smith d. 18 Oct 1825.

Smith Family Bible
Philadelphia, 1808

John Smith b. 20 Dec 1796.
Rebecca Keen b. 13 Apr 1769.
Margaret Smith b. 6 Apr 1799.
Henry Smith d. 4 Oct 1798.

Rebecca Smith mar. John Keen as his 2nd wife.
Rebecca Riley mar. a Smith. John Keen was her 2nd husband. They had 3 dau. -
Rebecca, Eliza and Mary who mar. William Bryant. They had a dau.,
Emma Bryant.

Mary Sayre's Bible

David Sayre b. 3 Aug 1795.
Mary Kendal b. 9 Feb 1806.
David Sayre and Mary Kendal mar 2 Oct 1824.
Robert Sayre b. 24 Apr 1830.
Caroline Sayre b. 30 Sep 1831.
Ann Sayre b. 27 Oct 1833.
Edward Sayre b. 11 Sep 1835.
Henry Sayre b. 4 Apr 1839.
Margaret Sayre B. 1 Jul 841.
David Sayre, Jr, b. 18 Sep 1844.

Foster Sayre d. 23 May 1825, aged 2 mo.
Lorenzo Sayre d. 18 Aug 1828, aged 4 yrs.
John Sayre d. 20 Aug 1828, aged 1 yr.
Catherine Sayre d. 14 May 1838, aged 7 mo.
George Sayre d. 4 Sep 1847, aged 7 mo.
Robert Sayre drowned in the Cohansey River 3 Jul 1860.
David Sayre, Sr, d. 26 Apr 1876, aged 81 yrs.
Mary Sayre d. 26 Nov 1884, aged 78 yrs.

Caroline Sayre and Alfred Godfrey mar 24 Jan 1852.
Ann Sayre and Augustus Bradagan mar 25 Mar 1855.
Robert Sayre and Naomi Brooks mar Nov 1854.
Margaret Sayre and Jerome Young mar 13 Feb 1861.
David Sayre, Jr, and Annie Truitt mar 8 Mar 1874.
Henry Sayre and Phebe R. Tice mar 16 Mar 1882.

Peter Soullard, his Book, March ye 2_, 1751
Ruth Burgins Book, 1828

Will of Peter Soullard of Bridgeton, Cumberland County, 28 Aug 1776:

Wife Mary; son John; son Peter; daughter Elizabeth Foxe; daughter Mary
    Soullard; brother Elias Soullard.

Polly Soullard mar Josiah Parvin 30 Dec 1795.
John Soullard of Deerfield mar Hannah Mulford 4 Jan 1762.
John Soullard b. 1764, d. 17 Nov 1803.

Peter and Mary Soullard came to live in Cape May on April 19, 1750.
Peter Soullard mar. Mary Piate 20 Oct. 1738.
John, their son, b. ......

Mary, their dau., b. 21 Apr. 1740.

John Soullard, s/o Peter and Mary, mar. Hannah Mulford, 5 Jan. 1762.
Rachel, their dau., b. 16 Nov. 1762. bapt. Oct. following.
John, their son, b. 28 Nov. 1764, bapt. 5 Apr. 1768.

Townsend Bible
London, 1756

John Willis (?) b. 29 Oct 1695?
Martha his wife b. 20 Jul 1695?
James Willits b. 24 Oct mo, 1717?
Sarah Willits b. 14 Oct 1719?
Mary Willits b. 11 Jan 1721.
Jacob Willits b. 22 Jan 1724.
Isaac Willits b. 11 Oct 1727.
Hannah Willits b. 3 May 1730.
Rachel Willits b. 22 Apr 1737.

Isaac Townsend b. 10 Jun 1715.
Sarah his wife b. 14 Oct 1719.

We were married 6 Dec 1737/8 and our son Isaac T. was b. 27 Sep 1738.
Our daughter Hannah b. 22 Dec 1741?
Our daughter Lydia b. 23 Jul 1748.
Our son Mark b. 5 Oct (torn).

Mark Townsend b. 5 Oct 1750/56? and Elizabeth his wife was b. 20 Sep 1757.
Our daughter Hannah Tond. b. 17 Aug 1778.

Our son Jacob b. 7 Dec 1780.
Our son Mark b. 9 Apr 1783.
Our daughter Elizabeth b. 13 Nov 1786.
Our daughter Rebeckah Townd. b. 18 May 1789.
Our daughter Lydia Townd b. 16 Jan 1792.

Isaac Townsend, ye 1st, d. 25 Feb 1788, aged 74 years.
Isaac Townsend, Jr, d. 1 Jan 1780.
Hannah Willis d. 12 Jun 1793.
Lydia Townsend d. 16 Oct 1793.
Lydia Townsend, d/o Mark and Elizabeth Townsend, b. 27 Sep 1794 _____.
    (?)
Sarah Townsend, widow of Isaac Townsend, d. 24 Apr 1796, in her 77th yr.
Hannah Grigory d. 31 Sep 1794.
Jacob Townsend, s/o Mark and Elizabeth Townsend, d. 1 Mar 1797, in his 17th
    yr.
Sarah Townsend, d/o Mark and Elizabeth Townsend, b. 23 Aug 1797.
Ruth Townsend, d/o Mark and Elizabeth Townsend, b. 11 Dec 1801.

Our daughter Hannah mar. Rheuben Hilliard 5 Mar 1801.
Mary Hilliard, d/o Rheuben and Hannah Hilliard, b. 22 Feb 1809.

Mark Townsend d. 11 Aug 1811, aged nr 55 yrs.
Elizabeth Swain, widow of Mark Townsend, d. 10 Oct 1813, aged 56 yrs and 20
    dys.
Sarah Townsend, w/o Mark Townsend, d. 20 Jun 1842, in her 58th (?) yr.
Mark Townsend d. 25 Jan 1844, in his 61st yr.

Mark Townsend, s/o Mark and Elizabeth, b. 9 Apr 1783.
Sarah Townsend, formerly Bradway, w/o Mark Townsend, b. 23 Nov 1789.

Mark Townsend and Sarah Bradway mar 17 Nov 1808.

Aaron B. Townsend, s/o Mark and Sarah Townsend, b. 12 Oct 1809.
Hannah Ann Townsend, d/o Mark and Sarah Townsend, b. 7 Jul 1811.
Our son Mark b. 22 Jan 1816.
David B. Townsend, s/o Mark and Sarah Townsend, b. 10 Nov 1819 and d. 16
    Jul month, 1820, aged 8 mo, 5 dys.
Elizabeth Townsend, d/o Mark and Sarah Townsend, b. 21 Jul 1820.
Our daughter Sarah B. b. 4 Feb 1823.
Our daughter Elizabeth d. 18 Sep 1823, aged 3 yrs and nr 2 months.

Josiah Townsend, s/o Mark and Sarah Townsend, b. 11 Jul 1827.
Hannah Ann Townsend d. 7 Oct 1818, aged 7 yrs, 3 mo.

Rebeckah Townsend d. 29 Feb 1812, aged 22 yrs and 9 mo.
Ellwood Evans d. 6 May 1831

Permilia Edwards, d/o Jacob and Ann Edwards, b. 31 May 1838.
Rachel Garrison b. 16 Oct 1822.

Mark Townsend, Jr, and Rachel Garrison mar 25 Jul 1840.
Their children: William Harrison Townsend b. 25 Sep 1841; Sarah B. Townsend
    b. 27 Feb 1843; Mark Townsend b. 13 Jan 1845; Ruth J. Townsend b. 13
    Aug 1847; Josiah Townsend b. 10 May 1849 and d. 12 Aug 1850, aged 10
    mo, 7 dys.

Rachel Townsend d. 16 Aug 1850, aged 28 yrs, 10 mo.
Ruth G. (?) Townsend, d/o Mark and Rachel Townsend, d. 1853, aged 5-8-4.
The s/o Mark and Sarah Townsend d. 23 Sep 1853.
Sarah Townsend , w/o Mark Townsend, d. 16 Aug 1889, in her 76th yr, lacking
    one day.
Mark Townsend d. 18 Nov 1899, aged 83-9-20.

Ebenezer Miller b. 15 Sep 1725.
Ruth Wood b. 16 Jan 1732.

Ebenezer Miller and Ruth Wood mar 15 Sep 1751, old stile.
Their children: Hannah Miller b. 14 Apr 1753, NS, about 9th hour in the
    morning; Ebenezer Miller b. 18 Jan 1761, about 11 pm and d. 16 of the
    month following, about sun setting; Priscilla Miller b. 9 Jul 1763, about 11
    pm.

Mark Townsend, s/o Mark and Rachel Townsend, b.3an. 1845 and d. 19 Jul.
    1913, in his 68th yr.
Phebe B. Townsend, d/o Jemarah and Mary Blissard. d. 5 Nov. 1920.
Mary B. Townsend b. 2/21/61.
Walter B. Townsend b. 8/22/62.
Mark Townsend, of D. C., and Phebe B. Blissard, of Halleyville, mar. in 1864.

David Bradway, s/o Edward and Elizabeth Bradway, b. 27 Jan 1761.
Hannah Bradway, d/o Aaron and Sarah Bradway, b. 30 Mar 1764.
They married 6 May 1788.

Their children: Sarah Bradway b. 23 Nov 1789; Edward Bradway b. 1 May
1791 and d. 14 Sep 1792; Ann Bradway b. 20 Sep 1793 and d. 1 Dec 1793;
Tacy Bradway b. 20 Sep 1794; Joshua Bradway b. 21 Feb 1797; David
Bradway b. 26 Aug 1799; Aaron Bradway b. 27 Jun 1801.

Hannah Bradway, w/o D. Bradway, d. 8-4 mo 12 (???), aged 30 or 38 yrs and
16 dys.
Aaron Bradway d. 29 Aug 1804.

David Bradway mar Rebecca Jeffries 29 Aug 1804.
Hannah Bradway b. 15 Nov 1805 and d. 15 Jan 1806.
Rebecca, w/o David Bradway, d. 12 Mar 1806.
David Bradway and Hannah Fogg mar 30 Dec 1807.
Josiah Bradway b. 21(?) Feb 1812 and d. 7 Sep 1812.
David Bradway d. 28 Dec 1820, aged 59-1-1.
Joshua Bradway d. 4 Jan 1823, aged 25-10-13.

On a separate piece of paper:
Mark Townsend and wife Elis4
John Willis, wife Martha3 1725
Mark Townsend, wife Elizabeth 1730
Mark Townsend, wife Sarah Bradway 1809
William Harrison Townsend, Rachel 1843
Joseph Townsend, s/o Rachel
Sara Townsend d. 16 Aug 1886, in her 76th yr.

Taylor – St Aubert Utter Bible

Solomon Taylor b. 1 May 1755.
Mary Shaw b. 1 Jan 1748.
Priscilla Taylor b. 10 May 1755.
Maria Taylor b. 12 Feb 1780
Solomon Taylor, Jr, b. 28 Aug 1782.
Electa Taylor b. 26 Jan 1785.
Dorothe Taylor b. 14 Aug 1788.
Edmund Taylor b. 21 Jun 1792.
Sidney C. Hempsted b. 20 Jun 1804.

Solomon Taylor d. 22 Dec 1809.
Mary Taylor d. 21 Sep 1824.

Edmund Taylor d. 25 May 1793.
Dorothy Utter d. 8 Dec 1833.
Electa Taylor d. 4 May 1854.

William Webb Bible

William Webb and Elizabeth Sawquill mar. ....
William Webb, s/o William Webb and Elizabeth Sawquill, mar. Elizabeth
    Morss, dau. of Jonas and Abigail Morss, 13 May 1816.
Mary Webb, d/o William and Elizabeth Webb, mar. William Clark, s/o David
    and Susan Clark.
Jonas Webb, s/o William and Elizabeth Webb, mar. Elizabeth Johnson, d/o
    William and Rebecca Johnson.
Nathaniel H. Webb, s/o William and Elizabeth Webb, mar. Mary L. Johnson,
    d/o William and Rebecca Johnson.
Hannah Webb, d/o William and Elizabeth Webb, mar. John Leeds, s/o Andrew
    and Armenia Leeds.
Elizabeth Webb, d/o William and Elizabeth Webb, mar. Samuel R. Midleton,
    s/o Jesse and Mary Midleton, 18 Apr. 1852.
Abby Webb, d/o William and Elizabeth Webb, mar. James Leeds, s/o Andrew
    and Armenia Leeds.
Rachel Webb, d/o William and Elizabeth Webb, mar. ......

Children of William and Elizabeth Webb: Sylvester Webb b. 10 Feb. 1785;
    Rachel Webb b. 19 Sep. 1786; Mary Webb b. 5 Feb. 1789; William Webb
    b. 28 Jan. 1791; Elizabeth Webb b. 14 Jan. 1793; Elener Webb 11 Feb.
    1795; Jacob Webb b. 13 ..... 1797; Rosel Deputy Webb b. 30 Sep. 1799;
    Silvester Webb b. 24 Feb. 1802; Rebeca Webb b. 7 Mar. 1804; John Webb
    b. 7 Aug. 1807; Hannah Webb b. 17 July 1809; Isaac Webb b. 7 Sep. 1810;
    Gideon Webb b. 22 Nov. 1812.

Nuel Johnson, s/o James and Elizabeth Johnson, b. 4 Oct. 1813.
Nathaniel Johnson, s/o James and Elizabeth Johnson, b. 6 Apr. 1816.

Elizabeth Webb, w/o William, d. 22 July ....., aged 73-4-17.
William Webb d. 14 Feb. 1846, aged 99 yrs, 1 dy.

Children of Richard and Mary Robins: Elizabeth Robins b. 15 Mar. 1805; Sarah
    Robins b. 9 July 1807; Tempy Robins b. 5 Mar. 1809.

24 Mar. 1810, Elizabeth, Sarah and Tempe, all three, were taken off by a remarkable and lamentable stroke of fire.

William Webb, Sr., Bible

William Webb, Sr., b. 13 Feb. 1747, d. 14 Feb. ......, aged 99 yrs. and 1 dy. old. He mar. Elizabeth Suaquill, of Sweden, who d. at the age of 75-5-15. His brother, Sylvester Webb b. 18 Feb. 1758.

Rachel Webb, b. 19 Sep. 1786, mar. James Dennight.

Mary Webb, b. 5 Feb. 1789, mar. Richard Robbins.

William Webb, Jr., b. 28 Jan. 1791 and d. 12 Dec. 1880. He mar. (1st) 13 May 1816, Elizabeth Morse, d/o Jonas and Abigail (Smith) Morse (Morss), b. 14 May 1788 and d. 31 Oct. 1857.

Elizabeth M. Webb, b. 14 Jan. 1783.

Elener Webb, b. 17 Feb. 1795.

Jacob Webb, b. 13 Mar. 1797.

Rosel Webb, b. 30 Sep. 1799.

Silvester Webb b. 24 Feb. 1802.

Rebeca Webb b. 7 Mar. 1804 and mar. John Collins.

John Webb b. 7 Aug. 1807 and mar. Maria Marsh.

Hannah Webb b. 17 July 1809.

Isaac Webb b. 7 Sep. 1810.

Gideon Webb b. 22 Nov. 1812.

INDEX

Phebe Smith, 9, 10
Thomas, 9
William, 9
ARRELL
Mary, 85
William, 85
ASHMEAD
L. and Company, 55
ASHTON
Ann, 64
ATKINSON
Abigail, 59
Benajah, 59
Clayton C., 59, 60
Elizabeth, 42
John, 59, 60
John C., 59
Joshua E., 59
Mary, 59, 60
ATLANTIC CITY, NJ,
90
AUSTIN
Ann, 12
Ann Lloyd, 12
Edward, 6, 11, 12
Hannah, 11, 12
Henry W., 12
John W., 12
Lydia, 6, 11, 12
Margaret W., 12
Mary Ann, 12
Mary Ann Weber, 12
Mary Augusta, 12
Rebecca, 12
Samuel, 6, 11, 12
Sarah, 6, 11, 12
Sarah Ambler, 12
William, 12
William W., 12

AVIS
Edward Dubois, 99
Emma M., 99
Hannah, 127
Hannah Louise, 100
Harriet Melvina, 100
Levi Janvier, 99
Mary Emma, 100
Neal Dow, 100
Sarah A., 99
Sarah Frances, 99
Theodore Cuyler, 100
William, 99
AVOS
Hannah J. Holton, 94
AXTON
Amea, 15
Elizabeth, 15
Jonathan, 15
AYARS
Clemmans P., 13
Edmund, 13
Elmer, 13
Elmina, 13, 41
Esther, 13
Esther D., 13
Ezekiel J., 13
Joseph, 13
Lydia, 13
Margaret, 13
Phebe, 90
Robeson, 13
AYERS
Clemmans P.l, 13
Elmer, 13
Esther D., 13
Lydia D., 13
Rebecca J., 13
AYRS
Esther, 141

BACON
Benjamin, 8
Beulah, 8
Charles, 8
Ennoch Allen, 8
Rachel, 8
Rebecca, 8
BAFSETT
Sarah, 35
BAIRD
S.J., Rev., 71
BAKER
George M., 2
Ruth, 2
Ruth S., 2, 3
BALLINGER
Benjamin, 100
Elizabeth, 95, 96,
97, 100
Henry, 96
Hope, 100
Isaac, 96, 100
J.G., 96
Jacob, 100
John G., 96, 97
John Goff, 96
John Groff, 97
John R,, 89
Joshua, 96, 100
Josiah, 100
Mary, 96, 97, 100
Mary Edwards, 96
Mary Ellen, 97
Mary Jane, 96
Mary Shin, 95
Naomi, 100
Reuben, 96
Richard Clark, 97
Samuel, 95, 96
Samuel E., 97
Sarah Ann, 96, 97

190

James, 161
Lydia, 161
CASTRO
Abel, 168
Abijah, 169
Andrew, 168
Ann, 169
Aquilla, 169
Azariah, 168
Cynthia Julia Emilia, 169
David, 168
Druzilla, 169
Elizabeth, 168
Emilia, 169
Firman, 169
Francis Marion, 169
George Washington, 169
Hannah Ann, 169
Jacob, 169
James Madison, 169
Jeremiah, 168
John, 168, 169
Jonathan, 168, 169
Lidea, 168
Mary Elizabeth, 169
Nancy Jane, 169
Purthenia, 168
Sarah, 168
Sarah Ellenor, 169
Saybreath Caroline, 169
Thomas, 169
Thomas Johnson, 169
William, 168, 169
CATHCART
William, 161
CATTELL
Sarah Gilmore, 65
Thomas W., 65

CAVMER
Ann, 70
CAXTON
William, Rev., 72
CECIL COUNTY, MD, 65
CENTRALIA, OK, 84
CHAMBER STREET, NEW YORK CITY, 86
CHAMBERS
Charles, 133
Mary, 58
CHAMPNEYS
Benjamin, 113, 114
Elizabeth, 113
John, 113, 114
Joseph, 113, 114
Rebecca, 113, 114
Sarah, 113
CHARD
Eliza, 95
CHATTEN
Hannah, 20
James, 20
Nixon, 20
William Penn, 20
CHATTIN
Anne, 20
Arabella S., 21
Bernice, 20
Daniel Jones, 20
Elizabeth, 20
Georgianna, 20
Hannah, 20, 21
Hannah Maria, 21
James, 20, 21
James Allinson, 20
John, 20
Montezuma, 20
Rachel, 20

Rebecca, 20, 21
Rebecca Ann, 20
Sarah Maria, 20
William James, 21
William P., 21
William Penn, 20
CHEESMAN
Hope, 14
CHESTER TWP, 7
CHEW
Arabella S., 21
Charles H., 21
Edward, 21
Henrietta, 21
Jesse, 21
Jessey, 21
Joseph K., 21
Joseph R., 21
Keziah, 21
Maria, 21
Mary, 21
Mary A., 21
Sinnickson, 21
CHISPEN
Sarah Jane, 120
CHRIST CHURCH AND ST. PETER'S, 86
CHURCHTOWN, NJ, 51
CINCINNATI, OH, 81, 84
CLARK
Ann, 26
Cornelius, 26
David, 89, 151, 182
Elizabeth, 26, 27, 71
Elizabeth Woolman, 130
Jane, 150

Sarah Ann, 33
Walter, 33
Walter D., 33
GUARWARD
Ann, 8
GUINN
Eadeth, 113
GUNDY
Elmer Stanley, 166
HAAS
Mary, 162
HABERMEYER
Anna Belden, 19
HADDONFIELD, 2
HAINES
Ann, 8
Elizabeth, 8
Mary, 61
William, 8
HALL
Ann, 34, 35, 36, 52,
74, 138
Benjamin S., 138
Benjamin Seeley, 138
Charlotte, 34, 74
Clement, 34, 35,
53, 74, 137, 138
David, 35
Deborah Kay, 74, 138
Edward, 36
Elizabeth, 35, 36, 137
Hannah, 5, 36
Isaac Kay, 34
Issac Kay, 74
Jane S., 138
John, 35, 36, 137,
138
John G., 138
Joseph, 34, 74,
137, 138
Josiah, 36

Lewis M., 35
Lydia, 35
Margaret, 34, 74,
138
Margaret H., 138
Margaret Morris, 34,
74
Margert M., 138
Margret, 137
Mary, 35, 36
Morris, 34, 35, 74,
137, 138
Nathaniel, 35, 36
Prudence, 34, 74, 137,
138
Rebecca, 34, 74,
138
Rebecca K., 73
Rebecca Kay, 34, 138
Rhoda, 34, 74
Samuel, 36
Sarah, 14, 34, 35,
74, 85, 137, 138
Stephen, 36
Susannah, 35
Thomas, 35
William, 5, 35, 36
HALLOWS PARISH,
93
HALSEY
Abigail, 34
Charity, 34
Charles Fithian, 34
Hannah, 34
Jesse, 33, 34
Kitturah, 33
Kiturah, 34
Sarah, 34
HALTON
John, 119
Mary, 119

Thomas, 119
HANCE
Anne, 28
HANCOCK
Abigail, 121
Ann, 63, 103, 121,
122
Benjamin, 103, 121,
122
Claaricy, 63
Clarissa, 121
Cornelia, 144
Daniel P., 103, 122
David, 121
Edward, 62, 63, 103,
121, 122
Elanor, 36
Eleanor, 38, 77, 82
Eleanor C., 37
Eleanor Caroline, 36,
82
Elizabeth, 103, 121,
122
Elizabeth Ann, 63,
121
Elizabeth Goodwin,
32
Elizabeth N., 144
Ellen Maria, 144
Gilbert, 103, 122
Hannah, 103, 121,
122
Henrietta Elizabeth,
36, 38, 84
John, 36, 37, 77,
82, 84, 103, 122
John F., 63
Joseph, 121
Mary, 32, 34, 36, 37,
77, 82, 84, 103, 121,
122

Elizabeth, 135
Esther, 136
Ezra, 110, 111
Hannah, 135
Hannah Ann, 110
Jane, 40, 136
Jane Smith, 136, 138
John, 41, 110, 111,
135, 136
John G., 136, 138
John Gibbon, 136
Margaret, 136, 138
Mary, 41, 110, 111
Rachel, 135
Samuel, 110, 111
HOLMES
Hannah Potter, 151
John, 111, 150, 151
Lewis Bush, 151
Mary Clark, 151
Mary P., 151
Sarah Ogden, 59
HOLTON
Bella May, 93
Carrie Vanneman, 93
Ella Kitturah, 93
Ellen M., 93, 94
Hannah, 94
John, 93
Mary, 93
Samuel B., 94
Samuel Borden, 94
HOOFMAN
Mary Ann, 58
HOOVER
Hannah, 29
HOPEWELL, 45
HORNER
Hannah, 49
HORTON
Hannah, 93

Hannah Jane, 93
Harriet Amanda, 93
Mary, 93
R.H., Rev., 84
Samuel, 93
Samuel Borden, 93
HOTCHKISS
B.B, Rev., 151
HOTCKIN
Rev. Mr., 152
HOUSE
Anna, 40
Elmina, 41
Frances Blackwood,
41
George, 41
Jacob, 41, 111
Jonathan, 41
Margaret, 40
Mary, 41
Sarah, 41
William, 40, 41
HOUSEMAN
Elmina, 41
John, 41
Jonathan, 40, 41
Mariam, 41
HOWARD
Joseph, 113
HOWELL
Clarissa, 74
Ebenezer, 74
Harrriet, 73
Mary A., 74
Mary C., 72
Sara Ann, 166
William W., 166
HOWEY
Anna, 59
HUDDY
Syndonia, 47

HUFF
Bertha Marie, 166
Elizabeth Jane, 160
Isaac, 160, 166
Isaac D., 159
Isaac Doty, 160, 166
Maria, 160
Sarahann, 160
HULICK
Abbyhale, 41
Abihall, 42
Ann, 41, 42
Cornelius, 41, 42
George, 41, 42
Hannah Porter, 41, 42
Jacob, 41
John V., 172
Mahalah, 41
Mahalath, 42
Margaret, 41
Mary, 41
HULINGS
Abraham, 86
Priscilla, 86
HUNT
James B., 53, 54
Lydia R., 53, 54
William M., 53, 54
HURLEY
Elizabeth B., 61
HUSTED
Caroline Taylor, 147
Henry, 158
Mary, 147
HUTCHINSON
Ann, 139
HUTHUISON AND
DWIER, 52
INGHAM
Harriet, 73
Jonathan, 73

IRICK
General, 166
Job, 166
John, 166
Mary, 166
JAGGERS
Artillia, 150
Attillia, 151
Benjamin, 150, 151
David, 150, 151
Deborah, 150
Jane Clark, 151
Joseph, 150
Joseph F., 151
Louisa Burch, 151
Louisa Bush, 151
Lucy Ann, 150
Martha, 150
Martha Bush, 151
Mary, 150, 151
Mary B., 150
Mary W., 151
Mary Westcott, 151
Violetta, 150
JAMES
Hetty H., 52
Mary, 52
Mary H., 52
Rebecca, 4
Samuel L., 52
Uncle, 52
JANVIER
G.W., 114
G.W., Rev., 66
George W, Rev., 19
Rev. Mr., 66
JAQUETTE
Henrietta G.S., 84
William Alderman, 84
JEFFRIES
Rebecca, 181

Sarah, 4
JERSEY CITY, NJ, 95
JOHNSON
Abraham, 141
Adaline, 131
Amelia, 131
Ann, 12, 43
Benjamin, 131
Catherine, 43
Christianna, 131
Edward D., 26, 27
Elizabeth, 43, 131,
141, 182
Elizabeth Taylor, 27
Emma Ann, 131
Esther, 131
Harrison, 66
Isaac, 43, 131, 133
Isabella, 43
James, 131, 182
James Dallas, 72
John, 71, 131
Joseph, 131
Margaret, 72
Margaret Morgan, 73
Martha, 131
Mary, 131, 133
Mary E., 131
Mary L., 182
Matilda, 131
Mayhew, 43
Nancy, 43
Nathaniel, 182
Nuel, 182
Rebecca, 131, 182
Rhoda S.E., 27
Robert, 72, 73
Robert G., 72
Samuel, 43, 131
Samuel M., 43
Sarah, 131

Sarah T., 142
Sauyberry, 131
Susan, 134
Thomas, 131
William, 131, 182
JONES
Charles, 43
Elizabeth, 6, 42,
43
Elizabeth C., 43
Hannah T., 42
Jeremiah, 50
Jesse, 42, 43
Jonathan, 42
Mary, 42
Owen, 6, 42, 43
Owen L., 43
Rebecca, 50
Sarah, 6, 42, 43
Susanna L., 50
Thomas, 50
William, 42, 50
KAY
Ann, 34, 74
Joseph, 34, 74
Rebecca, 34, 74, 138
KEASBY
Ann, 45
Anthony, 44, 45
Artemefia, 45
Artemefis, 45
Bradway, 44, 60
Dezil, 44
Edward, 43, 44
Edward Quinton, 45
Elizabeth, 44
Hannah, 44, 45
Hannah Foster, 45
Jane, 44
Jesfe, 44
Kezia, 44

218

Phillip J., 173
Rebecah, 140
Rebecca, 141
Richard, 147
William, 147
POWERS
Emily S., 123
PRESBYTERIAN
CHURCH, 19
PRESCOTT
Edward G., Rev., 51,
80
Edward Goldsburg,
Rev., 76
PRESTON
Abagail, 147
Freelove, 147
Isaac, 147
John, 147
Levi, 147
Martha, 147
Mary, 147
PRIOR
Lavinia D., 18, 19
QUACKENBUSH
Mattie, 156
QUINTON
Edward, 44
Prudence, 44
Sarah, 44
Temperance, 44
QUINTON, NJ, 39, 90
RAMBO
Sarah, 103
RAMSEY
Amelia, 64
John, 139
RANDOLPH
Asa, 140
Elizabeth, 72
RAUB

Catherine, 168

RAY
Benjamin, 131
Johnson, 131, 132
Samuel, 131
Sarah, 104
William, 131
Zaccheus, 131
READ
Mary, 23
REDSTREAKE
Sarah, 23
Sarah S., 23
REED
Aubrey, 116
Aubrey C., 117
Blanch L., 117
Caroline H., 117
Elija, 159
Eliza, 117
Elizabeth C., 116, 117
Ethel K., 117
Evaline D., 116, 117
Georgianna, 116
James, 106
James Aubrey, 117
James M., 116, 117
Louisa W., 117
Mary, 117
Matlock, 116
Matlock R., 117
Miranda, 159, 160
R. Matlock, 117
Sally, 159
Victory L.W., 116
REEVES
Arthur, 106
David, 52
Hetty, 52
Mary, 99, 106
Sarah, 97
Stephen, 97

Naomi E., 100
Peter, 139
Richard P., 100
Robert, 100, 101, 117,
  118
Samuel, 117, 139
Susannah, 117
Thomas, 118
William, 117
SPROGELLS
Ludonick, 79
STANLEY
Mary, 89
STEEPER
Christopher, 113
Clarence M., 113
STEIN
Abigail, 147
STEINMETZ
Annalyze, 166
STEPHENSON
C.S., Rev., 84
STETSON
Martha, 103
STILES
Margaret, 20
STINSON
Charles G., 113
STOCKTON, MO, 83
STOTTSENBERG
Enoch C., 61
STOTTSENBURG
Isabell, 61
STOUGHTON
Augustus Bissell, 76
Cylinda Bissell, 76
Mary S., 76
Mary Sinnickson, 76
Oliver B., 76
Olivor B., 76

STRAHAM
Andrew, 15
STRATTON, 36
Abagail, 148
Abigail, 149
Alexander, 148
Arabel, 83
Benjamin, 147, 148,
  149
Charles Preston, 148
Daniel, 37, 82, 83,
  84, 85
Daniel P., 37,
  83, 84, 148
Daniel, Rev., 18, 19,
  38
Edgar, 148
Eleanor, 149
Eleanor C., 37
Eleanor Caroline, 38,
  85
Eleanor H., 84
Eleanor Hancock, 37,
  83
Eleanor Leake, 148
Eleanor Yorke, 37, 83
Elizabeth, 148
Ellen C., 37, 38, 83,
  84
Freelove, 148
George, 148
Gilbert, 148
Henrietta Gibson, 83
Henry, 37, 83, 148
Jane, 148
Jessie T., 84
John, 148, 149
John Quinton, 37
Jonathan, 148
Jonathan D., 27

Joseph, 28
Joseph Barnes, 83, 84
Joseph Buck, 148
Levi, 148
Morris H., 37, 38,
  83, 84
Morris Hancock, 37,
  83
Nathan, 148
Nathan L., 148
Preston, 148
Rebecca Barnes, 83
Robert, 148
Sarah, 27
Sophia Neal, 148
Thomazine, 148
William L., 27
STRAUGHAN
Ann, 41
STREEPER
Alinda Louise, 114
Almarin Brooks, 114
Catherine, 114
Christopher, 114
Clarence Mulford,
  114
Mary, 114
Rollins Foster, 114
STREET
Ann Ogden, 59
Mary, 29, 78
STREETER
Elvira, 159
STRETCH
David, 78
Elizabeth, 16, 19, 40,
  125
Hannah, 78
James, 16, 125
Joel, 78
Jonathan, 78

Luke, 175, 176
Mark, 40, 78
Mary, 53, 78
Nathaniel, 78
Rachel, 16
Samuel, 175
Sarah, 56
SUAQUILL
Elizabeth, 183
SUMMERILL
Elizabeth, 93, 94, 118
Furman, 118
Hannah, 93, 94, 118
Hannah Jane, 118
John, 118
Jonathan, 118
Joseph, 118, 119
Mary, 93, 118
Naomi, 118
Paul, 118
Rebecca, 118
Samuel, 118
Thomas, 93, 94,
  118, 119
Wiliam, 119
SUMNER AND
  GOODWIN, 100
SUTTON
Ann, 112
Margaret B., 112
William, 112
SWAIN
Elizabeth, 179
SWAN LAKE, SD, 69
SWEET
Catherin, 174
Delia, 174
Elvira, 174
Jno. M., 174
Lebbeus, 174
Louisa M., 173

Louisa Maria, 174
SWING
Abraham, 92
Christianna, 92
Hannah, 92
Jeremiah, 92
Jonathan, 91
Jonathan Luis, 92
Leonard, 92
Michael, Rev., 149
Nathaniel, 92
Rebecca McQueen, 91
Rev. Mr., 152
Ruth, 92
Ruth Lawrence, 92
Samuel, 92
Sarah, 92
TATNALL
Samuel A., 6
TAYLOR
Benjamin F., 147
Benjamin Franklin,
  146
Caroline, 146
Dorothe, 181
Edmund, 181, 182
Electa, 181, 182
Enoch, 26
Enos, 146
Ethan, 146
Harriet, 146
Harriet L., 147
Henry S., 147
Henry Sheppard, 146
Isaac Henry
  Williamson, 146
John E., 26, 27
John Newton, 146
Lydia, 149
Maria, 27, 181
Mary, 146, 181

Mary S., 146
Nancy Jane, 146
Priscilla, 153, 181
Rhoda S., 27
Rhoda S.E., 26
Rhoda Westcott, 146
Richard Pearson, 27
Sarah, 27, 152
Solomon, 181
William, 146
William Henry
  Harrison, 146
TEAL
Margaret, 94
THACKERY
Ruth, 161
THACKRAY
Sarah E., 43
THEALL
Isabell, 174
THOMAS
Rachel C., 14
THOMPSON
Aaron H., 109
Andrew, 23, 26,
  27, 43
Ann, 48
Ann D.C., 27
Ann F., 27
Anna, 27
Benjamin, 110, 111
Clark Holmes, 27
David A., 27, 48
Edith, 6, 109
Elizabeth, 29, 69,
  110, 111
Encie Louise, 167
Hannah, 110
Isaac, 69, 110
Jacob, 29
James, 69, 109

Mary, 132
VANLIER
Ann, 140
Michal, 140
VANMETER
Almira C., 91
VANMETER
Ann, 107, 108
Benjamin, 91, 107, 108
Edward, 19
Elizabeth, 108
Enoch, 108
Erasmus, 91
Hannah, 91
Hannah F., 45
Hannah McQueen, 91
Harriet, 108
Israil, 107
John, 108
John McQueen, 91
Margaret Jane, 66, 67
Mariah, 108
Marmaduke, 107, 108
Mary, 91
Nathan, 107
Rachel Moore, 107
Sara, 107
Sarah, 115
William, 107
VANNAMAN
Edith, 109
Hannah, 109
Martha, 109
VANNEMAN
Anna, 30, 31
Charles, 30, 31
Darcus, 102
Dorcas, 102
Elizabeth, 102
George, 30

Hannah, 101, 102
Henry, 101, 102
Israel, 102
Issac, 30, 31
John, 30
Joseph, 30, 101, 102
Kezia, 30, 31
Marget, 101
Mary, 30, 102
Ovid, 102
Persis, 102
Pheby, 102
Philadelphia, 101, 102
Rebecca, 30
Rebecca C., 30
Samuel, 102
Sarah Ann, 30
Susanna, 30
VANNOSTRAND
Maria, 166
VANNOSTRANDT
Jacob, 166
Javcob Jacobse, 166
John, 166
VENDEGRIFT
Sarah, 132
VERNON
Anne, 68
Harriet, 68
James, 68
VICARY
Margaret, 51
WADDINGTON
Ann, 40
Eliza M., 78
Martha, 40
William, 40
WAITHMAN
John, 171, 172
Lydia, 171, 172
Lydia Y., 171

Rachel, 171
Thomas, 171, 172
WALDRON
Johannes, 156
Mary, 156
Resolved, 156
WALES, 65
WALKER
Ellen Hann, 108
John, Rev, 64
William, 71
WALLACE
Benjamin, 123
Martha, 123
WALLEN
Dorcas, 164
John, 164
WALLIN
Dorcas, 165
Hannah Ann, 165
John, 165
Lydia, 165
Mary, 165
Ruth P., 165
Sallie, 165
WALTON
George, 86
Henry, 86
Henry Durell, 86
Henry P., 87
Henry Pemberton, 86, 87
Joseph, 86
Lydia, 86
Lydia T., 87
Margaret, 87
Mary, 87
Mary Arrell, 86, 87
Rachel, 86
William, 86, 87

Heritage Books by Anna Miller Watring:

Accomack County, Virginia, Marriage References and Family Relationships, 1620–1800

Bucks County, Pennsylvania, Church Records of the 17th and 18th Centuries,
Volume 2: Quaker Records: Falls and Middletown Monthly Meetings
Anna Miller Watring and F. Edward Wright

Bucks County, Pennsylvania, Church Records of the 17th and 18th Centuries,
Volume 3: Quaker Records: Wrightstown, Richland, Buckingham,
Makefield And Solebury Monthly Meetings

Civil War Burials in Baltimore's Loudon Park Cemetery

Early Church Records of Monmouth County, New Jersey

Early Quaker Records of Philadelphia, Pennsylvania,
Volume 1: 1682–1750

Early Quaker Records of Philadelphia, Pennsylvania,
Volume 2, 1751–1800

King George County, Virginia, Marriage References
and Family Relationships, 1721–1800
Anne M. Watring and F. Edward Wright

Loudon Park Caretaker Records, A–B, 1853–1986
Anna M. Watring, E. Charles Miller, and R. Scott Johnson

New Jersey Bible Records:
Volume 1, Atlantic, Burlington, Cape May
and Gloucester Counties

New Jersey Bible Records:
Volume 2, Salem and Cumberland Counties